Golf's
Greatest
Championship

Golf's Greatest Championship

THE 1960 U.S. OPEN

Julian I. Graubart

DHF

DONALD I. FINE BOOKS
New York

Donald I. Fine Books
Published by the Penguin Group
Penguin Books USA Inc., 375 Hudson Street,
New York, New York 10014, U.S.A.
Penguin Books Ltd, 27 Wrights Lane,
London W8 5TZ, England
Penguin Books Australia Ltd, Ringwood,
Victoria, Australia
Penguin Books Canada Ltd, 10 Alcorn Avenue,
Toronto, Ontario, Canada M4V 3B2
Penguin Books (N.Z.) Ltd, 182–190 Wairau Road,
Auckland 10, New Zealand

Penguin Books Ltd, Registered Offices:
Harmondsworth, Middlesex, England

First published by Donald I. Fine Books, an imprint of
Penguin Books USA Inc.

First Printing, May, 1997
10 9 8 7 6 5 4 3 2

LIBRARY OF CONGRESS CATALOGING-IN-PUBLICATION DATA
Graubart, Julian I.
    Golf's greatest championship : the 1960 U.S. Open / Julian
I. Graubart.
        p.   cm.
    Includes bibliographical references and index.
    ISBN 1-55611-489-3
    1. United States Open Golf Championship Tournament—History.
I. Title.
GV970.G73   1997
796.352'66—DC21   96-49708
                                                              CIP

Printed in the United States of America

This book is printed on acid-free paper. ∞

To Mom and Dad
with Love

Golf may be . . . a sophisticated game.
At least, it is usually played with
the outward appearance of great dignity.
It is, nevertheless, a game of considerable passion—
either of the explosive type
or that which burns inwardly and sears the soul.

— ROBERT TYRE JONES, JR.

Acknowledgments

THE INFORMATION IN THIS BOOK WAS OBTAINED THROUGH FACE-TO-FACE and phone interviews with the people named below and from the newspapers, magazines, and books listed in the bibliography. Reporters from several dozen newspapers came to Denver's Cherry Hills Country Club to cover the 1960 U.S. Open. Those whose articles provided some of the book's details about the championship are listed in the bibliography alongside the newspapers they represented.

Interviews with the following golfers contributed to this book and to my pleasure in writing it: Jerry Barber, Tommy Bolt, Jack Burke, Jr., Billy Casper, Charles Coody, Bruce Crampton, Bill Ezinicki, Dow Finsterwald, Jack Fleck, Doug Ford, Bob Goalby, Fred Hawkins, Lionel Hebert, Howie Johnson, Gene Littler, Billy Maxwell, Arnold Palmer, Gary Player, Bob Rosburg, Paul Runyan, Doug Sanders, Charlie Sifford, Mike Souchak, Bob Verwey, and Claude Wright.

Several officials and long-time members of Cherry Hills Country Club opened their doors and memories to me: club manager Joe Vincent and members Dick Braun, Bill Hewit, Bill and Jean Kindel, and Steve Knowlton. So did Babe Aranjo, who caddied for Mike Souchak at the 1960 Open; Ralph

Moore, retired *Denver Post* reporter; and Dick Haskell, executive director of the Massachusetts Golf Association.

Andy Mutch of the United States Golf Association's Golf House was particularly helpful in my early research. Phil Stambaugh of the Senior PGA Tour helped connect me with the players. Sherry Major of the Professional Golfers' Association of America sent me articles I needed on the 1958, 1959, and 1960 golf seasons.

Rebecca Lintz of the Colorado Historical Society sent me some videotape from the telecast of the 1960 U.S. Open. Staff members at the following libraries helped me unearth relevant details: Library of Congress (Newspaper and Current Periodical Room), Washington, D.C.; Martin Luther King, Jr., Memorial Library, Washington, D.C.; Fort Worth Public Library, Fort Worth, Texas; and Denver Public Library, Denver, Colorado.

Becky Geanaros assisted mightily with permissions and photos. Bruce Geanaros photographed me more flatteringly than I thought could be done.

Many family members, friends, and business associates provided much appreciated encouragement, support, and understanding, chiefly my brother Ron; aunts Doris Graubart and Marilyn Sokoll; and friends and colleagues Dan Alpert, James Appleby, Eric Anderson, Joe Bonnarens, Jim Caro, Jane Diao, Wally Etienne, Mark Evans, Linda Faison, Nina Fales, Ann Franke, John Gans, Ronnie Ghelardi, Joel and Linda Harteker, Melissa Kahn, Steve Marks, Susan McLaughlin, Evelina and Jim Moulder, Elaine Papazian, Everett Potter, and Pam Sparr.

The book would not have been possible without the wise counsel of four people: Donald Fine, my editor; Nina Graybill, my agent; Ron Shectman; and Tim Wells.

1960 U.S. Open Pairings
Saturday, June 18

8:00 A.M. and 12:30 P.M.	Rex Baxter–Chick Harbert
8:06 A.M. and 12:36 P.M.	Lloyd Mangrum–Art Wall
8:12 A.M. and 12:42 P.M.	Bob Watson–Lionel Hebert
8:18 A.M. and 12:48 P.M.	Dave Marr–Frank Stranahan
8:24 A.M. and 12:54 P.M.	Stan Dudas–Doug Ford
8:30 A.M. and 1:00 P.M.	Frank Boynton–Henry Ransom
8:36 A.M. and 1:06 P.M.	Bob Harris–Ken Venturi
8:42 A.M. and 1:12 P.M.	Huston LaClair, Jr.– George Bayer
8:48 A.M. and 1:18 P.M.	Dutch Harrison–Charlie Sifford
8:54 A.M. and 1:24 P.M.	Dave Ragan–Don Whitt
9:00 A.M. and 1:30 P.M.	Ben Hogan–Jack Nicklaus
9:06 A.M. and 1:36 P.M.	Gary Player–Julius Boros
9:12 A.M. and 1:42 P.M.	Paul Harney–Arnold Palmer
9:18 A.M. and 1:48 P.M.	Bob Goalby–Dick Stranahan
9:24 A.M. and 1:54 P.M.	Johnny Pott–Bob Shave, Jr.
9:30 A.M. and 2:00 P.M.	Mike Souchak–Doug Sanders
9:36 A.M. and 2:06 P.M.	Dow Finsterwald–Jack Fleck
9:42 A.M. and 2:12 P.M.	Jerry Barber–Bruce Crampton
9:48 A.M. and 2:18 P.M.	Billy Casper–Ted Kroll
9:54 A.M. and 2:24 P.M.	Don Cherry–Sam Snead
10:00 A.M. and 2:30 P.M.	Jackson Bradley–Sam Penecale
10:06 A.M. and 2:36 P.M.	Dave Douglas–Walter Burkemo
10:12 A.M. and 2:42 P.M.	Al Feminelli–Al Mengert
10:18 A.M. and 2:48 P.M.	Claude Harmon–Bob Goetz
10:24 A.M. and 2:54 P.M.	Jim Turnesa–Cary Middlecoff
10:30 A.M. and 3:00 P.M.	Harold Kneece–Bob Verwey
10:36 A.M. and 3:06 P.M.	Bob Rosburg–Howie Johnson– Bill Johnston

PAR AND YARDAGE

HOLE	PAR	YARDAGE	HOLE	PAR	YARDAGE
1	4	346	10	4	444
2	4	410	11	5	563
3	4	348	12	3	212
4	4	426	13	4	385
5	5	538	14	4	470
6	3	174	15	3	196
7	4	411	16	4	402
8	3	233	17	5	548
9	4	430	18	4	468
OUT	35	3,316	IN	36	3,688
			TOTAL 71		7,004

Cherry Hills Golf Course – 1960

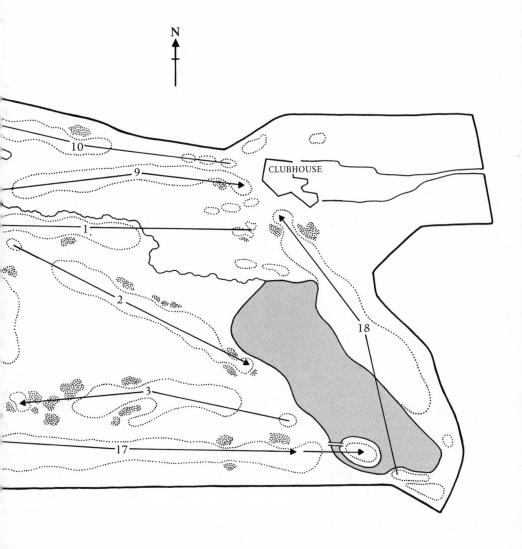

Prologue

ARNOLD PALMER WON HIS FIRST MAJOR CHAMPIONSHIP, THE MASTERS, and two other tournaments in 1958, and for the first time he was the leading money winner on the Professional Golfers' Association of America tour. It was an outstanding year, but, to Palmer, it represented only a modest beginning toward all he hoped to accomplish in the game. He had far loftier goals and was impatient to press on.

The 1959 season began full of promise. In January he won the Thunderbird Invitation in Palm Springs, California. Five strokes behind third-round leader Jimmy Demaret, he closed with a scorching 62, his lowest round as a professional. It was his 12th victory in four years on the tour, the most wins recorded by any of the so-called Young Lions.

And yet, in the eyes of golf fans and writers, Palmer didn't particularly stand out. He was still one of a handful of talented golfers of his generation—Gene Littler, Mike Souchak, Billy Casper, Dow Finsterwald, and, lately, a cocky kid named Ken Venturi. Like the best of their immediate predecessors—Cary Middlecoff, Lloyd Mangrum, Doug Ford, Jack Burke, Jr., and Tommy Bolt—neither Palmer nor any of his peers had been able to unseat the legendary Old Guard players, Ben Hogan and Sam Snead, even though Hogan had all but retired and Snead had curtailed his tournament schedule.

It had been five years since Hogan's majestic 1953 season, and golf fans watched for a successor. One was on the horizon, not yet quite recognized. It would take the 1960 U.S. Open to fully establish his presence. But first there were miles of championship fairways to live and die on.

CHAPTER 1

STANDING ON THE 12TH TEE IN THE FINAL ROUND OF THE 1959 MAS-
ters, defending champion Arnold Palmer held a slim two-
stroke lead on the field. Arnold, going with his six-iron on
Augusta National's famous par three over Rae's Creek, tried to
draw his ball safely into the heart of the shallow green, but it
didn't draw and plopped into the water. After taking a drop in
front of the creek, he pitched a tad too firmly and watched as
his ball bounded off the green into a tangly lie. A five was now
the best he could hope for; but after failing to hole a nine-foot
putt he stalked off the 12th hole with a triple-bogey six. Suddenly, the two nearest contenders, Cary Middlecoff and Stan
Leonard, were back in the hunt.

A year earlier it was on the 475-yard 13th hole that
Palmer had laid claim to the title. As Bobby Jones, legendary
golfer and Masters founder, watched from a nearby hill, Arnold selected a three-wood for the perilous second shot. Risk
be damned; he was going for the green. It was Palmer's way.
Settling into a sidehill stance, he swung hard and the contact
was true. The ball soared over the stream that cuts in front of
the green and landed 18 feet from the pin; Palmer sank the
putt for an eagle three.

Jones called the three-wood one of the two greatest shots he had ever seen. "The same exhilaration came over me as when I watched Sarazen from that same mound in 1935," he said. Gene Sarazen had holed his fairway wood (on the par-five 15th hole) for a double-eagle two and gone on to win the tournament.

This year of 1959 at the 13th, Palmer recovered impressively from his staggering triple-bogey, making a birdie four. With a confident par at 14 followed by another birdie at 15, he regained his lead and held on to it through 16. But then on the 17th green he missed a three-footer for his par, and on the 18th he missed a four-foot birdie putt. He had stumbled at the worst possible moment.

Meanwhile, Art Wall, who had entered the final round six strokes behind leaders Palmer and Leonard, was on the most amazing final-nine binge in Masters history: a 15-foot putt for a birdie at 13; at 14, using his putter from the apron, he sank a 22-footer for birdie; a putt for eagle at the 15th just spun out and he tapped in for his third straight birdie. A safe par at 16 was followed by another birdie at 17 with another 15-foot putt. Only then, leaving the 17th green, did he realize just how far he'd come: a par would beat Palmer by one stroke and might hold up against Middlecoff, who was a few holes behind him.

At the 18th tee Wall, an underrated journeyman who was off to his finest year on the PGA tour, hit his best drive of the tournament, and a nine-iron left him 12 feet below the hole. On his walk to the green he heard a distant roar—Middlecoff had eagled the 15th—and decided he had better not play it safe for a par. After careful study, he stroked his putt straight into the cup—his fifth birdie in the last six holes—for a 66. Middlecoff, failing to get the one birdie on the final three holes that he needed to tie Wall, fell one stroke short. It was the last time the great post-war golfer was in contention for one of the major championships.

4

* * *

MONTHS PASSED BEFORE PALMER could put the disappointment of the 1959 Masters behind him. His considerable pride was wounded. Ever since he was a sprig romping about the Latrobe, Pennsylvania, golf course where his father was the pro and greenkeeper, he had world-class plans for himself as a golfer. He fantasized attaining the stature of his idol, Bobby Jones, of winning the Masters, the British Open, the PGA Championship, and the U.S. Open. Early successes as an amateur—first as a schoolboy in Pennsylvania, then a three-time Atlantic Coast Conference titleholder at Wake Forest College in North Carolina, and ultimately the 1954 U.S. Amateur champion—made such dreams within reach.

After winning the Amateur and then turning pro, he won the Canadian Open in 1955, his first full season on the tour, and improved steadily each year. In 1956 he won two tournaments, and in 1957, four, the most of any player that year. A few times when he fell too far behind the leaders, he withdrew from the tournament—considered a cardinal sin in professional golf. But Palmer played an attacking, bold game— shooting directly at pins, putting aggressively—and he came to believe that if he could just stay in touch with the leaders he could catch and beat them.

And how he loved the exhilaration and attention that came with winning dramatically. It was just like when he was a little boy, showing off at Latrobe Country Club with his sawed-off lady's driver, challenging members to give him a nickel if he hit his ball over a ditch. "He'd be yelling, 'Watch me! Watch me! Watch me, Pap!' " his father, Milfred "Deacon" Palmer, recalled. "You'd get so sick of him you'd feel like hitting him a lick." The boy swung so hard that often his feet would go out from under him.

As a brawny adult, 5 feet 11 inches, 177 pounds, he took the same ferocious cut as he did as a youngster. Standing far from the ball, he had a fast, flattish swing. It was hardly elegant, but the results were impressive. Palmer was one of the tour's longest drivers, and when his tee ball stayed straight, he usually was a threat to win.

Two weeks after the Masters, at the tour stop in Houston, Palmer squandered a comfortable lead in the third round, coming home in 39. The last day, needing to get down in two from the apron of the 72nd green, he chipped five feet beyond the hole and missed the return putt. Making it would have gotten him into a play-off with Julius Boros and Jack Burke, Jr. Even after he won the Oklahoma City Open three weeks later—this time he protected his third-round lead—he hardly sounded like the victor. "Who did you fear most heading into the last round?" a reporter asked him. "Myself," he answered.

At the Western Open in July, he came undone again. In the first 11 holes of the last round, Mike Souchak made up five strokes on Palmer, the co-leader after three rounds. On the last hole, now tied with Souchak, he exploded out of the greenside bunker, his ball coming to rest three feet from the pin. He then stepped up and missed the putt, admittedly a tricky side-hiller.

Toward the end of the summer, saying he felt overgolfed, Palmer took off a full ten weeks from the tour. He and his family—wife Winnie and daughters Peggy and Amy, ages three and one respectively—returned home to western Pennsylvania and the three-bedroom ranch house they had built overlooking the golf course he grew up on. There he consulted with his lifelong golf instructor, Pap, who was still the club pro.

Returning to the tour in mid-November, he tied for seventh at the Lafayette Open. Two weeks later he captured the year's penultimate tournament, the West Palm Beach Open, for his third win, and then tied for third the next week at Coral Gables. Although he had closed out the season strongly and had finished 1959 fifth on the money list, 30-year-old Arnold

Palmer regarded the season a loss—he had failed to win any of the major championships—and he swore to make amends.

ON APRIL 29, THE day before the 1959 Colonial National Invitation began, 46-year-old Ben Hogan informed the golfing world that he could still summon the skills of the incomparable shotmaker he once was. Playing his final practice round, he shot the lowest score ever produced on the long, exacting Colonial Country Club—a 63. And in so doing he conquered, at least for a day, the "yips"—the nervous, herky-jerky putting that sometimes in recent years had made the greatest golfer of his era seem a pathetic figure.

Now running a successful golf-club–manufacturing business in Fort Worth, Texas, and playing in only a select few tournaments each year, the reclusive elder statesman had attracted little attention in pretournament commentary. After all, the last time he had won a tournament on the tour was in 1953, and the 1958 Colonial had ended ignominiously for him. Still solidly in the running at the final hole, he had hooked his drive into the trees, hit a tree with his second shot, flew the green with his third, and took three to get down. With that double-bogey six he finished three strokes behind the winner, Tommy Bolt.

The fact remained, however, that in most respects Hogan was still Hogan—arguably the finest ball-striker and golf-course strategist in the game's history and a competitor whose concentration was so profound that some found it eerie. Besides, in the tournament's 12-year history, he had won four times. That record, and now his record-setting 63, reminded everyone why Colonial Country Club, located in his hometown, was coined "Hogan's Alley."

After the first round, Hogan left little room for doubt that he was still to be reckoned with. Not only did he shoot a 69, which placed him only two strokes behind the leader, Lionel

Hebert, but he had a run-in with a movie cameraman who distracted him on the 15th green. Hogan had three-putted for a bogey and was still seething later in the locker room. It was like old times. "I asked him twice to quit, then the third time I ordered him to stop," he muttered to Harry Gage of the *Dallas Morning News.* "Those guys think we're playing these tournaments just for them."

In the second round Hogan exhibited the consistent excellence for which he was famous. His scorecard contained 3 birdies and 15 pars for a 67, matching Hebert for the low round of the day. Alone in second place, still trailing by only two shots, he followed his old habit and declined to visit the press room—Hogan presented himself to the writers only when he was the leader.

Round three, played in winds gusting up to 40 miles an hour, jumbled the list of leaders. Ben's 77 was a sad, sloppy affair, but not much worse than the others' rounds, so he was lucky to find himself only three behind the new leader, Ted Kroll, after 54 holes.

The next day Hogan played in the last threesome with Kroll and Fred Hawkins, who was four strokes back. Kroll fell out of the picture on the back nine, and Hogan and Hawkins came to the final hole tied for the lead. Hawkins, a golfer much better than his record on the tour suggested—one win in 12 years—bogeyed 18. Hogan ran a 40-foot birdie putt 3 feet past the hole. While the spectators watched transfixed, the familiar figure in the customary white, flat, linen cap stood an agonizing full 20 seconds over the ball before he could get his putter started. The ball stopped on the lip. There would be an 18-hole play-off the next day.

Hogan downplayed his missed putt, but, in fact, it revealed the glaring weakness in his game. Whereas his confident tee-to-green play was still something to behold, his hesitant putting was so appalling that one could hardly believe it was the same golfer on the green. Back in the 1940s, when he was "Bantam Ben" in the press because of his modest stature—5 feet 8 inches, 140 pounds—his rock-steady putting was an asset that contributed to his piling up victory on victory. But ever since the terrifying car crash in 1949, his peripheral vision had declined, and the man had grown to hate this facet of the game; he literally feuded with it. As he grew older and his putting skills eroded, he burned with outrage that what happened on the greens mattered so much. "There are two games of golf," he declared. "One is the game of golf; the other is putting."

After the fourth round at Colonial, Ben, now less of a bantamweight at 155 pounds, was obviously weary. As always since the collision that nearly took his life, the question surfaced: Could his legs carry him another 18 holes?

"Oh, sure," he answered after a long pause. "It's just that I've got a lot of things I need to do. And I'm sure Fred would like to be on his way." Hogan, dubbed the Hawk for his cold, piercing stare, had mellowed somewhat since the accident, but it's questionable whether Hawkins, or anybody else, fell for such uncharacteristic insouciance.

On a muggy, windy Monday, the Hawk finished off his opponent with machinelike efficiency. He jumped in front on the 4th hole, where he sank a 15-footer for a birdie. An eight-foot birdie putt at number 7 extended his lead to four strokes. The players then halved each of the final 11 holes: Hogan 69, Hawkins 73.

The U.S. Open was only a month away, and Ben said he hoped his fifth win at Colonial was "an omen of things to come." Another win in the Open would make five, one more than the record shared by turn-of-the-century pro Willie Anderson and Bobby Jones. Surely he wouldn't have many more chances to capture the game's preeminent championship.

Although Colonial marked Hogan's first victory in six years, the *New York Times* minimized it. A story ran on the third, and last, page of its sports section, carrying the sour subhead: "Hogan Plays It Safe After Taking 4-Stroke Lead in First 7 Holes." Other coverage was much warmer and included an Associated Press photo of Ben's mother, Clara, hugging her son on the 18th green. Two photos accompanying a *Sports Illustrated* story captured the serene pleasure of the former champion savoring what no longer came easily. "It has been an awfully dry spell," he said.

TWO WEEKS LATER, SAM Snead, 11 days shy of 47, countered with the most spectacular round of his life, a 59. The first sub-60 round in tour history, it was a flourish befitting the career of the tour's biggest winner. Like his old rival, Ben Hogan, Sam turned the trick on native ground—the Greenbrier in White Sulfur Springs, West Virginia. And like Ben, he won his "home tournament" (formerly the Greenbrier Invitational, then called the Sam Snead Festival) for the fifth time.

Samuel Jackson Snead, of Ashwood, Virginia (population 400), first came to the Greenbrier in 1936 when he was 23. Before that he repaired clubs, cleaned up, and ran errands at the Cascades, a golf course in Hot Springs, three miles from home. For this, his first job in golf, he received no salary, his only payment being a basic lunch and whatever cash he could bring in giving lessons in his spare time. But it was the Depression, and the job provided a start in golf at the wonderful course where he had caddied as a boy. Best of all, it was a job that enabled the raw recruit to practice on a real golf course.

As Sam recalled in *The Education of a Golfer*, one evening he was out behind the caddie shack cleaning mud off some golf balls when Freddie Martin dropped into his life. Martin, the manager of golf at the Greenbrier, located just across the border in West Virginia, had seen the young Snead playing in the Cascades Open that day. Sam, using an incomplete, mismatched set of battered clubs, shot a 70 and finished in second place. Billy Burke, the 1931 U.S. Open champion, had to scramble to win. But what had really impressed Martin was a swing as graceful as Bobby Jones's that sent the ball prodigious distances. On one 330-yard hole, Sam went through the green with his tee shot.

"You've got a golf swing that's amazing," Martin said. "Where'd you learn it?"

"Nowhere much," Sam replied. "In a hayfield over home. That's in Ashwood, up the road a ways."

"Which of these Virginia pros has been working with you?"

"Not any pro. I never had money for lessons or greens fees; just watched my brother, Homer, and practiced in the back pasture."

In short order Martin asked Sam to fill an open position he had for a golf professional at the Greenbrier. The pay would be 45 dollars a month plus room and board and any money he could earn teaching the Greenbrier's well-heeled guests. Would he accept the offer? "Mr. Martin, I don't know how fast you move," Sam answered, in his country drawl, "but when you get back to your pro shop, the first sight you're going to see will be me."

Sam collected his few belongings at home that night and, along with his motley assortment of clubs, arrived at his new job the next morning. And so began an association with the Greenbrier that was to continue, with only a couple of interruptions, into his 80s.

Martin encouraged Snead to test his game against the best players, and in the fall of 1936 Sam headed to Florida. He won $108 in the Miami Open, and he accepted $500 to endorse Dunlop golf equipment. The green peckerwood from the hills of Virginia thought he'd struck it rich. Back in 1934 he'd met Johnny Bulla, a tall, young West Virginian, at a tournament in Louisville, Kentucky, and the two hit it off instantly. Now he hooked up with Bulla, who also was trying his luck on the tour, and the two drove cross-country in Johnny's jalopy to

11

join the golfing circuit in Los Angeles. They would split expenses and—if the doubtful Snead had his way—whatever prize money either should win.

The tour—in those days called the tournament circuit or just the circuit—was a patchy series of mostly low-budget, casually run tournaments, a succession of vaudeville stops zigzagging across America. Several tournaments couldn't weather the Great Depression; others were forced to cut back their prize money.

The established events were a handful—the Los Angeles, Texas, Western, North and South, and Metropolitan opens—plus the two major championships, the National Open (as the U.S. Open was called) and the PGA Championship. The Augusta National Invitation, soon to be known as the Masters Tournament, had just begun in 1934. With the major championships providing the foundation, a summer circuit of more than a dozen events was now attracting the top players of the country—at least those who could get away from their club jobs.

The pro ranks featured 15 to 20 marvelous golfers—Craig Wood, Paul Runyan, Ralph Guldahl, Denny Shute, Johnny Revolta, Tommy Armour, Gene Sarazen, Jimmy Thomson, Harry Cooper, Horton Smith, Ky Laffoon, Vic Ghezzi, Henry Picard—plus an itinerant cadre of hustlers and hangers-on. Future greats Byron Nelson and Ben Hogan, acquaintances from their boyhood caddying days in Fort Worth, waited in the wings.

Tournament golf was a tough life. To thrive on the circuit you had to have a large tolerance of risk, a sense of adventure, and a golf game, because if you couldn't finish in the top four or five places each tournament, you couldn't earn a living—at least not from prize money alone. Walter Hagen and Gene Sarazen, the biggest stars of the twenties, made most of their money giving exhibitions. For the others, gambling on the golf course between tournaments and around the card table provided opportunities for reward as well as recreation. The goal most of the players on tour shared was to make a name for themselves in hopes of attracting a plum position at one of the country's top golf clubs. But they stayed out on the circuit as long as possible, driving their big Buicks and Packards great distances in two- and three-car caravans, mostly because they loved the game.

Snead started winning tournaments at once and was relieved that Bulla had rejected his proposal to split their winnings 50-50. After finishing sixth at the Los Angeles Open, Sam won both the Oakland and Bing Crosby tournaments, and by the end of 1937 he had added three other victories to his record.

The arrival on the national stage of this hillbilly golfing prodigy created a sensation. How could this hayseed who'd never taken a golf lesson, who'd never competed in amateur tournaments, who'd run around barefoot on his folks' little cow-and-chicken farm possibly play as he played? Was he for real? Fred Corcoran, the tournament manager of the PGA and soon Sam's business manager, assured everyone that he was very much for real. "He's the best swinger of a golf club I've ever seen," he stated flatly.

Corcoran, a Boston Irishman, was the ideal front man for the PGA and Sam alike. He knew all there was to know about the game; he was blessed with great instincts for news and publicity; and he had the gift of gab. In Snead he had a completely fresh personality who wove backwoods anecdotes into his naturally picturesque, earthy vocabulary. The press ate it up. And in Snead he had the kind of bigger-than-life golfer the struggling pro circuit badly needed if it was to spark the interest of prospective tournament sponsors such as civic and business groups and golf resorts. The press instantly dubbed Fred's man "Slammin' Sammy Snead," and golf fans, longing for a hero to replace the retired Bobby Jones and Walter Hagen, embraced him.

In 1938 Sam won eight tournaments. A group of his peers, socializing in a hotel lobby one night, couldn't get over the year he had had. All agreed: no golfer would ever top his earnings of $19,399.49.

Over the next 20 years, as new stars replaced the great players of Sam's generation, the Slammer stayed at the top of his game. To his fans he seemed to change hardly at all. Well, he did go bald, but his trademark straw hats with their colorful cloth bands more than compensated. He was the same wonderful physical specimen that came out of the hills of Virginia—5 feet 11 inches, 185 pounds, with the same 33-inch waistline and gymnast's flexibility. He could reach into the cup to retrieve his ball without bending his legs, and—as he loved demonstrating—he could kick one leg high enough to reach the top of a door frame while keeping the other touching the floor.

His golf swing remained fluid and graceful, seemingly devoid of all tension. It had the same beautiful tempo as the day Freddie Martin first set eyes on it. Years later, when Snead was almost 70, golfer Gardner Dickinson said, "Sam was born warmed up. If you cut him, 3-In-One oil would come out, not blood."

From the late thirties to the late fifties, Sam Snead won more golf tournaments and more prize money than anyone else. He won more than 100 tournaments in all—including the PGA three times, the Masters three times, and the British Open once—and about $400,000. He won everything he wanted to win, except the biggest championship of all—the U.S. Open.

It looked as though he had clinched his first one, the 1937 Open, until Ralph Guldahl caught fire and Snead had to settle for second place—still, an auspicious beginning. In 1939 he butchered the last hole, taking an eight when a mere par five would have brought him the crown. Although nothing in his long career would ever approach the infamy of this championship, more Open anguish lay ahead.

By the fifties it seemed as though he was doomed to experience heartbreak at the Open again and again. Apart from his second-place finish in 1937, he was runner-up in 1947, 1949, and 1953. Each June his fans and the press wondered, Is this the year the Slammer can finally overcome his Open jinx? And every June he endured the same old questions and gave it his best effort, but the answer still came back no.

In 1959 Sam Snead was the game's biggest star, constantly in demand—traveling to tournaments, to golf exhibitions, to televised golf appearances, to business functions. During spring and summer Sam returned from his travels to his home base, the Greenbrier.

On May 16, when he walked off the 18th green with his phenomenal score of 59, Freddie Martin was waiting for him with tears in his eyes. Back in 1936 he had predicted that one day Sam would break 60 in a tournament; lately he had predicted a U.S. Open title. Sam walked over to Freddie and gave his old friend the last ball he played during the round. The two men faced one another and communicated silently.

IN LATE SEPTEMBER TWO of the favorites met in the finals of the 1959 U.S. Amateur championship: 35-year-old Charlie Coe, an oil broker from Oklahoma, and 19-year-old Jack Nicklaus, an Ohio State University junior. The championship was played at the Broadmoor in Colorado Springs, Colorado, on a lovely course located 6,400 feet above sea level. Playing a level of golf as rarified as the course's elevation—especially considering the pressure of a 36-hole match-play final—the opponents came to the home hole all even.

Coe, the defending champion, and Nicklaus each placed their drives in excellent position to approach the Broadmoor's 18th green 430 yards in the distance. Charlie, using his eight-iron, struck his ball too hard and it ran off the back of the green to the bottom of a small bank. Could his young opponent capitalize on the opening? Nicklaus lofted a nine-iron that stopped nine feet below the hole.

Coe's ball lay in tangly rough and the pin was only 20 feet from the back apron, yet he had to get up and down in two to stand any chance of halving the hole. With his sand wedge, he floated his ball ever so softly just onto the back of the green. It rolled toward the pin—directly toward the pin—and stopped one revolution short of the hole. The two teammates from the States' recent victorious Walker Cup team exchanged wry smiles; the 4,000 spectators gasped. As the crowd settled down, Nicklaus examined his nine-footer, a tricky uphill putt with a slight left-to-right break near the hole. He stroked his ball into the center of the cup.

The new U.S. Amateur champion, the youngest winner in 50 years, was little known to the public. But he had been building a record, and few in the world of amateur golf were surprised by his victory.

Jack took up the game at age ten. At 13 he started to play in tournaments, and in the next few years he won almost all the junior championships of any consequence. At the same tender age of 13 he broke 70 for the first time. He would never forget that day at his home course, Scioto Country Club, in Columbus, Ohio. Playing with his father, the two standing on Scioto's 18th green in the gloaming, Jack squinted at the 35-foot eagle putt he needed to make for his 69. He holed it.

In 1955, at 15, he qualified for his first U.S. Amateur championship but lost his first-round match. Bobby Jones, a prodigy in his own day but now incapacitated by a painful spinal disease, drove over to watch him from his golf cart, departing when he realized his presence might have been contributing to the boy's disappointing play. At 16 Jack won Ohio's Open championship. At 17 he qualified for his first U.S.

Open; he missed the cut by ten strokes, shooting 80-80 at Inverness in Toledo, Ohio.

The next year, 1958, he won the Trans-Mississippi, one of the top amateur tournaments in the country. In June he survived the cut at the U.S. Open and finished tied for 41st—an amazing achievement for an 18-year-old (though only the fourth best finish by an amateur that year).

Three weeks later he played in his first regular PGA tournament, the Rubber City Open. Outwardly unfazed by playing with the likes of newly crowned Open champion Tommy Bolt, former Open champion Julius Boros, and the tournament's eventual winner, Art Wall, Jack finished tied for 15th. The always controversial Bolt had just been fined $500 and put on indefinite probation by the PGA for quitting the Pepsi Open— the latest in a string of citations he had received for flinging his golf clubs, breaking his golf clubs, cussing, and stalking off the course in the middle of tournaments. Years later, Nicklaus acknowledged that the only time he ever felt intimidated on a golf course was during a round in this tournament in which Bolt kept badgering him.

By 1959, though, it was clear that not much could intimidate this kid Nicklaus. In January he was named to the Walker Cup team—then, more so than today, the dream of all young golfers. That May, in the practice round at Muirfield, Scotland, he drove the 15th green—a distance of 397 yards—and in the competition he won both his foursomes and singles match. He returned home a perceptibly more seasoned competitor, as his subsequent victory at the U.S. Amateur confirmed.

Several fortunate circumstances, in addition to his innate ability and considerable early tournament experience, contributed to the resounding arrival of Jack Nicklaus. Although he didn't look it, the husky 5-foot 11³/₄-inch 210-pounder actually was a very good athlete—quick, well coordinated, and strong as a bull. Taking after his father, Charlie, he loved sports

17

and he loved to compete, particularly in basketball (he was a star on his high school team), but also in baseball and football.

From the start Jack received instruction at Scioto from Jack Grout, one of the country's best-trained teaching professionals. Grout had uncommon insight as a teacher, thanks in no small measure to his golfing lineage. He had been an assistant pro to Henry Picard, a top player in the thirties who possessed one of the game's finest swings; Picard in turn had learned from Alex Morrison, one of the early masters of technique whose theories were years ahead of their time. (Grout also spent time as assistant pro at Glen Garden Country Club, the Fort Worth, Texas, golfing birthplace of Ben Hogan and Byron Nelson.)

Grout's new pupil took part in Scioto's weekly lesson for junior golfers and from time to time a private lesson was arranged. Soon the boy was as passionate about golf as he was about basketball. Jack dwarfed the other kids not only in size and power but in his voracious appetite for practice. Here was a game in which he didn't have to rely on the fickle interests of the other kids to play. He'd regularly hit 300 balls on the practice range—*after* playing 18 holes.

The swing that evolved was colossal, if unorthodox—a low take-away with a wide arc; an upright backswing with a strong body turn, the right elbow jutting away from the body as the hands reached a high position at the top; a powerful lateral leg drive on the downswing, the clubhead reaching maximum speed as the clubface struck the ball. Jack hit the ball so hard that a number of times the insert on his driver burst.

Jack was also fortunate in the father he had. Charlie Nicklaus, a Columbus pharmacist, encouraged and supported Jack—and punished him when he needed his comeuppance—but he was not one to force practice on his son, as parents of talented kids often did and do. He nurtured Jack's growth as a golfer but even more so as a sportsman. The two were very close.

Add to the mix: young Jack Nicklaus had an abundance of intelligence, ambition, and desire for perfection. What a synergy of golfing attributes and experience!

From all this, early on, came confidence, and with confidence came the marvelous poise that he displayed at the Broadmoor against the more experienced Coe. Ultimately, with his poise grew the ability both to outthink his opponents down the stretch when the pressure was greatest, and to make swing adjustments when his mechanics went awry. Bobby Jones, who won his second U.S. Open championship at Scioto, once told Charlie Nicklaus that the ability to correct swing problems during a tournament was the key to his becoming a champion, and this comment, relayed to Jack, made a deep impression.

Like Jones, his boyhood idol, Nicklaus intended to remain an amateur. And like Jones, his overriding goal was to win the U.S. Open. He was determined to be the first amateur to do so since Johnny Goodman in 1933.

IN JANUARY 1960, the first month of the new golf season, Arnold Palmer's name barely strayed onto the tournament leader boards. Three other pretenders to the throne last occupied by Ben Hogan, and one little-known veteran, fared far better.

Palmer's best friend on the tour, Dow Finsterwald, captured the year's first tournament, the Los Angeles Open; Arnold, beaten by a stroke by the low amateur, Phil Rodgers, was scarcely mentioned. The next week, 43-year-old Jerry Barber, a club pro making one of his periodic forays onto the tour, surprised everyone with his first victory since 1954, the Yorba Linda Open. Palmer finished in seventh place, collected $610, and headed off to the Monterey Peninsula for the season's third event.

Played in furious rain and wind, the Bing Crosby National Professional-Amateur (or "the Crosby," as it was universally known) was taken by Ken Venturi; Palmer finished in the pack. Mike Souchak won the following week in San Diego, edging 24-year-old Johnny Pott in an exciting stretch drive by one stroke; Arnold improved to a tie for seventh.

Next it was on to Palm Springs, California, for the Desert Classic, the tour's first 90-hole tournament. It was here, the year before, that Palmer had closed with a torrid 62 to grab his first 1959 title. This year, after 72 holes, a Palmer was leading, but it wasn't Arnold. Forty-one-year-old Johnny Palmer, winner of a half-dozen tournaments from the late forties to mid-fifties, led Arnold by one stroke.

The Associated Press reported that the two men were not related, which even the casual sports fan soon would know. On the last day, the younger Palmer, buoyed by a six-under-par 66 in round four, came back with a 65 to win his first tournament of 1960. Encouraged but wary of overconfidence, Palmer stayed with the golfing caravan as the California portion of the winter tour concluded and the Southwest leg began.

The Phoenix Open featured the season's second victory by a veteran who had been winless for many years, Jack Fleck. One of the game's more curious figures, Fleck had emerged from obscurity in 1955 to win the U.S. Open—defeating Ben Hogan, in an 18-hole play-off no less. It was his first tour win. The Phoenix Open, in February 1960, became his second and it followed the same 18-hole play-off route. Palmer, despite shooting a third-round 66, finished in 13th place.

The next week, in Tucson, Arnold shot the low nine-hole score of the year, a 29, in the first round, but finished tied for seventh. Don January, a lanky 30-year-old Texan, was the winner. On to San Antonio for the Texas Open, the eighth tournament of the year.

With rounds of 69, 65, and 67, Palmer entered the last day of the Texas Open with a four-stroke lead. He extended his cushion to six strokes with an even-par 36 going out. This was fortunate for him, because as the wind whistled and the temperature plummeted into the 40s, he came home with a shaky 39, though he still held on for a two-stroke victory. Suddenly the 1960 season was looking up. With this, his second win of the year, he had already earned $20,211, some $5,000 more than anyone had ever won at this point in the season.

Arnold stayed with the tour for the ninth consecutive week as it headed to Baton Rouge, Louisiana. For the second tournament in a row he managed a four-stroke lead in the first 54 holes. This time, however, he closed with an airtight 68 to bury the nearest competitor seven strokes behind him. For once, Palmer's putting, which had failed him so miserably in 1959, was exemplary. In his final-round 68 he holed a 15-footer for a birdie at the 6th hole, a 30-footer for an eagle at 8, and 15- and 25-footers for birdies at 14 and 16 respectively. Next stop, Pensacola.

When the PGA tour moves to Florida each March, professional golfers start thinking about the Masters. Somewhat akin to baseball's spring training, with which the Florida tournaments coincide, this is a time to hone your swing, build your confidence, and get competition-tough. In 1960 four events remained to be played before the year's first major championship: the Pensacola, St. Petersburg, and De Soto opens in Florida, and the Azalea Open in North Carolina.

Playing the Pensacola, for the first time in three weeks Palmer did not enter the final round in front; he stood two strokes behind the leader, Joe Campbell. Campbell soon tumbled from the top but Palmer, languishing at one over par after three-putting the 8th, couldn't get his game in gear. Then, suddenly, he found the groove on the soft Pensacola Country Club greens.

Over the next eight holes he one-putted seven times and collected four birdies. At number 17 he learned that he was one stroke behind the leader, Doug Sanders, who had shot a dazzling 34-31—65. Arnold needed one more birdie on the final two holes for a tie. At the 17th green he left himself a 12-foot birdie putt and holed it. A par now and he'd be alive to duel Sanders in a play-off. On the final green, faced with a 30-footer for birdie, Palmer holed that one, too. In a flash he had stormed to his third straight victory.

The win, his fourth of the season, was the fifth in 12 starts. The last time anyone had been this hot on tour was 1952, when Jack Burke, Jr., had won four tournaments in succession.

Palmer's streak, though, ended the next week at the St. Petersburg Open. George Bayer—golf's biggest hitter and, at 6 feet 5 inches, 250 pounds, its biggest man—defeated Jack Fleck in a sudden-death play-off; Palmer finished in fifth place. The following week the inaugural De Soto Open was won by Sam Snead, playing in his first tournament of the year. It was his first victory since his fabulous win at the Greenbrier the previous May. Palmer finished tied for fifth.

While many of his peers then traveled up the coast to Wilmington, North Carolina, for the Azalea Open (won by former National Collegiate Athletic Association champion Tom Nieporte), Arnold finally took the week off to rest and prepare for the Masters.

SOMEHOW, EACH APRIL the Masters invents an ingenious plot, setting in dramatic motion a cast of stars and unknowns. Or maybe it just seems that way because even a humdrum Masters still bears the dual imprint of greatness—Bobby Jones and Augusta National.

In 1956 the protagonist was Ken Venturi, a stylish, 24-year-old amateur who led after each of the first three rounds, only to suffer a terrible attack of nerves and take a 42 on the final nine holes. A hot Jack Burke, Jr., edged him by one stroke.

In 1957 tour star Doug Ford shot the lights out with a

final-round 66 to top the headliner Sam Snead. The climax came on Ford's final swing—an explosion shot out of the sand that landed in the bottom of the 72nd hole. Two weeks earlier Ford had correctly predicted the winning score, 283, as well as the champion.

In 1958 rising star Palmer prevailed over playing partner Venturi for his first green jacket, aided by a controversial imbedded-ball ruling at the 12th hole, his bold three-wood on number 13, and some untimely three-putting by Venturi.

The 1959 Masters was still fresh in everyone's memory. Palmer's foibles there and his recent tour domination heightened anticipation over the upcoming championship and insured a large television audience. The only disappointment was that Art Wall would be unable to defend his crown because of a kidney infection and knee injury.

The bookies made Palmer the favorite at 6–1. He was the pick of most of the press, too, though some writers named Mike Souchak a co-favorite. Being the "favorite," a label athletes usually shun, didn't bother Palmer at all. "I sort of like it," he admitted to Bob Russell, writing for the PGA's *Professional Golfer* magazine. "I'm flattered that they picked me." Determined to live up to his billing, he arrived at Augusta National a week early to put in extra practice. The Masters would be his 13th tournament of the year, and feeling superstitious, he requested to be registered as player number 13.

A perennial scenario at the Masters, it seems, is that following the first round the spotlight shines on a long shot who's leading the tournament. Almost inevitably, the long shot returns to anonymity 24 hours later. At the 1960 championship, though, no underdog appeared. And among the top golfers of the day, only Gene Littler, the tour's lone five-time winner in 1959, and Cary Middlecoff, the 1955 champion, missed the cut.

Palmer birdied the first two holes of the tournament, shot a brilliant opening-round 67, and burst into a two-stroke lead.

Ken Venturi's quite different tour of Augusta, however, commanded equal attention. After shooting a flawless front nine of 31 and appearing full of backbone and spirit, he three-putted the 11th, double-bogeyed the 12th, and wilted precipitously. The parallels between his incoming 42 and his disastrous final nine in 1956 were uncanny. Few expected Venturi to be able to put back the pieces the next day, but he brought home a brave 69, stopping the muttering that he couldn't hack it under pressure and winning all-around admiration.

Only one man shot a lower score in round two: Ben Hogan. The Hawk, having opened with a mediocre 73, was delighted by his play, particularly on Augusta's glassy putting surfaces. "This was quite an event for me," he said of his 68. "I didn't three-putt a green!" Palmer held on to the lead by one stroke over Hogan and Dow Finsterwald despite shooting a disappointing one-over-par 73.

Finsterwald would have led by one were it not for a penalty he received—the first retroactive penalty in golf history so far as anyone knew. As he was preparing to take a practice putt during the round, his playing partner, Billy Casper, shouted at him to stop, that he would incur a two-stroke penalty. Finsterwald then recalled that he had taken a practice putt on a green the day before and immediately informed the officials. Disqualification was not out of the question, he knew, because, unaware of the two-stroke penalty, he had turned in an incorrect score. Upon completing his round, a 70—remarkable under the circumstances—he learned that he was being assessed a two-stroke penalty; his first-round 69 was now a 71, but he was still very much alive.

On day three the magic left Hogan's putter and continued to ignore Palmer's. Three times Ben missed putts of less than three feet, and he could only explain it in a curious yet somehow apt visualization of his battle with the yips. "Every time I stand over the ball I feel like the hole is filled with my corpuscles," he said. Despite near paralysis on the greens, he went around in even-par 72, thanks to strong tee-to-green play. Ben Hogan, in his prime, hit a beautiful controlled fade (a slight left-to-right turn in the ball's flight) off the tee, but this year he had adopted a slight draw (right-to-left movement on the ball) to maximize his driving distance on the long Augusta National course and it was working; he was walloping the ball far down the fairways.

Hogan remained one stroke behind Palmer, who shot a 72, too, no thanks to his own putting. "I've putted like Joe Schmokes two days in a row," he said. Meanwhile, four others joined Hogan at one behind the leader: Finsterwald (71-70-72), Julius Boros (71-72-70), Billy Casper (71-71-71), and Ken Venturi (73-69-71). Next, three shots behind Palmer, was Gary Player (72-71-72), a 24-year-old South African who had won the British Open in 1959. Even by Masters standards, the final round promised to be a dramatic one.

In 1960 the typical four-day PGA tournament averaged 25,000 in attendance. The Masters has never announced attendance figures, but the turnout the first three days of 1960 was huge—swelling from about 20,000 on Thursday, to 25,000 on Friday, to 35,000 on Saturday. The final round brought out some 40,000 spectators.

Hogan attracted perhaps the largest gallery, but no group was more boisterous than the one that accompanied the game's current darling, Arnold Palmer. The sports editor of the *Augusta* (Georgia) *Chronicle*, Johnny Hendrix, impressed by the sight of the multitudes tromping happily alongside their hero, dubbed them "Arnie's Army." In contrast, Hogan's followers were a reverent congregation worshiping at the master's feet.

Despite the adulation, a tired Hogan dropped out of contention in the final round, shooting a disappointing 76. Again, he hit greens in regulation, one after the other, but again his putting let him down. The prevailing opinion afterward was that if he could somehow improve his putting, even minimally, in the next couple of months, he would have a real chance for his longed-for fifth U.S. Open title. Casper, Boros, and Player faded with scores of 74, 75, and 74 respectively. And so the 1960 Masters had come down to three players—Finsterwald and Venturi, who were paired, and Palmer, who was playing an hour behind them with Casper.

The Finsterwald-Venturi twosome became, in effect, a scintillating match-play contest. On the first nine, Ken won the 2nd, 3rd, and 6th holes with birdies; Dow took back two of the holes with birdies of his own on 7 and 8. Neither player went over par on any hole. Palmer, meanwhile, had birdied the 1st hole but bogeyed two of the next four and lost his lead; a birdie at least brought him back to even-par 36. The to-and-fro Finsterwald-Venturi battle continued throughout the back nine, and the golfers arrived at the 18th tee, fittingly, all even. Dow landed in a bunker and missed a difficult eight-foot sidehill putt to save par. Ken parred the hole and finished at two-under-par 70 for the day and five-under-par 283 for the tournament.

As Palmer headed up the 11th fairway he received a lift from an unexpected source. In the corner of a scoreboard reserved for messages, the kids handling the job had posted lettering that read:

GO ARNIE
ARNIE'S ARMY

Coming to the 13th hole, he stood one stroke behind Venturi, but he had two good birdie chances coming up—the par-five 13th and 15th holes. To his chagrin, more disgust, he parred them both. Furious with himself after a poor chip at 15, he brusquely tossed his wedge to his caddie, Nathaniel "Ironman" Avery. Ironman, his caddie when he won in 1958, glared at Arnold and his scowl had a bracing effect. The exchange, Palmer told *Life* magazine, reminded him of the time when, as a teenager, he threw a club over a tree in a tournament and Pap warned him, "If you ever do that again I'll take your clubs away and you'll never play golf again."

Whatever, Palmer's way was really all uphill now. The last three holes at Augusta National are poor birdie prospects, particularly on the last day of the Masters. On number 16, a par three over water, Palmer put his three-iron tee shot on the green but 25 feet below the hole. Because of the slope of the green he couldn't even see the hole from where his ball lay.

Determined not to leave the uphill putt short, he decided to leave in the flag (an option no longer allowed today). His putt was too strong, but it ricocheted off the pin and came to rest two feet away. Had the pin been removed, the ball might have dropped, though most spectators agreed that it probably would have bounded out and finished well beyond the hole. In any event, Palmer putted out for his par. On to 17.

"Well, I've got to make two birdies," he told an official matter-of-factly, as though playing for a tie hadn't dawned on him yet.

Meanwhile, Venturi was being fitted with a green jacket and being briefed about the televised presentation ceremony. Along with Jack Nicklaus, who tied for low amateur of the championship, he was following events on television.

Arnold now hit a good drive at the 400-yard 17th hole, but his eight-iron pulled up 30 feet short of the hole, which was cut in the back of the green. The ball actually had much the same line as the three-footer he had missed there the year before. Two times he took his stance to putt, then backed away, distracted by spectators moving behind the green. A third time he huddled over the ball in his peculiar knock-kneed, pigeon-toed stance. This time he struck the ball firmly up the slight incline. It rolled right at the hole, reached the lip, hesitated momentarily, and fell into the cup. Palmer jumped into the air, ecstatic. The crowd exploded in cheers that went on and on. Venturi sensed a sickening fate at work and tried to prepare himself for the worst.

The Masters was tied with one hole left.

As spectators from the 17th hole ran to the 18th, desperate for any kind of view, others hurried back down from the elevated 18th green until both sides of the fairway were densely packed. The 420-yard hole, uphill much of the way, was playing into the wind. A par would be a very good score under the circumstances.

Standing on the 18th tee, Palmer set out to make par. He hit a strong, well-positioned drive and selected a six-iron for his 150-yard approach shot. As he prepared to hit the toughest shot of his career, he thought of his father's long-standing advice: "Just take it back slow and it will come off. Slow and deliberate."

Arnold hit a punch shot to keep the ball low into the wind. It landed two feet right of the pin and spun back six feet left of the hole. After reaching the green he had a moment to compose himself. As Casper putted out, he sat on the grass beside the green, staring moodily at the ground. Presently he got up, and as he lined up the putt he tried to catch a few breaths of fresh air, as though he were enjoying a pleasant day in the country, he said later.

This time he didn't deliberate. He aimed just outside the left edge of the hole, stroked the ball, and watched as it curled into the cup. Palmer retrieved it calmly and then, as though he suddenly realized what he'd done, started leaping in the air. Venturi had turned away from the television screen, but he heard the crowd's roar and staggered to a nearby room where his friend and instructor Byron Nelson waited.

IN THE WEEKS THAT followed the 1960 Masters, Arnold Palmer was celebrated across the land as the latest in a line of authentic sports heroes, with the likes of Babe Ruth, Jack Dempsey, and Bobby Jones. He was fawned over by the nation's power elite and idolized by its workingmen. The little boy who cried "Watch me! Watch me!" on his dad's golf course had grown up and gotten his wish. He commanded everyone's attention now, and he relished the spotlight.

The game of golf finally seemed to have found a candidate sufficiently talented and dramatic to succeed Hogan and Snead. Instantly Palmer came to be regarded as the sole heir to the throne. Fans and newspapermen, giddy that the long-awaited prince was so appealing, predicted unimaginable achievements for him as a champion, and soon the cocksure golfer announced equally fantastic goals for himself.

Arnold Palmer knew as well as anyone that if he were going to succeed Hogan, he would have to capture the championship of Vardon and Ouimet, of Hagen and Jones, of Nelson and Hogan—the United States Open.

The Open was and had to be his number one goal.

CHAPTER 2

In 1960 the United States Open was the preeminent golf championship in the world. The British Open, the oldest, was still considered the most significant by most of the major golfing nations—Scotland, England, Ireland, Australia, New Zealand, and South Africa—but it had been eclipsed.

Despite the advent of transatlantic air travel, few American golfers even entered the Open Championship. Whatever prestige might accrue to the winner wasn't sufficient to override the paltry prize money offered, most American pros believed. And many held the same parochial view as Sam Snead, the winner of the first post-war British Open: "Anytime you leave the U.S.A., you're just camping out."

Besides, the United States, the largest golfing nation with the richest professional tournament circuit, was home to the best players in the world and had been for more than a generation. Each year more of the world's finest golfers by far played in the U.S. Open than in the British Open—or any other championship, for that matter.

Of course, it wasn't always that way.

*   *   *

IN 1895, WHEN THE first U.S. Open golf championship was held, the British Open was already 35 years old. Golf had been played in Scotland for more than 400 years, and the first organized golf club, the Honourable Company of Edinburgh Golfers, was 151 years old.

In America, golf was first played in South Carolina in the 1780s, but the game really didn't take root for another century, when the earliest golf clubs were founded. The first permanent club was organized in Yonkers, New York, in 1888. It was named St. Andrew's, in homage to the Scottish golfing mecca thought of as the birthplace of golf. (For some reason the New York club added an apostrophe to its name.)

Only 11 golfers entered the inaugural American Open championship—ten professionals and one amateur. Few natives, other than the members of the clubs at which the pros were employed, had the slightest interest in the fact that Horace Rawlins, a 21-year-old Englishman who was an assistant pro at the host Newport (Rhode Island) Golf Club, had become the first U.S. Open champion. In fact, the 36-hole tournament—four times around the nine-hole course all in the same day—was essentially an afterthought. The main event in Newport was the first U.S. Amateur championship, and that had been completed the day before.

Amateur golf, played by the very well-to-do, was the only brand of golf that mattered at the time. So subservient were the professionals—and so insignificant was the National Open in its infancy—that when the 1901 Open ended in a tie on Saturday, the 18-hole play-off had to be postponed until Monday. The reason? Sunday play at the host Myopia Hunt Club, in South Hamilton, Massachusetts, was reserved for club members. Even in 1929, in the prime of Bobby Jones's career, the members of Winged Foot, in Mamaroneck, New York, kept open the East Course for play while the Open was conducted on the West Course.

The professionals who played in the early U.S. Opens were, plain and simple, hired hands. Most were Scottish or English immigrants who came to America to design and maintain the wealthy's new golf courses, make and repair their golf clubs, and teach them how to play. Sometimes they became their employers' show horses in money matches against other clubs' professionals. Even as entrants in the National Open, they were excluded from the clubs' dining and locker rooms. Such second-class treatment continued for years.

The U.S. Open attracted scant attention until 1900, when the greatest player in the world, Englishman Harry Vardon, entered the tournament. So did a second member of the "Great Triumvirate" then dominating the game, J. H. Taylor (James Braid was the missing member of the British trio). Vardon made the long journey not for the American tournament, however; he was already in the States playing a long series of exhibition matches to promote the Spalding Sporting Goods Company's new Vardon Flyer golf ball. Likewise, Taylor had crossed the Atlantic on business.

The championship, which by then was played over 72 holes in two days, was won by the masterful Vardon. His only competition was Taylor, who finished two strokes back in second place. In third place, American David Bell finished a distant nine shots behind the victor.

Watching Vardon in the Open and on his tour was an eye-opening experience for America's golfers—perhaps a bit demoralizing, too—so far advanced was his swing, his control of his fairway woods, and his shaping of shots. As the new century dawned the chasm separating the finest British golfer and the top American golfers could not have been more apparent.

Not until the 1911 Open did a native American, John McDermott, win the title, and he repeated in 1912. But it was the fairy-tale victory in 1913 of American amateur Francis Ouimet over British champions Vardon and Ray that first animated the public about golf and attracted widespread attention to the championship.

The U.S. Open, however, was still, by British standards, a minor event, and Harry Vardon and Ted Ray were entered only because they were in the States on an exhibition tour. It was Vardon's first trip to America since 1900; he hadn't bothered to defend his title in 1901, but nobody expected him to.

Vardon, 43, and Ray, 36, boasted a combined total of six British Open titles. Ouimet, a 20-year-old gardener's son from Brookline, Massachusetts, had little more to show for himself than a victory in that year's state amateur championship. A salesman in a Wright and Ditson sporting goods store, he would not even have competed—and he actually lived right across the street from that year's Open course, The Country Club—if his boss hadn't brought it up.

Francis knew and loved that golf course, one of the first and finest to be built in the country. As a boy, he cut across it on the way to and from school. When he was still too young to join his older brother, Wilfred, as a caddie there, he searched for lost balls, and when he had collected a sizable number the boys took them to a store where they could exchange them for a golf club. Francis studied the swings of the fine golfers who came there for tournaments, and later he would run home, pick up his club, and try to mimic what he saw.

Ouimet caddied at The Country Club from age 11 to 16, and at 20 he could still identify with youngsters wanting to do the same thing. So, before the Open, when the caddie he had lined up abandoned him for a famous player, he let himself be coaxed by a ten-year-old playing hooky into hiring him. The small, feisty boy was named Eddie Lowery.

Vardon and Ray finished the tournament tied for the lead and watched as first one contender, then another, fell short of the score they posted. One was a brash, 21-year-old assistant pro from Rochester, New York, named Walter Hagen. Although he was a U.S. Open rookie, when he arrived in Brookline he introduced himself to defending champion John McDermott and stated, "I'm here to help you boys take care of Vardon and Ray." And he almost did, too, finishing tied for fourth, three strokes back. One year later, having declined a professional baseball contract, he became the Open champion, launching a brilliant golf career that allowed him to cultivate the dashing style and formidable appetite for luxury that earned him the title "The Haig."

Ouimet came to the last four holes of the Open needing to shoot one under par to join the co-leaders in an 18-hole play-off the next day—not very promising considering the pressure of the moment, the rainy weather, and his mediocre six-over-par round. All the same, the local boy seemed to be the calmest person on the course. He parred 15 and 16, and at 17 his 12-foot birdie putt slammed into the back of the cup, popped straight up, and dove into the hole.

After a perfect drive on 18, his little caddie handed him an iron and instructed, "Keep your eye on the ball and hit it." Francis followed Eddie's directions, but his ball landed on soggy turf and stopped just short of the green. A nice chip left him with a four-foot putt, and without fuss he stepped up and canned it. The obscure Ouimet had earned a spot in the play-off! The spectators rushed forward and hoisted their hero on their shoulders, unconcerned about the long odds of the next day's battle.

Although the play-off was played in drizzly weather, a crowd that grew to 5,000 or more escorted the odd-looking threesome around The Country Club. Vardon, a gentle, stoic man with a neat little mustache, still had the most graceful swing in golf (the swing that is the model for modern players). At 5 feet $9^{1}/_{2}$ inches, 165 pounds, he had a medium build but unusually large hands and long fingers with which he popularized the overlapping grip.

If Vardon looked like Ouimet's kindly Uncle Harry, then

Ray was intimidating Uncle Ted. A bearish man of 6 feet 1 inch with a bushy, walruslike mustache, he smoked a pipe nonstop and wore a fedora on the course. He had an ugly swing—a swaying backswing followed by a lurching downswing—but he hit the ball a mile.

Then there was Ouimet. Slim, clean-cut, and modest, nephew Francis looked outmanned. But he knew the course, he knew his own game, and he was a surprisingly cool customer.

At the first tee, Francis led off. As might be expected, he was more than a little keyed up and was relieved not to dub his opening shot. But when he sank a three-foot putt to halve the hole with his opponents, he felt himself settle down. From there on out that September day he demonstrated his mettle.

After the front nine the three men were all square at 38. Ouimet edged ahead early on the home nine and, amazingly, it was Vardon who cracked first. At the 14th hole he hooked his tee shot into a troublesome lie—for Harry, a very uncharacteristic error. At 15, one stroke behind Ouimet, he smoked a cigarette, something he never did in a tournament. Ray, two behind Ouimet through 14 and frustrated with his play, double-bogeyed the 15th. That was that for him.

At the par-four 17th, still one shot behind Ouimet, Vardon decided to gamble on his tee shot. Trying to cut across the dogleg left to shorten his approach shot to the green, he hit another hook, landed in a fairway bunker, and took a bogey five. Ouimet reached the green in regulation and, 18 feet from the hole, chose to lag up to try for a safe two-putt. He stroked the ball. The line looked good. It rolled in! Pandemonium. Suddenly his lead was three strokes.

Vardon, pressing, crumpled at the home hole with a double-bogey six; Ouimet parred. He'd done it! Francis Ouimet, hitting shots heard round the golfing world, had pulled off a courageous upset. He finished in 72 strokes to Vardon's 77 and Ray's 78. It was the most amazing day in the brief history of the U.S. Open and of golf in America, and it changed the game forever.

The David and Goliath story of the ex-caddie defeating Britain's renowned duo in an 18-hole play-off sparked a riot of enthusiasm for the game in America. No longer could golf be identified as exclusively a rich man's game. In the next ten years the country's golfing ranks expanded from 350,000 to 2 million.

The 1913 Open also hinted that the wide lead in talent that British golfers had always held over their American counterparts was closing. In the twenties that gap disappeared. In team competitions U.S. amateurs won the first Walker Cup match in 1922 and the next eight repetitions; their professional brothers won the inaugural Ryder Cup match in 1927 and eight of the next ten biennial matches. As for the British Open, the finest American amateur, Bobby Jones, and the finest professional, Walter Hagen, seized the title for themselves. Between 1922, when Hagen became the first native American victor, and 1930, they won the championship seven times. These two hugely talented golfers and their vivid personalities helped make golf a national pastime.

Bobby, a man endowed with equal parts warmth and intelligence, good looks and dignity, was beloved on both sides of the Atlantic. By the time he returned home from England in July 1930 to a ticker-tape parade up Broadway, the United States had overtaken Britain as a golfing power and more than 5,000 courses dotted the American landscape. Of course, he brought back with him the British Amateur and Open titles, and he pushed on that summer to capture the American half of the Grand Slam—first the Open at Interlachen in Minneapolis, Minnesota, and then, protected from his overly adoring gallery by a barrier of 50 Marines, the Amateur at Merion Cricket Club outside Philadelphia. In November, at age 28, he retired from competitive golf.

Jones, together with the earlier U.S. Open champions,

Vardon, Ouimet, and Hagen, cleared a passage from national indifference to international acclaim for golf in America. The United States Open, at last a bona fide major golf championship, was on the way to becoming *the* major golf title.

Now it was as though Sam Snead were trying to put the Arnold Palmer hysteria into proper perspective. A Sam Snead perspective. The week after the 1960 Masters the ageless Slammer won the 79th official tour event and the 105th professional tournament of his career. It was his seventh Greater Greensboro (North Carolina) Open victory. Twenty-two years earlier he had won the inaugural tournament.

In comparison, Palmer's Masters title brought his tour record to 18 wins. Although the younger man was the most prolific winner of his generation, understandably Sam wasn't quite ready to accept the notion that Arnold was destined to become the greatest golfer in history, as many enthusiasts were predicting.

The surprising aspect of Snead's victory was that nobody seemed in the slightest surprised by it; nobody made much of the fact that a 47-year-old had just won his second tournament in only three 1960 outings. Less than a year removed from his phenomenal 59 at the Greenbrier, Sam Snead was no longer capable of inspiring awe.

Sam's victory was extremely popular, but he left Greensboro's fervent golf fans with a rather bitter aftertaste. In accepting his winner's prize of $2,800 he told the startled spectators that the reason the top stars bypassed the tournament was that the Starmount Forest Country Club had barely improved since the thirties. (A different theory circulating was that certain players stayed away in protest, believing that Snead was receiving money to appear, which the tour prohibited; Sam denied it.) Afterward, the unrepentant Snead informed club president Edward Benjamin that his course was "lousy" and he ought to "get wise" and fix it up. A month later the club announced that Snead was banned from playing there in the future.

Although the legendary golfer had never ceased to be well loved since he emerged from the Virginia backwoods, the incident revealed a quality that those who knew him well were not exactly unfamiliar with. Sam could be a delightful performer, hamming it up for his gallery when he was winning or playing for the cameras or simply feeling cheerful; but don't approach him when he wasn't, many fans discovered.

When Sam suddenly went from having nothing to having plenty, he feared that people would take advantage of him, some of his friends observed, but others said the dollar seemed to hold an inordinate sway over him long after he ceased to need more money. (Hogan, too, was accused of greed by some when he was the game's biggest star.) Sam had long been a figure of fun on tour as the biggest tightwad around; so when Jimmy Demaret concocted a tale that he buried his money in tomato cans in his backyard, many people actually believed it.

By 1960 cash streamed in from multiple sources—the Wilson sporting goods company, television golf shows, golf exhibitions, Sam Snead School of Golf franchises, golf concessions at the Greenbrier and Boca Raton resorts, and fees that he charged amateurs to play with him. Prize money from tournaments was the only diminishing source of income—not because he could no longer win but because, after two decades as a full-time tour vagabond, he was playing in fewer and fewer tournaments.

Even in the weeks before the 1960 National Open, Snead stayed away from the tour. Most pros like to enter a tournament or two shortly before a major championship to sharpen their game under the pressure of competition, but Sam simply showed up at the Open site, Cherry Hills Country Club in Denver, Colorado, three days early for his practice rounds. For much of his first tour of the course he kidded with the fans; on the practice range, within earshot of a *Rocky Mountain News* reporter, he joked when a caddie shagging balls for him let one get through: "Looks like old Ted in left field." Sam and baseball great Ted Williams were pals and business partners who loved to rib one another.

In past years rigorous preparation had carried Snead ever so near the mountaintop without reaching it. Now, he decided, the time for such exceptional effort was over. He was playing it strictly low-key.

"I don't get excited about the Open anymore," he said a couple of weeks before the championship. "I've found out it's not a life-or-death matter. I figure I'll still get by if I never win it." In the weeks after taking his infamous eight on the final hole of the 1939 National Open, Snead's weight dropped 30 pounds to 151 and he feared a nervous breakdown was imminent. Now he insisted, "It hasn't become a psychological matter with me. It's not that important anymore."

Many, though, including former Open champion Ed Furgol, were skeptical about Snead's new mental attitude. "Winning the Open is 60 percent psychological for anybody in this field," he observed a couple days before the championship began. "But with Sam it has to be 90 percent psychological. That's because he wants to win it so bitterly."

One wouldn't have known it by looking at the Slammer, though. On Tuesday, June 14, two days before round one, Sam laughed at references to his infamous U.S. Open jinx. "I'm gonna stay loose for this one," he said. "No more nerves." All the same, he acknowledged, "Sure, this might be my last big chance," and he vowed to "really turn it loose."

On Wednesday, it appeared as though he didn't have a care in the world. At the Cherry Hills players' buffet, he cleaned off two servings of baked chicken and stuffed peppers, topped off the meal with gelatin, a lemon tart, and iced tea, and said casually, "I need to lose ten pounds. I'm 195 now without a sweater on. I'm carrying a lot of excess baggage."

Despite his dearth of tournament activity, the oddsmakers placed him among the favorites at 7–1, and a surprising number of his peers predicted he would finally drop whatever baggage from 1939 he secretly still might have been carrying.

ARNOLD PALMER'S LIFE CHANGED dramatically after his heroics at the Masters. Overnight he became not only the game's biggest star but the country's as well. He turned up everywhere in print and in person, yet he showed no sign of ever wearing out his welcome. Even those whose view of golf was equivalent to Winston Churchill's—that it was like chasing a quinine pill around a pasture—had to admit this guy was the genuine article.

But what made him so? Writers and broadcasters lavished hundreds of thousands of words on the topic. There was something so vital about him, the commentators all noted. He was passionate about excelling at his trade but without Hogan's grimness and need to separate himself from the world. He was an athlete, yes, but first he was a performer. Take him away from his audience, his Army, and he wasn't Arnie. Snead was a performer, too, but he lacked Palmer's warmth and immediacy. Hogan played for himself; spectators were irrelevant.

Indeed, Palmer possessed the ideal package of golfing and personal attributes to become the people's hero: he won often, he won coming from behind, he exuded an all-American appeal, and he expressed vividly and boyishly his great enthusiasm for the contest.

Arnold Palmer having a bad round was a crime; it was like Marlon Brando giving a flat performance. But even then, the golfer was captivating to watch, grimacing over his ineptitude, struggling with it, trying to ignite a spark, pleading with the powers that be to intervene, to let him be Arnold Palmer.

And when the spark caught and the first birdie flamed into a blaze of birdies, the excitement was palpable. All that mattered now was the next shot. He would rush to his ball, select the club needed for a bold shot, toss aside his cigarette, hike up his trousers a last couple times, plant those strong legs in his wide stance, peek up at the flag, and whale into that ball with a fury. In 1959 golf was still the proverbial humblin', never-to-be-tamed game. In 1960, with Palmer's emergence, it seemed as though it could be tamed after all.

After the Masters, Arnold took off two weeks during which he played only 27 holes of golf. He played the first 18 the day after his triumph, a round with President Dwight D. Eisenhower at Augusta National. "I hear you're a good putter," the President said in delightful understatement. Much of what they chatted about is unknown, but it seems likely that Cherry Hills Country Club would have come up; Ike was a member of long standing who loved the course, and Arnold had never played there. The two men took to each other immediately and started a friendship that was to grow over the years. The other nine holes Arnold played back home at Latrobe Country Club.

During the rest of his hiatus, golf took a back seat. Reporters from *Time*, the *Saturday Evening Post*, and *Life* descended on the Palmer household to do feature stories on America's new darling. Arnold also appeared on the *Perry Como* and *Masquerade Party* television programs and made cigarette commercials. When he returned to the tour at the end of April he nearly picked up where he left off. Birdieing two of the last four holes, he finished the 72-hole Houston, Texas, tournament tied for the lead with Bill Collins; the next day, however, he lost an 18-hole play-off by two strokes.

In the six tournaments that lay ahead before the Open, Arnold Palmer did an amazing thing—he went winless. At the Tournament of Champions, in the first week of May, he tied for fifth; the surprising Jerry Barber handily won his second event of the season. Julius Boros took the next tour stop, the Colonial National Invitation—a good omen for him, since in

8 of the past 12 years the Open champion had finished in the top five at Colonial; Palmer, in tying for 22nd, missed the top five for the first time since the Phoenix Open in February. Defending champion Ben Hogan hit more greens and made more birdies than the winner, but he was undone by his putting, as at the Masters, and ended up in eighth place.

Arnold took a breather the following week, during which two tournaments were held: the Sam Snead Festival, won by 26-year-old tour rookie Dave Marr, and the Hot Springs (Arkansas) Open, captured by the streaking Bill Collins. Palmer rejoined the tour the next week for the first "500" Festival Open in Indianapolis, Indiana, a tournament actually played during the Indianapolis 500 auto race on a course that included several holes *inside* the Speedway's oval track.* For the first time in some two years, Palmer missed the cut.

June arrived. It being Open month, with only two tour stops remaining before the championship, Ben Hogan re-emerged from Fort Worth. At this point in his career anytime he competed was special, and Tennessee's golf fans were thrilled that the Hawk had decided to enter the Memphis Open.

Right from the outset it was apparent that although this was only Hogan's third tour event of the year, long hours back home on the practice range had brought his game to championship fettle. With opening rounds of 66-66, he shared the lead. The next day he slumped to a 73, but luckily he fell only two strokes behind the leaders. In a final-round 68 he holed a clutch birdie putt on the 18th hole to finish tied at the top with Tommy Bolt and Gene Littler.

Although Ben found himself in another cursed play-off, at least it wasn't a sudden-death showdown as expected. Bolt

* Doug Ford, considered the fastest player on the tour, was a fitting winner (he was identified once as the one who always looked as though he was playing through the group he was with).

had learned while playing the 16th hole that his wife, Mary Lou, who had been ill since giving birth the previous November, had undergone surgery at a Memphis hospital. The officials decided to hold an 18-hole play-off the next day so that Tommy could visit her without delay. Happily, the operation was successful. As for the play-off, it was a thriller.

Bolt dominated play on the front nine, leading Littler by three strokes and Hogan by four and reminding golf fans that he was much more than just a club-throwing ogre. But then on the 12th hole Bolt's approach flew the green and he lost a stroke. Hogan sank an 18-foot eagle putt on the next hole, closing the gap to two strokes, and gained another shot at 14 when Tommy missed the green and bogeyed. Littler, with a long, silky, repeating swing that earned him the nickname "Gene the Machine," consistently reached the greens in regulation but couldn't buy a putt, and by now it was a two-way contest between Bolt and Hogan. The duo halved the 15th. At 16, Ben hit a great pitch and made his short birdie putt. The match was square.

It looked as though Ben might take command after his tee shot at the 186-yard 17th hole settled 20 feet from the pin. But Tommy, a brilliant and imaginative shotmaker in his own right, choked up on a two-iron and almost aced the hole. Ben missed his birdie bid; Tommy canned his, a seven-footer. When the Hawk's ten-foot birdie putt slid by the final play-off hole, the 42-year-old Bolt had his 14th career victory (his last had been the 1958 U.S. Open).

Bolt's ten-year playing career had been stained by one hotheaded fiasco after another, many of them triggering reprimands and fines and new rules from the PGA. His tantrums had earned him the interchangeable noms de guerre "Thunder" Bolt and "Terrible" Tommy Bolt. Then there was the more literary moniker, "The Terrible-Tempered Mister Bolt," coined by *Stars and Stripes* (and later *Washington Star*) reporter

Merrell Whittlesey while watching Tommy's antics in a GI tournament after the war.

By mid-1960, still on probation with the PGA, Tommy had kept his magisterial nose clean for two years. Now his win in Memphis reminded many close to the tour just how good he could be when he was on his game and when he controlled his temper. Over the years golf fans and writers had all but ignored Bolt, the topflight golfer. Though he had few peers among the post-war pros as a brilliant shotmaker with a sweet swing, he was treated as a sideshow figure—"Thunder Bolt, the marauding invader of the royal and ancient game." A clotheshorse with rich tastes and a flair for the bold—none of those muted Hogan blues and grays for him, he said—even his attire attracted more comment than his golf game.

In the fifties, other golfers erupted from time to time into a thoroughly embarrassing tantrum. Big George Bayer, for one, got so furious with himself at the 1957 Kentucky Derby Open that on one hole he chipped his ball all the way down the fairway with a seven-iron, took a score of 17, and collected a $200 penalty and 90-day probation from the PGA. But spectators joined Tommy's gallery solely to see whether he'd blow his top that day. Some tried to goad him into a tirade. "Throw it! Throw it!" they would yell after he missed a putt. From time to time he complied, and as a result Tommy Bolt anecdotes proliferated. Some of them were true.

It's a fact that he packed up in utter exasperation during the second round of the 1957 U.S. Open—and in many lesser tournaments. But did he really withdraw from the Houston Open one year because it was raining and the prize money wasn't enough to replace the fancy threads that were getting soaked? Did he really fling his putter 50 yards into the distance after *sinking* a sizable putt the day after the PGA instituted a 100-dollar fine for club-throwing? "I did it because it was my rule and I didn't want anybody else in the world to be the first one fined," he reportedly said later. And did he really bend over and break wind in the direction of a fan who was taunting him? Irascible, irreverent, and impossible; witty, entertaining, and generous—Tommy Bolt belonged to a line of larger-than-life sportsmen that included Walter Hagen and, later, Muhammed Ali.

Tommy also was one of the only pros who wasn't in the least intimidated by Ben Hogan. He even had the temerity to poke fun at Hogan. Perhaps as a result, and perhaps also because they shared the same hardscrabble childhood, Ben enjoyed Tommy's company as he did few others' on tour. With Tommy, Ben displayed a pleasing sense of humor. One time he and Tommy, playing at Colonial, bickered playfully over whether an approach required a four- or a five-iron. Bolt hit a five-iron 20 feet from the flag; Hogan then stepped up and put his four-iron closer.

"See, Tommy, it was a four," the Hawk said.

"But you hit it fat, Ben."

"Yes, but the shot called for a fat four," Hogan replied.

Although Tommy treated Hogan as just one of the boys, he idolized him as a golfer. "He's the only one I've ever been to for a golf lesson—in 1955," Bolt stated many years later. He had been hooking the ball, so Hogan adjusted his left hand, with lucrative results—wins that year in San Diego, Tucson, and St. Paul.

To Bolt, no golfer could touch Hogan, even at age 47. After his Memphis victory he said, "That Hogan is tough coming down the stretch. I don't like to play him at all." Then his thoughts shifted to the Hawk's ultimate goal. "The National Open is coming up and the little man is playing very well. I better get my money down on him."

Bolt had one of the more impressive recent Open records himself—a tie for seventh in 1952, a tie for sixth in 1954, a tie for third in 1955, and the championship in 1958. Following his bracing triumph, Tommy Bolt looked like a good bet himself.

*   *   *

As BOLT, HOGAN, AND Littler were battling one another in Memphis, Arnold Palmer was making the casual acquaintance of Cherry Hills Country Club. Having sat out the Memphis Open, Palmer flew unannounced from Pittsburgh to Denver early on Sunday, June 5. Several hours later he arrived at the club in a taxi and exchanged greetings with Mike Souchak, who was at work on the practice tee. The two, joined by club pro Ralph "Rip" Arnold and member Jim Stalder, soon made a jovial circuit of the course trailed by a small gallery.

At the 17th hole, a long par five with a small island green, Souchak (pronounced SOO-chak) goaded Palmer into going for the green in two. "You can make it, easy," Souchak said. "I'll try," a grinning Palmer replied, reaching for his three-wood. The shot looked good at first, but it splashed into the water and Souch burst into laughter. Afterward Palmer praised the course for its pristine condition, predicting that even though it would toughen up over the next ten days, a record score of 275 would be needed to win the Open. Hogan's 276 had stood up since he had won the 1948 championship at Riviera Country Club near Los Angeles.

Turning to his own chances, Palmer sounded guarded. "My game isn't as sharp as it was from January through April. I haven't been playing well lately, but then I usually taper off after the Masters. Now I feel like playing again. Only time will tell."

Later Palmer and Souchak, along with Rip Arnold, appeared at a local charity affair involving the news media, and they were a big hit providing a few golfing pointers.

The next day Palmer played a second practice round, then headed off to Oklahoma City to defend his 1959 title. Souchak flew to Lexington, Kentucky, for an exhibition, then continued on to Oklahoma. Both men would be back in Denver in less than a week.

CHAPTER 3

A RECORD 2,472 GOLFERS REGISTERED TO QUALIFY FOR THE 1960 U.S. Open, the U.S. Golf Association announced May 14. For almost all of them—golf professionals and amateurs with a handicap not exceeding two strokes—winning was out of the question. Simply qualifying for one of the places in the 150-man field was the supreme goal; doing so would be the accomplishment of a lifetime.

The first hurdle the hoi polloi faced was a one-day, 36-hole local qualifying tournament on May 23 or 24. Only 490 golfers would advance to the second stage, another 36-hole grind on June 6 or 7.

The USGA exempted a fortunate few from this dual survival course. Twenty-two golfers—by no means all the top players of the day—merely had to show up in Denver for the championship: the last five Open winners (in order from 1955—Jack Fleck, Cary Middlecoff, Dick Mayer, Tommy Bolt, and Billy Casper); the 1959 titleholders of the PGA (Bob Rosburg), U.S. Amateur (Jack Nicklaus), British Open (Gary Player), and British Amateur (Deane Beman) championships; the head professional at Cherry Hills (Rip Arnold); and the '59 Open's ten lowest scorers and those tied for tenth, excluding

JULIAN I. GRAUBART

the last five Open winners (Claude Harmon, Mike Souchak, Doug Ford, Arnold Palmer, Ernie Vossler, Ben Hogan, Sam Snead, Dick Knight, Dow Finsterwald, Fred Hawkins, Ted Kroll, and Gene Littler).

A broken elbow sidelined Mayer, the 1957 Open winner, leaving 21 passing directly into the championship and almost 2,500 competing for the remaining 129 openings. Forty-eight of the entrants received a partial pass. All former U.S. Open, U.S. Amateur, PGA, and British Open champions; the 1959 Ryder and Walker Cup team members; the 20 lowest scorers in the 1959 Open and PGA; and the top 20 money winners on the 1960 tour were excused from local qualifying; they advanced automatically to the second stage known as sectional qualifying.

In Denver, one of 56 sites nationwide hosting the local trial, a Cherry Hills member was the top qualifier in a field of 159. Amateur Claude Wright, a two-time Colorado amateur and four-time Denver city champion, shot a one-over-par 72 at Denver Country Club in the morning and then a four-under-par 68 at his home course in the afternoon.

Much to the chagrin of Joe Dey, the USGA's executive director, another Cherry Hills member, Harold "Potts" Berglund, had insisted on entering. Berglund was the Open's general chairman, the preoccupied commander of more than 1,000 paid and volunteer workers who were handling one aspect or another of the tournament. Although he missed the cut by two strokes, he shot the first hole in one of his life and it did him a world of good: "He slept well for the first time in a year," his wife reported. In all, 30 of the 159 golfers advanced to sectional qualifying.

Nationally, the major casualty of the first qualifying round was Jim Ferree, a tour regular. He fainted while playing in 90-degree heat and 75 percent humidity in Little Rock, Arkansas, and failed to finish. John Brodie, star quarterback of the San

Francisco 49ers and a struggling part-timer in his second year on the tour, also failed to advance.

Robert T. Jones III, the son of Bobby Jones, was a happier story. Stocky and blond like his famous father, the 32-year-old bottling executive from Pittsfield, Massachusetts, led qualifiers in Albany, New York, with rounds of 71 and 74. As a boy he had really thrown himself into the game, but winning the 1941 Atlanta City Junior Championship and a few club championships constituted the limits of his competitive success.

Like his father in his early tournament career, Bob III blew his stack when he was not playing well, but the younger Jones never mastered his short fuse as did the elder. In recent years he had qualified three times for the U.S. Amateur but each time had lost his first-round match. In the 1959 Amateur he had the misfortune to draw Jack Nicklaus and was trounced, 7 and 6. "I'm just a weekend golfer but I'd like to play in at least one Open," Jones said after clearing his first hurdle in Albany.

Sam Snead's old sidekick, Johnny Bulla, led the local qualifying field in Phoenix. Virtually retired from the tour, Johnny was living, and selling real estate, in the Arizona capital. Two weeks later, calling himself "the youngest 46-year-old golfer alive," he qualified for his 20th Open in style, repeating as the medalist (the player with the lowest qualifying score in a tournament) in the Denver sectional. Johnny just hung around the area for the next week waiting for the Open practice rounds to begin. "Haven't got anything to do back home," he said cheerfully. One stroke behind him was Jim English of nearby Littleton, Colorado, a former state champion and the low amateur in the 1959 U.S. Open. Claude Wright, the Cherry Hills member, finished in a tie for the final spot and birdied the first play-off hole to advance to the Open.

Because more and more golfers were trying to qualify for the Open each year, the USGA had introduced this two-tier qualifying system the year before. It had received a chorus of complaints, particularly from older tour members such as Ernest "Dutch" Harrison.

A year earlier Dutch had been the medalist in his local qualifying rounds, only to be eliminated in the sectional stage. This year, after repeating as the low qualifier in his local test, the colorful 50-year-old pro made it clear that he regarded having to play the initial rounds as beneath his dignity. "I don't see much reason for two qualifying trials, especially when I look at the list of players exempt from local qualifying," he said, adding, "I'd like to play some of those fellows for a living."

Some men hustled in dark, smoke-filled pool halls on the bad side of town; Dutch Harrison hustled under sunny skies, enjoying the fresh air at posh golf courses. Although he had won some 20 tour events stretching back to 1939, he was best known for his wagering and gamesmanship. According to Tommy Bolt, Dutch could have been another Hogan had he concentrated on his golf rather than on the daily double at the local track. More often than not, the native of Conway, Arkansas, came out on top, though on one memorable occasion, in 1937, predator became prey.

He and a pal were hanging around a course in California, waiting for the next pigeon to flutter within their grasp. Soon enough, a raw hatchling ambled over and asked if he could join them for a game. Hearing the youngster's country drawl, Dutch figured this one was money in the bank. Out on the course, every shot, every bet Dutch threw at the stranger, the kid matched or bettered.

After the round, as Harrison and his buddy were making an unexpected withdrawal from their wallets, the stranger said, "Sure do thank you fellers. Say, what time you gonna be here tomorrow?" Dutch replied, "Son, you work your side of the road; we'll work ours." Years later he would say, "That is how I met Sam Snead."

Since 1954 the "Arkansas Traveler," as he was called, had

been a club pro at Old Warson in St. Louis, Missouri, and only infrequently played the tour. This year, in sectional qualifying, he hung on for one of the six places available at St. Louis's grueling new Robert Trent Jones course, Bellerive. "They just want to make a fellow work hard," Dutch concluded.

No one worked harder to qualify for the '60 Open than Davis Love, Jr. (In a few years he and his wife, Penta, would bring into the world Davis Love, III, a golfing whiz who never would have to practice like his dad did.) On Memorial Day the index finger on his left hand was crushed by a car bumper, requiring a dozen stitches. A doctor who examined him told him he would not be able to play golf all summer. But the members of Mountain Ridge Country Club in West Caldwell, New Jersey, where Love was an assistant to pro Wes Ellis, contacted a specialist for a second opinion. Both Ellis and Love had passed the initial qualifying test. With one week remaining before the sectional round, club members were pulling hard for both men to make the Open.

Love, a nervous, intense man of 24, wanted badly to play in Denver. He used to live there, and that was where he first made a mark in golf, winning the Colorado State Junior Amateur title in 1953 and 1954. Afterward he headed off to the University of Texas, where he played on the golf team coached by a masterful teacher named Harvey Penick.

In 1958, now a pro, Love went out on the tour. Despite practicing hour after hour, sometimes until his hands bled, he failed to cause a ripple. After more than a year the best payday he had to show for his travails was 353 dollars at the 1959 Rubber City Open. By 1960 his golfing woes had taken a toll on him emotionally. Early in the year he confessed to Jim Gaquin, who covered the tour in the PGA's *Professional Golfer* magazine, "I freeze when I go to take the club back. I can't explain it." In April, Ellis, another Penick team alumnus and a two-time winner on the tour, began his club job at Mountain

Ridge, and Love accepted an offer to join him as an assistant pro.

The medical specialist the Mountain Ridge members contacted rebuilt Love's mangled finger and designed a splint that would immobilize it. This doctor did not prohibit Davis from playing but warned him not to use any club with which he normally would take a divot. So much for iron play. In order to continue his bid for the Open, Love exchanged his five-, six-, and seven-irons for corresponding woods, and practiced at scooping the ball off the fairway. Only nine fingers gripped the club; the tenth stuck straight out. He worked hardest on his putting, which he knew would have to be extra sharp to compensate for his physical limitations.

In the morning round of the sectional, held at the 1959 Open site, Winged Foot, Love shot a remarkable 75. Although the score placed him in the middle of the 81-man field, with only the top 21 scorers going on to Denver, it gave him a reasonable chance. Between rounds, his specialist and a nurse tightened the stitches in his finger.

Meanwhile, Wes Ellis's 68, capped by a 90-yard wedge that went into the last hole for an eagle two, made him the low scorer in the morning action, and he breezed home with a 71 to finish second among the qualifiers. Robert T. Jones III, however, wasn't nearly as sharp as he had been in Albany. It quickly became apparent to him that the 1960 National Open would not be the occasion to experience firsthand the championship his father had captured four times. Gene Sarazen, a contemporary of his dad's, had entered at Winged Foot, but the Squire was forced to withdraw because of an ear infection.

As for Love, somehow in his afternoon round he improved on his morning score. A 73 put him in a four-way tie for the 21st, and final, qualifying spot. Having already endured 36 holes with a throbbing finger and a bag full of unfamiliar clubs, he now had to face three men in a sudden-death playoff. One was Vic Ghezzi, winner of the 1941 PGA Championship at Cherry Hills. At the first extra hole, as the others failed to better par, Love canned his birdie putt. His diligence on the practice green—and his stubborn courage—finally was rewarded. Davis Love, Jr., was going to his first U.S. Open, and, man, did he ever earn it! The members of Mountain Ridge could not have been happier; two of their pros had qualified for the Open. But nobody was prouder than Davis Love, Sr., back home in Denver, when he received his son's call with the wonderful news.

THE LOW-HANDICAP AMATEURS and the club professionals who qualify for a U.S. Open have accomplished what thousands of golfers can only dream of. Back home they're the winners of their local, state, and regional championships. They are such highly skilled ball-strikers that their friends and family insist they could clean up on tour anytime. But, in truth, they couldn't.

Although an amateur or a club pro might fantasize about playing his best in the Open—the way he played that magical day at his home club when every approach shot covered the flag, every makeable putt fell—he'd have to repeat that memorable round three more times to stay within reach of the leaders. The chances of that are nil, particularly on the long, difficult courses selected for the U.S. Open, made harder still by the way the USGA sets them up.

Bill Ezinicki, the 36-year-old pro at Hillview Country Club in North Reading, Massachusetts, had enjoyed his share of great days in golf by the time he qualified for the 1960 Open. He won the New England PGA in 1956 and 1958, the New Hampshire Open in 1958, and the Rhode Island Open in 1958 and 1959. When he tried his hand on the PGA tour for a few winters earlier in the fifties, however, the highlights were few—top-ten finishes at New Orleans, Baton Rouge, and Phoenix—and the prize money sparse.

But, then, Ezinicki had gotten a late start. Born in Winnipeg, Manitoba, he first loved hockey, and in 1944 he reached the pinnacle of Canada's premier sport, the National Hockey League. Though a soft-spoken gentleman on the golf course, he was a terror on ice with the Toronto Maple Leafs. "He was the kind of player you could immediately despise with a passion," recalled Dick Haskell, executive director of the Massachusetts Golf Association and a Boston Bruins season ticket holder in the 1940s.

When "Wild Bill" Ezinicki skated out on the ice, legs bulging with tape he wore like armor, bodies started flying. The 5-foot 9-inch, 170-pound right wing led the NHL in penalty minutes two seasons running, 1948–49 and 1949–50. But he was far more than just a hatchet man.

In the second game of the 1947 Stanley Cup final against the Montreal Canadiens, Toronto coach Hap Day assigned him the job of shadowing the legendary right wing Maurice "Rocket" Richard. After one collision too many, the familiar "Rocket's red glare" exploded into rage. He chopped Ezinicki over the head with his hockey stick and got himself suspended for the next game. The Maple Leafs went on to win the final and, with Ezinicki continuing to attract more than his share of opponents' attention, retained possession of the Stanley Cup for the next two years as well.

Despite his NHL success, Ezzie couldn't wait for the off-season, when he would spend his hockey earnings traveling to amateur golf tournaments from one end of Canada to the other. A self-taught player, he improved steadily and became one of his country's finest amateurs. In the 1947 Canadian Amateur, then played at match play, he advanced all the way to the finals. He lost, but it took one of the best amateurs of the day, Frank Stranahan, to beat him. That year he qualified for his first U.S. Open.

By the time he retired from the NHL in 1955 he had become a golf professional. The father of three, he settled into the club pro's existence outside of Boston, where he had played part of his hockey career. "I love golf more than hockey," he said on the eve of the 1960 Open. "In golf, you have no coaches to set the pattern; you have to determine what you are going to do yourself." The championship would be Ezzie's fourth Open. He had yet to make the cut.

Bill Spiller, who qualified for the Open for the first time in 1960 at age 47, got an even later start in the game than Ezinicki. And being black, he faced many more obstacles along the way. Spiller was born in the rural town of Tishomingo, Oklahoma. He attended an all-black Texas college on a track scholarship, earned a degree in education, and entered teaching.

Unable to find a decent paying job at home, he moved to Los Angeles, where his mother lived. There he took a job as a redcap at the train station and started playing golf. Within a few years he had won all the black tournaments in southern California and was playing in events sponsored by the United Golf Association, the shoestring national black tour.

The white tour was another matter. A clause in the PGA of America's constitution, adopted in 1916, limited member-ship to Caucasians only. Before 1948 the only tour events from which blacks were not excluded were the Los Angeles Open, World Championship of Golf, Western Open, and U.S. Open. But because blacks were unwelcome even in men's clubs at public courses, they were hampered in obtaining the official handicap needed to enter their country's national championship.

What happened after the 1948 L.A. Open prompted Spiller, a proud, intelligent man, to fight back. He and Ted Rhodes, the finest black golfer, both finished the tournament in the top 60, which at the time guaranteed entry into the next tour event. The sponsor nonetheless refused them a spot in the field, so they sued the PGA for $250,000 for denying them the right to work in their chosen field.

Subsequently they dropped the suit when the PGA's attorney promised their lawyer that they'd be allowed to play on the tour. Little changed, though. Sponsors of open tournaments (competitions that both amateurs and professionals may enter) who wanted to bar black golfers like Spiller, Rhodes, and Charlie Sifford simply renamed their events "invitationals."

In 1953, after Spiller threatened to sue the PGA again, the organization amended its constitution to allow sponsors to invite any golfer to play in their tournament. That year Spiller, now age 40, played in ten tour events. It was a start but no more. He still could not become a PGA member, so even a job in a pro shop was out of reach; and he still could not get a PGA player's card, so he was dependent on invitations to play the tour. In his sporadic appearances on tour, his best finish was a 21st place in the Labatts Open in Montreal, Quebec.

In 1960, while caddying for a friend of California Attorney General Stanley Mosk, Spiller was encouraged to write to the elected official. He did, and after an investigation had confirmed the tour's virtual lockout of black golfers, Mosk told the PGA point-blank: If you want to hold another tournament in the state of California you won't discriminate against entrants based on race.

In May, beyond his prime but still game, Spiller made the cut in the local qualifying round for the 1960 U.S. Open. Then, in the sectional round, played June 7 in Napa, California, he survived the cut by the barest of margins. With only 10 of the 36 entrants earning an Open berth, he finished in a five-way tie for the last four spots. A sudden-death play-off was held, and on the first hole San Francisco's Ed Castagnetto double-bogeyed.

Less than a week later, Bill Spiller was practicing at Cherry Hills Country Club in Denver. Described in Denver's *Rocky Mountain News* as an unattached (meaning he had no club affiliation) Negro golfer from Los Angeles, Spiller was asked his prediction about the Open. The winning score will be a 278, and the winner undoubtedly will be Bill Spiller, he replied. After many long years of anonymity and exclusion, that he was feeling somewhat feisty was surely understandable.

If qualifying for the 1960 U.S. Open was a signal achievement for apprentice Love and journeymen Ezinicki and Spiller, it was little more than a formality for the day's established touring pros. Compared with Spiller, for example, Jerry Barber breezed through the Napa sectional, coming home in third place behind Eric Monti and Ken Venturi. But watching him after he completed play, you'd never have known it. In fact, he looked as menacing as a bespectacled 5-foot 5-inch, 135-pound man of 44 can look.

Trying to expedite play, USGA officials had sent out twosomes at six-minute intervals, which Barber felt was rushed. The golfer mastered his irritation until he came off the course in the afternoon, but then he made a beeline at two officials, Bob Hanna and Ray Fisher.

"What do you think we are, race horses?" he said, as spectators eavesdropped and *San Francisco Chronicle* reporter Joe Wilmot scribbled away. "You'd think we were dancers at the Paladium," he went on. "First we're whirled around the dance floor and then whacked on the bottom and told to get off. You guys did a poor job running this affair." Hanna and Fisher, dignified in their conservative USGA outfits, stared uncomfortably into the distance until the storm had passed.

The episode received no national coverage, even though Little Jerry Barber, as he was called in the press, was the 1960 tour's biggest surprise. (Years later, the American media would have turned the incident, and the antagonists, into a cause célèbre.) Before 1960 he had won only twice in 13 seasons as a part-timer, the last time in 1954. But in the first five months of the current season he had already won two tournaments and taken second place in two others.

The day in which Barber lectured the USGA officials belonged to another qualifier, Art Wall. At the Oklahoma City sectional he shot a sensational 65-63—128—to lead 34 qualifiers. Wall had missed nine weeks of the season because of illness, and having returned less than a month earlier, he was hoping mainly to continue to sharpen his game and work himself into shape. Instead he turned in a score three strokes better than any previous qualifying total of which the USGA had record and set a new Twin Hills Country Club course record. "I've been making progress the last few weeks, but nothing like this," he said, shaking his head in amazement. He needed only 44 putts over the 36 holes.

A gentle, self-effacing man, Art was a bit embarrassed about all the attention he had received since capturing the 1959 Masters and PGA Player of the Year award. Before 1959, he still was virtually unknown to the casual fan even though he had won seven tournaments during his ten years as a professional. He'd also achieved a certain notoriety because he used the highly uncommon baseball bat grip (Bob Rosburg was the only other well-known pro who shunned the standard overlapping or interlocking grip) and he had an uncanny knack for manufacturing holes in one—34 at last count. Just a week before his Masters victory, en route to winning the Azalea Open, the PGA's Jim Gaquin overheard one spectator comment to another, "Say, isn't that Art Wall over there?" "No," the companion replied. "That's his brother, Finster Wall."

Two days after dominating the 1960 Oklahoma City sectional, Art entered the city's annual PGA tour event, the final tune-up before the U.S. Open. By tournament's end there could be no doubt that he had returned to top form. He finished in second place, and the winner, Gene Littler, needed a birdie on each of the last three holes to beat him by a stroke. Littler, one of the Memphis play-off participants the week before, and Wall immediately joined Arnold Palmer as the favorites at Cherry Hills.

Opinions about Littler were strangely contradictory. On the one hand he was recognized as one of the top young players of his generation, with the wins, the swing, and the putting stroke to support this appraisal. On the other hand he was treated as a failure, because he hadn't yet won even one of the many major professional championships predicted for him. Earlier in the season he told Gaquin, "It's funny, but a lot of people seem to feel sorry for me. Last year was my best year, but I'm still getting sympathy. People pat me on the shoulder and say, 'Don't worry, Gene, you'll get going before long.' " All he had done was win five tournaments, the most on the 1959 tour!

Palmer played his best golf in weeks. He shot three rounds in the 60s and finished in third place, two strokes behind Littler. After an opening round of 68, he vowed he would not shoot a higher score the rest of the tournament—a remark he rued later, fearing it had come across as boastful. Mike Souchak came home in fifth place, his second strong finish in a month.

Because of the timing of the Oklahoma City tour event, the Open sectional qualifier there boasted the largest contingent of touring pros. Advancing along with Wall were several foursomes of established and emerging stars, including Lloyd Mangrum, Julius Boros, George Bayer, Jay and Lionel Hebert, Doug Sanders, Paul Harney, Bob Goalby, Dave Marr, Bruce Crampton, and Mason Rudolph.

Four-time British Open champion Peter Thomson and tour pros Don January, Gardner Dickinson, Tommy Jacobs, and Bill Collins all failed to qualify. Collins's misfortune was just one more demonstration of the game's fickleness—playing the best golf of his life, the 32-year-old former Marine had won two of the past six tournaments. A bigger casualty was 1956 Masters and PGA champion Jack Burke, Jr., who fell on the first hole in a six-man play-off. And yet far more surprising than either Collins or Burke was Bob Verwey, a 19-year-old South African. He *survived* that six-way shoot-out.

The youngest player on the tour, Verwey appeared to be on borrowed time when he stumbled into the play-off with a double-bogey on the 36th hole. But then, on the third extra hole, he landed his approach shot two feet from the cup, insuring an Open spot. Escaping from precarious situations was getting to be old hat for Bob, a happy-go-lucky lad. Two weeks earlier, in his local qualifying round in Richmond, Virginia, he had survived a three-way play-off for the last qualifying spot by holing a 20-foot birdie putt.

Verwey was one of a half-dozen South African golfers who had made the long journey to the States that season to try their luck on the American tour, and he was not the only kid. Bryan Roelofsz and Retief Waltman were contemporaries, and Gary Player, a fellow Johannesburg native with three years of tour experience, was only 24.

Bob first met Gary when he was ten years old. Gary had phoned the Verwey residence to speak with Bob's older sister, Vivienne. Bob hung up on him, as he did all her suitors. He soon discovered that it would take far more than a prank to discourage Gary Player.

Gary's mother had died of cancer in 1943, when he was eight years old, leaving Harry Player, a gold-mine foreman, to provide and care for Gary and his older sister, Wilma; an older brother, Ian, was off fighting in the war in Italy. Harry was a disciplined, resolute fellow who refused to complain about his lot. His son Gary acquired these traits, which later would serve him so well as a golfer. The father, a low-handicap golfer, bought his son a set of clubs and took him out on a course when he was 15. The boy parred the first three holes and, despite suffering a sudden reversal of fortune, made up his mind to master the game.

Gary would transport his clubs from the family's working-class neighborhood in the Johannesburg suburb of Booysens to the Virginia Park course just outside the city. There the dark, intense young man caught the eye of the club pro, Jock Verwey, Bob's father, and the pretty, petite Vivienne. The two Verwey kids and Gary became friendly and played a good deal of golf together. In 16 months Gary was a scratch golfer, meaning he could par every hole.

After Gary completed his schooling, the senior Verwey put him to work as his assistant, gave him lessons, and took him into his home. Bob and Gary ended up rooming together for three years. Often, as the boys lay awake in bed, Gary would talk about his golfing dreams, how he was going to be the greatest golfer in the world, and Bob believed.

"He was my idol at the time," Verwey recalled. "I didn't ever not think he was going to do it. He wanted to be a champion golfer more than anything in the world."

Player worked furiously on his game eight hours a day. He also began an exercise regimen that burned off body fat and sculpted his physique into near-classic proportions. Confident and impatient, at 17 he suddenly turned pro although he had not yet even won an amateur tournament.

Two years later, with money his father had borrowed, Gary left South Africa for England to pursue his life's mission. Player hardly set the British golf world afire, but he did manage to meet expenses, a solid accomplishment considering the day's anemic tournament purses. The next year, 1956, he returned to Britain, won the first significant tournament of his career, the Dunlop, and finished fourth in the British Open.

When he defeated Bobby Locke, South Africa's greatest golfer, in a special 108-hole match in 1957, people at home were certain they'd discovered the next international star. More impartial observers, however, were dubious. What they saw seemed more like a flash in the pan. Player had a faulty grip, an overly wide stance, and an ugly, flat swing, the club wrapping around his neck at the top of the take-away fol-

61

lowed by a lunge into the ball to produce maximum distance. That he was winning at all was baffling—unless you watched carefully. The newcomer chipped and putted masterfully.

Player first came to America in March of 1957 in search of stouter competition and better prize money. After all, he had another mouth to feed—that of his bride, Vivienne Verwey. Although the 21-year-old golfer already was a seasoned world traveler, New York City was more than he had bargained for. There alone, in a hotel room 30 stories up, he felt overwhelmed. "I called my wife and said she'd have to come over. I couldn't handle all of this alone," he remembers. That season he played in 11 tournaments and won $4,300—not much, certainly, but compared with what he would have earned in Britain for the same record, not bad, either.

When he returned to the U.S. tour in 1958, not only was he better prepared emotionally, but he was much improved technically. Back home he had overhauled his swing so that he looked like a different golfer. Now employing a mainstream upright swing and a narrower stance, Player was set to go. In April he won his first American tour event, the Kentucky Derby Open, in Louisville; in May he extended Sam Snead to five play-off holes before bowing in the Greenbrier Invitational; and in June he finished second to Tommy Bolt at the U.S. Open. Between the spring and the fall, when he left for Australia, he entered 16 tournaments and finished in the top ten 11 times.

Only his driving—his auto driving, that is—wobbled during the year. After Player won in Louisville, he drove the car of fellow pro Paul Harney to the next tournament, the Lafayette (Louisiana) Open. He barely made it, according to Jim Gaquin in *Professional Golfer*. Along the way, Gary drove on the wrong side of the road, he used his shoelaces to tie down windshield wipers that were flapping away uncontrollably, he got stuck in the mud, and he saw his golf career flash before his eyes when the car hood popped up while he was on the road. Finally, a suspicious police officer stopped him. "Officer, I'm not drunk," he protested, his appealing South African accent helping his case. "I just don't know what I'm doing."

Player's U.S. record in 1959 was spottier, with only two top-ten showings: a tie for seventh in the Masters and for second in Memphis. Nonetheless, he believed firmly that he now had the game to win the championship of greatest significance to his countrymen, the title that Bobby Locke had captured four times, the British Open.

After his first two rounds at Muirfield, Scotland, a 75 and a 71, his faith seemed questionable. He languished eight shots out of the lead, and nobody was picking him to be the one who would hoist the claret jug after the championship's 36-hole conclusion—other, that is, than Player himself. That night, dead serious, he told a couple of close friends that he would win. The next day he shot rounds of 70 and 68 and became, at 23, the youngest man to claim the Open Championship since Young Tom Morris in 1868.

Meanwhile, as Player started to make it internationally, Bob Verwey, his young friend—and now his brother-in-law—was home in Johannesburg grooming himself to follow in his idol's footsteps. Bob certainly did not have Gary's austere work ethic on the practice range but he loved the game, he had it in his blood, and he showed considerable promise.

In 1958, at age 17, Verwey qualified as an amateur for his first British Open. Soon he turned pro, and in the first professional tournament he entered in South Africa he finished second. In early 1960, as the growing Player family—Gary, Vivienne, and one-year-old Jennifer—prepared to catch up with the American golf tour, Bob decided to join them.

In April, not long after arriving, he finished in the money for the first time at the Greater New Orleans Open. Purely by coincidence, Verwey played the last round with Player and compatriot Harold Henning, leading Gary to quip, "I came all the way from Johannesburg, South Africa, to get away from these blokes, and here they are playing with me." At the moment the American tour must have seemed like Xanadu, especially to Bob Verwey, a teenager who had just won 775 dollars. In early June, buoyed by passing his Open qualifying exams, he tied for sixth place in the Oklahoma City Open and departed for the National Open with a fresh 1,300-dollar stake.

Player performed considerably better on the American tour in the spring of 1960 than he had in the 1959 season but not well enough to win. He tied for 6th place in the Masters, finished 5th the next week at Greensboro, tied for 9th in New Orleans, tied for 4th in Houston, tied for 11th at Colonial, came in 7th at the Sam Snead Festival, tied for 11th at the Indianapolis 500 event, and tied for 17th at Memphis (but only five strokes behind winner Bolt).

As his fellow pros headed down to Oklahoma City for the Open sectional qualifier and the city's tour event, Gary drove with his wife and infant daughter the more than 1,000 miles to Denver. Player was one golfer who would not need to get acclimated to hitting a golf ball at the city's mile-high elevation; Johannesburg lies 6,000 feet above sea level. But hungry for his second major championship, he was anxious to get out on Cherry Hills. With the Open still nine days away, he became the first exempt player to arrive.

Jay Hebert, a tour regular who almost never sat out a tournament, also skipped Oklahoma City for some extra preparation in Denver. He needed rest as much as practice, he noted, having played in 14 consecutive events. A week before the Open, he drilled irons off Cherry Hills's practice tee as Player and Johnny Bulla, alone among the name golfers, practiced out on the course.

CHAPTER 4

The 1959 GOLF SEASON THAT JACK NICKLAUS CONSUMMATED WITH HIS stirring U.S. Amateur victory over Charlie Coe was hard to believe. The young man had played in 30 matches and won 29 of them, capturing the North and South Amateur, the Trans-Mississippi Amateur, and the Grand Challenge Cup at Sandwich, England, along the way. Only the British Amateur, in which he lost in the quarterfinals, eluded him.

In the autumn of 1959, with nothing left to conquer, the 19-year-old returned to the college student's life as an Ohio State University junior—studying to become a pharmacist like his dad, cheering on his beloved Buckeyes football team, and quaffing Blatz beer at the rathskeller with his Phi Gamma Delta fraternity brothers. He may have been the National Amateur champion, but his frat mates called him Blob-o and named him chairman of a hallowed observance known as "Hell Week."

A few days after his 20th birthday in January of 1960, accompanied by his father, he traveled to New York City as one of the guests of honor at the National Golf Awards dinner. There he had the opportunity to chat with two of the country's most celebrated amateur golfers: Bobby Jones, the greatest in history, and Vice President Richard Nixon, surely one of the worst. As described by Ray Cave in a *Sports Illustrated* profile later that year, Jack was excited but not starstruck. While talking with the vice president, he called across the Plaza Hotel banquet room, "Hey, Dad! Come here! I want you to meet Dick Nixon."

Back in Columbus, with spring still two months away, he headed over to Scioto Country Club to start to prepare for the coming golf season. Shielded somewhat from the winter's cold by a crude hut, he blasted shot after shot onto the snow-covered practice range.

Jack played well in the spring of 1960 but was little noticed outside the narrow worlds of amateur and college golf. In March he and his Walker Cup teammate, Deane Beman, won the International Men's Four-Ball title in Hollywood, Florida. At the Masters the next month, as Palmer became the pro tour's supernova, Nicklaus quietly shared low-amateur honors with Billy Joe Patton; 11 strokes back, he finished tied for 14th place. Bobby Jones said he exhibited "the finest potential of any young player in years."

A brief college golf season concluded in late May with Jack finishing second in the Big Ten conference championship, two strokes behind Purdue University's John Konsek. The season had been fun but beside the point for Nicklaus. He was looking ahead to the U.S. Open. Two weeks later, during practice rounds at Cherry Hills, he suddenly commanded national attention.

Even allowing for added carry in Denver's thin air, Nicklaus's club selection on the 7,004-yard course was incredible. He played almost all the par-four holes with a wood and a wedge or nine-iron, including the uphill, 430-yard 9th hole. On the 548-yard, par-five 17th hole, which everyone laid up on in two, he cleared the moat fronting the green with his second shot, a seven-iron. "Look at that," his pal Beman said, shaking his head. "Multiply that advantage by four or five

times a round, which would be 16 to 20 times in a tournament, and you see what an advantage he has over most of us."
And nowhere was that superiority in length more noticeable
than when displayed alongside the 5-foot 7-inch, 140-pound
Beman, an uncommonly short hitter.

Tour star Jay Hebert was equally dazzled. "I just saw the
best round of driving in my life," he said after playing companion Nicklaus shot a 66 the Saturday before the Open. After
completing another nine holes, though, Jack had mixed feelings. "Missed putt after putt," he said, his seven birdies in 27
holes notwithstanding. "But I was hitting the ball better than I
have all year."

Beman, who played a half-dozen practice rounds with
him at Cherry Hills (leading some writers to refer, quite
ineptly, to the inseparable duo as Snow White—Nicklaus's
Walker Cup nickname—and his Little Bitty Buddy), concurred. "It's a sin for anybody to be playing as good as Jack,"
Beman said. "He could win it."

Even with Nicklaus's studious, extremely thorough on-
course preparation, he squeezed in some fun in the days leading up to the Open. Jack let the ham in him come out on the
practice tee for the delectation of onlookers investigating his
vaunted power. Fellow collegian Konsek, a serious young man
headed for medical school, observed his friendly rival knocking balls over the fence on the fly. "Sure, Jackie'll turn it on
now and then to wow the people," he told Bill Searby of *Newsday,* a Long Island, New York, newspaper. "But that's only part
of it. He has all the shots. He sure could [win the Open]."

As for the small, crew-cutted Beman, he was desperate to
make it into Open Saturday. In his first appearance in the
British Amateur, in 1959, he became the youngest, at age 21,
ever to win the venerable championship. Now appearing in his
fifth U.S. Open, he had yet to survive the cut.

Ken Venturi, playing the course that Saturday for the first
time, holed his wedge to the opening green for an eagle and

67

proceeded to shoot a 31 going out. "That shot came a week too early," he said, grinning.

BEN HOGAN DID NOT show up for his tee time at Cherry Hills on Thursday, June 9. Admittedly worn out from five rounds of golf at the Memphis Open, culminating in the Monday play-off, he postponed his arrival a day. "It was hot and I was wringing wet after every round," he explained to the Denver newsmen. Still, with six days remaining before the Open, he was among the earliest to settle in at Denver for the duration.

On Friday, he played his first practice round, joined by Jay Hebert and Cherry Hills officials Potts Berglund and Joe Dyer. Hogan started out indifferently, but on the home nine, chipping and putting beautifully, he made four birdies. He had no illusions about his one-under-par 70, however. "Today doesn't make much difference," he remarked to *Rocky Mountain News* sports editor Chet Nelson, strolling from the final green. (Shrewd players like Hogan don't worry about scoring well in practice rounds; they sometimes intentionally shoot away from the flag to familiarize themselves with expected difficult pin placements.)

Having casually sampled the course, Hogan turned to business as he entered Rip Arnold's golf shop. "Rip, I want to play a couple of rounds all by myself," he said. After tee times were set up and Hogan had departed, Arnold said, smiling, "He's getting ready. I picked him months ago and I'm sticking with my pick." To Arnold, Cherry Hills was a "placement course." The golfer who could position his tee shots where he'd be presented with the best approach to the green would have a decided edge, and that golfer was Hogan, he believed.

The next day's Denver newspapers played up Hogan's appraisal of the course as too easy for a National Open. It was in immaculate condition, the Hawk noted, but the fairways were unusually wide and the rough so short it hardly punished a bad tee shot at all. The players were going to embarrass the USGA with their low scores, he predicted. Two-time Open champion Cary Middlecoff wasn't buying it. "Hogan's using that old psychology again," he said with a smirk. "I've seen that headline before at other Opens."

For years Hogan had been accused of trying to influence the USGA to toughen the Open course to the point where only he and a few top players could hope to score well on it. Probably the most brutally difficult course in Open history was Oakland Hills Country Club in 1951, and Ben seized the championship at the Birmingham, Michigan, layout with the greatest round of his life, a three-under-par 67 (only one other round in the entire tournament was under par, a 69 by runner-up Clayton Heafner). But the "Monster," as the course was called, was more than even he bargained for, and at the trophy presentation he said, with an edge to his voice, "I'm glad I brought this course—this monster—to its knees."

In Denver, Ben might very well have been trying to psyche the USGA officials, but he was not the only player to characterize Cherry Hills as not difficult enough for the Open. The USGA's Joe Dey, expecting the usual chorus of complaints, was tickled. "A player actually came up to me today after he'd played a practice round over an Open course and complained that he thought it played too easy," he told *Newsday*'s Searby. "What a switch!"

Dave Marr, a veteran of three Opens, predicted the scoring record would fall, an observation that was supported by many entrants' practice rounds. Frank Stranahan, a monomaniacal golfer and fitness devotee who tapped into his family's Champion Spark Plugs fortune to enter tournaments around the world, posted a 66. Doug Sanders one-putted 11 greens and shot a 67; Palmer powered to a 67; and Venturi turned in a 68, as did Finsterwald despite a heavy head cold. Others were also belittling the test of golf that the course posed—a strange phenomenon, because contestants perennially criticize Open courses as "tricked up"—that is, made extremely onerous by the way the USGA sets them up.

The typical refrain is twofold—first, that the rough is so high and the landing areas so narrow you don't dare use the game's main weapon, the driver, on your tee shots; and second, that the putting greens are so hard and fast and the pin placements so difficult that it's impossible to hold approach shots and foolhardy to aim for the flag from the fairway or to take a run at the hole from the green. In a word, Open courses reward the conservative, prudent golfer, the critics complain.

To this refrain, the USGA responds with its own: Open courses don't embarrass champions, they reveal them. Golfers worthy of the national championship must be able to drive the ball accurately, land it on greens in regulation, and putt it true, the organization counters.

So each year it selects one of the country's finest golf courses—one that requires competitors to use all 14 clubs in their bag, to execute a variety of skilled shots, and to make strategic choices from among difficult options—and its officials prepare the course with certain uniform features that enforce these values. Putting greens are made unnervingly fast, the primary rough stands about five inches high, and fairways average only 30 yards in width. Anticipating an upcoming Open one year, Gene Sarazen said, "The fairways are so narrow the player and his caddie will have to walk them Indian file."

At the Open, if a player mishits a shot he almost certainly will pay by losing a stroke. If he tries to avoid the consequences of the error, disaster can strike suddenly, testing composure to the limit. For example, all but the strongest men who drive into the rough on a par-four hole will be unable to advance their second shot all the way to the green. If they try to do so without success, they may land in a patch of rough protecting the greens that the USGA cultivates to penalize a scrambling style of play. And even if they reach the green on the fly, they won't be able to stop the ball there because the deeper the rough, the harder to apply backspin—particularly on a putting surface so hard that ball marks are a rarity.

So most Open contestants punch their ball safely back onto the fairway, content to reach the green in three. No time to relax there, however. If they go after that par putt even a touch too firmly and miss the hole, they may need two more putts coming back. Then, muttering to themselves, they arrive at the next hole, a par five, let's say, and wonder, Should I use my driver and go for the green in two or should I play cautiously with a three-wood?

Under the intense pressure of the U.S. Open, this scene plays out regularly. It's the same exasperating experience amateur golfers face every weekend—one error begetting another. The difference, though, is that on an Open course a single-digit handicapper would be hard-pressed to break 100, never mind 90.

Even seasoned professionals are unlikely to avoid stretches of purple play, unless, like Hogan, they hit virtually all their tee shots in the fairway and all their approach shots on the green. That's the Open in a nutshell—fairways and greens. And for almost everyone who ever played in the national championship, that was more than challenge enough. When a golfer wins the U.S. Open, he knows that he has excelled in his profession's supreme trial.

Which was why Jerry Barber dismissed assessments of Cherry Hills as being exceptionally soft. "They haven't changed the size of the cup, have they? It's still $4^1/_4$ inches in diameter and this is the U.S. Open." Jay Hebert shared Barber's historical perspective. Predicting a four-under-par 280 would win the title, he said, "Find me somebody who wants to bet on 275 and we'll go to the bank right now. This is the U.S. Open, don't forget."

Hogan in his prime defied the Open's harsh conditions. In

the second round of the 1954 Open he told Bill Campbell, the fine amateur with whom he was paired, that he had prepared so exhaustively for the championship that the tournament was an anticlimax. There at the 16th hole of Baltusrol Golf Club's Lower Course, in Springfield, New Jersey, he uttered the strange words, "I am bored."

In 1960, on the Monday before the Cherry Hills Open, boredom was a luxury he no longer enjoyed. For one thing, he couldn't shake a headache he had had since arriving, the result, most likely, of the mile-high elevation. The club was providing oxygen for the contestants, and 38 of them, including Hogan, were taking 12 to 14 liters a day.

A bigger problem for Hogan, though, was his putting. He shot another practice round of 70 but his putting teetered. So he did what you'd expect of a golfer so fussy that he actually measured new golf balls before using them to insure that they were perfectly round: he took the offending club in to the equipment repair shop. Middlecoff, an occasional Martini drinker with Hogan, was there to straighten his own two-iron, which was bent in transit to Denver. He watched for a while as the Hawk filed down the head of his putter, then asked, in mock concern, "Gosh, Ben, are you hitting them that bad?"

Hogan didn't take Middlecoff's bait, but later he was too proud to let pass doubts that were circulating about his stamina. "If I make the cut for the final 36 holes and then don't play well, I won't blame the distance," he said. "Never in my life when tournament rules required the playing of 36 holes in one day have I failed to play the second round in a lower score than I made on the first 18." Actually, there were a few notable exceptions, including two of his four Open victories, 1948 (he went 68-69 the last day) and 1950 (72-74). But his message was clear: if I am in contention on Saturday, watch out!

The day before the Open, accompanied by Claude Harmon, Hogan took the unusual step of practicing on another golf course. The two veterans traveled to nearby Columbine

Country Club, away from all the hubbub. They still had some serious work to do, but they knew all they needed to know about Cherry Hills.

BY TUESDAY MORNING, PREDICTIONS of low, perhaps record, scoring in the championship had subsided as the greens firmed up and Cherry Hills's clumpy bluegrass rough thickened. "I can hear it coming up through the ground," Ken Venturi cracked to Dan Jenkins, sports editor of the *Fort Worth Press*. Some of the tour's big boxing fans, like Snead, turned instead to predicting the winner of the upcoming heavyweight championship bout. Most picked Sweden's Ingemar Johansson to flatten Floyd Patterson and retain his crown in their rematch at New York's Polo Grounds. (Just the opposite happened.)

Under the mounting tension, players no longer were complaining about overly spacious fairways; somehow, the fairways didn't seem so wide anymore. Indeed, as Dey confirmed, they actually ranged between a snug 28 and 35 yards—namely, they were typical U.S. Open dimensions. The exception was the 18th fairway, which was 45 yards wide. Yet, because it tilted toward a large pond, it actually played as though it were much narrower. What all the fairways had in common was that they were immaculate, velvety carpets. (They were so pristine that one contestant reportedly said he felt guilty about taking a divot.) In the absence of rainfall, tee shots ran and ran, placing a premium on control.

A second feature that made the course play tougher than it first appeared was its putting greens. In the style of America's older golf courses, the greens were small and sloping, with subtle, hard-to-read breaks. Unless tee shots were very well positioned and approach shots high enough to hold the firm greens, short birdie putts would be few. And how makeable those short ones would be would not become apparent until the player reached the green and surveyed the USGA's pin placement for the round.

And, third, while the opening holes were easy compared with what the contestants had faced at the previous two Open sites, Southern Hills and Winged Foot, Cherry Hills's home stretch compensated for them to a large extent in their difficulty. The course's main weakness was that its front nine, at only 3,316 yards long, was simply too short. Because of the extra distance the ball traveled in the rarified mountain air, the five par-fours in the first seven holes could be reached with a driver or fairway wood and a short iron (for some players, just a nine-iron or wedge).

This stretch of short, benign holes gave hope to second-echelon players to shoot a low score, and it expanded the usual number of contestants who had a legitimate chance to win the Open. But starting with the 233-yard, par-three 8th hole, having lulled golfers with its nonthreatening invitation to shoot for birdies, the course abruptly withdrew its gracious hospitality. As a whole, then, although Cherry Hills did not provide quite as stiff a confrontation as some other classic Open courses, it did provide a challenge worthy of the championship.

The entire 150-man field had checked in before the Tuesday 8:00 A.M. deadline, with four exceptions: three obscure alternates named to replace golfers who had withdrawn from the tournament and one Thomas B. Bolt, delayed, reportedly, by bad weather. When he arrived later in the day, rather than being contrite about his tardiness, he was irritable. Almost before he pulled up to the course, he complained that he had a bad cold, his hands were swollen, and Denver's elevation made him queasy. Nonetheless, he managed to get a practice round under his belt without incident.

As he was changing his shoes, *Newark* (New Jersey) *Evening News* correspondent Des Sullivan reported that someone called over the locker, "Going to play your usual jolly game here, Tommy?" "Nobody ever won a tournament being jolly," he growled. Midway through his practice round the next day, Bolt fired his caddie.

Relations hit the skids, said Don "Fuzzy" Seyfried, a 46-year-old veteran caddie from Los Angeles, at the 3rd hole. "After leaving number 2 green, I handed him the ball and his driver and took a little shortcut to get a bit down the 3rd fairway. After he'd hit and caught up he raised cain about me not walking with him." Later in the nine, Bolt started to lag way behind the other players. "He just acted funny," Seyfried said. At the turn, Bolt severed their 27-hole-long relationship. "This is the first time I've been fired by a pro," Fuzzy stated.

At lunch, Bolt said, "My hands are swollen. My head is swollen. I think it's the altitude." A doctor was summoned and Tommy received penicillin.

In the afternoon, winds blew at 30 to 40 miles per hour and dried out the course, making its par 71 increasingly formidable. No rain had fallen since Sunday, and a repeat of dry, breezy weather was forecast for opening day. The USGA scrapped its plans to roll the greens, judging them to be fast enough. Lloyd Mangrum, the gruff 1946 Open champion with the riverboat gambler's mustache, concurred; he described them as "little spots of concrete."

Maybe Julius Boros, the player with a U.S. Open record in the 1950s that was second only to Hogan's, was right when he remarked a day earlier, "Weather will be the determining factor. If it rains and the course gets soft, the scores will be low. If not, I have a hunch 280 will be good enough." After a final nine-hole tune-up on Wednesday, Bob Rosburg reached the same conclusion with his own meteorological analysis. "A total of 280 should win," he told the *Toronto Daily Star*'s Gordon Campbell. "That's figuring on one windy day and a couple of good days. It's short, but it's a good course."

* * *

Back from Oklahoma City, the ubiquitous Arnold Palmer stopped off at the Cherry Hills transportation tent to pick up a courtesy car. "And what is your name, sir?" asked Mrs. Grant Hartman, soon recognizable as the tournament's most red-faced volunteer.

Just a couple days before the Open, Palmer, Ken Venturi, and Bob Rosburg seemed more interested in cutting up and ribbing one another in the contestants' lounge than in getting out on the course to practice. "Arnold Palmer eats ketchup," Rosburg intoned, referring to a new television commercial. "Now all the kids want it instead of ice cream." Asked by a reporter which of the three was going to win, Palmer answered, "Anybody can win here except Jerry Barber." Venturi, picking up on the straight line, said, "Yeah, not enough traps."

After going on like this for a while, they finally were ready to play a practice round—not that anyone had reserved a tee time. Ken said, "We'll horn in on somebody. It'll be okay. We've got Palmer with us." As they headed out, Bob said, smiling, "Maybe we can cut in front of Hogan."

Palmer was feeling much more bullish about his game than only a week earlier. He had led in Oklahoma City at the midway mark with rounds of 68 and 66, and despite a sloppy third round of 75 he finished only two strokes behind winner Littler thanks to a final-round 67. His come-from-behind bid for the title fell short, but it bolstered his confidence. On the day before the Open, Palmer played only nine holes at Cherry Hills. "If I don't know this course now, I never will," he said.

The increasingly familiar Palmer gameness shone off the course, too. The weekly edition of the *Saturday Evening Post* that coincided with the Open carried an article by the charismatic star (as told to Will Grimsley) bearing the unabashed title "I Want That Grand Slam." In it Palmer admitted that after his great start to the season, his sights were trained on winning each of the four major professional championships—maybe even in the same year. "The odds against it must be at least 1,000 to 1. Yet I feel confident that, with a little luck, it can be done. I want to be the man to do it."

As the bookmakers saw it, after the U.S. Open he'd be halfway there. Even though Palmer's career record in the Open was not spectacular—he'd registered two top-ten finishes in seven championships, including a fifth-place tie in 1959—they rated him the man to beat at 5–1 odds (up from 4–1 a couple days earlier). Hogan was alone at 6–1, and Finsterwald and Venturi joined Snead at 7–1. Wall, Boros, Littler, and Casper followed at 8–1, and Middlecoff was listed at 9–1.

Casper, the defending champion, sounded like a long shot when he confessed to the *Fort Worth Press*'s Jenkins a few days before the Open, "I haven't gotten fired up for a tournament since [the '59 Open]." Earlier in the week, when others were practicing diligently, Billy had gone fishing.

Also listed on Open eve, but at longer odds, were Jerry Barber, Gary Player, and several others having solid years on tour: Doug Sanders, who arrived in Denver with no wins but six top-five finishes; streaky, long-hitting Mike Souchak; and the mercurial Tommy Bolt. Bob Rosburg was placed in this group even though he had played infrequently in 1960 because of a hand injury and stomach disorder. One man the oddsmakers discounted was Jack Fleck, despite a position on the top-ten money list for the year.

Meanwhile, 33 members of the press contingent participated in a straw poll on the expected winner. Palmer received a plurality of nine votes, followed by Wall with eight, and Littler with five. Only one reporter, Merrell Whittlesey, chose Snead; no one picked Hogan. As for Jack Nicklaus, as impressively as he had played in practice, a favorite he wasn't—except in the eyes of the *New York Times*'s golf writer, Lincoln Werden, who picked the kid to win. As Nicklaus related in a

May 1994 *Golf* magazine interview, his father informed him that the odds on his winning were 35–1.

"Would you like to make a bet on that?" Charlie Nicklaus asked.

Jack replied, "You're damn right I would. I'll have 20 bucks of that."

"Do you want place or show?"

"Hell, no!" said Jack. "I want to win."

ON WEDNESDAY EVENING, JUNE 15, the last practice rounds concluded. Ready or not, 150 golfers had tee times to play the same 18 Cherry Hills Country Club holes the next day. Somehow though, the golf would feel, and be, completely different. "You may take it from me that there are two kinds of golf," Bobby Jones wrote in his 1927 autobiography, *Down the Fairway.* "There is golf and tournament golf, and they are not at all the same."

The tournament's field of 128 professionals and 22 amateurs could not have been more distinct, more intriguing. Represented were the Old Guard, with legends Sam Snead and Ben Hogan presiding; the electrifying Young Lions, starring Arnold Palmer and Ken Venturi; and the Forgotten Middles, featuring perennial Open contenders Julius Boros and Tommy Bolt.

Then there were the once all-but-forgotten Jack Fleck and Jerry Barber, whose dormant careers reawoke magically on the winter tour; the international contingent, headed by South Africa's Gary Player; and the most talked-about amateur in 30 years, Jack Nicklaus.

And finally, standing tall, were the Open's annual cast of overachievers—the Bill Ezinickis and Bill Spillers, the Davis Loves and Bob Verweys—who had survived two 36-hole qualifying rounds for the precious chance to test their mettle alongside the game's elite.

As the sun set behind the eastern slope of the Rocky Mountains and the evening's breeze grew chilly, a few players took their final swings on Cherry Hills's practice range. Others on the putting green superstitiously waited to hole several balls consecutively before calling it a day.

CHAPTER 5

It was 8:00 A.M., and Jack Koennecker had the honor of teeing off first in the 60th National Open. Though an unpleasantly early hour for some fun-loving pros, it wasn't for Koennecker. If he were back home at Twin Orchards Country Club in Prairie View, Illinois, he'd have been up for two hours already, orchestrating his club's busy golf program.

Early arrivals at Cherry Hills Country Club were rewarded with a heavenly summer morning, the air still and cool, the sky cloudless. From the club's elevated first tee Koennecker looked out over the quiet course, the snowcapped Rockies in the distance, and then his eyes settled on the first fairway. The hole provided just the kind of gentle welcome a nervous 45-year-old club pro might hope for. Only 346 yards away, and moderately downhill, lay the 1st green, a swale crossing its middle. A jagged line of poplars and pines bordered the left side of the fairway; Little Dry Creek, the right. The strategy was self-evident: keep your tee shot—a three-wood or long iron—in the fairway, leave yourself far enough from the green to produce good spin with a wedge, and hope to plant your ball within birdie distance of the hole.

What a moment this was for Koennecker! Although he

did not take up the game until age 26, he had qualified for the Open nine or ten times before. Yet this was only his second appearance because of his busy club schedule; the other came back in 1948, the year Hogan won his first Open. There was no way he was going to miss this one, though. As with Davis Love, Jr., the Open marked his homecoming. A former Colorado University baseball star and pro at Denver's City Park Golf Club, Koennecker last played in Denver in 1951 when he won the city's Metro tournament. His father and mother and a son and two small grandchildren lived in Denver. His gallery was small but fervent.

Koennecker planted a tee between two big red wooden tee markers shaped like cherries, and belying his nerves, he sent his tee shot 260 yards down the middle of the fairway, landed a wedge 18 inches from the hole, and tapped in for an easy birdie. Then his game, having just soared so effortlessly, immediately fell to earth. Koennecker had no choice now but to battle, one shot at a time, against being overwhelmed. Battle he did, but he still lost eight strokes to par the rest of the way and finished with a 78.

Young Bob Verwey went off at 8:32 A.M. along with tour pros George Bayer and Johnny Pott. The giant Bayer, who once drove past the flag on a 445-yard hole in Tucson, reached the 1st green with his tee shot and three-putted for par. Pott parred the hole more conventionally. Verwey drove short of the band of rough fronting the green, hit a wedge to ten feet, and canned his birdie. "That was the start to my first U.S. Open," he recalled many years later with a laugh. Verwey's first round, a 75, though a commendable showing for a 19-year-old rookie, would make qualifying for the championship's final two rounds a tall order.

Ed Furgol, the first former Open champion to tee off, contrived a surprising round of 71—surprising because he did it with wonderful putting. It was inept putting that had hastened the end of his playing career only three years after winning the

1954 Open, but in round one he needed only 23 putts, the fewest of the day. Even in his victorious Open he had averaged 35 putts a round. "If I putted like I did today I would have run away and hid from the field," he told the press afterward. Furgol now held a club job, at Pittsburgh's Westmoreland Country Club, in which he carried a grueling teaching schedule to supplement his income. But then Furgol's life—inside and outside the game—always had been hard.

Ed's parents, Polish immigrants, both worked in the cotton mill in the family's upstate New York home of New York Mills. When Ed was 11 he smashed his left elbow in a playground fall. The broken arm was never set properly—Furgol believed he received shoddy medical care because of his working-class pedigree—and the boy was left with an arm permanently bent at the elbow and withered above the joint.

The disability led to years of cruel remarks, and when he took up golf as a teenager it forced him to improvise a bizarre swing that prompted further ridicule of its own. At age 17 he left high school and found work as a metal polisher to contribute to the family finances. He played in his first tournament at 20, the city amateur in Utica, New York, and gradually built a respectable amateur record over the next seven years.

Ed turned pro in 1945 after winning the prestigious North and South Amateur tournament. Friends thought he was crazy. He and his bride, Helen, traveled 175,000 miles over the next three years, driving wherever a golf tournament offering prize money was on. He produced a solid record—a tie for first with George Fazio in the 1947 Bing Crosby tournament was 1 of 19 top-ten showings that year—but just breaking even in those days was a constant struggle. When his game soured and a high tournament finish seemed like a thing of the past he felt like a shadow in the presence of the other pros, he would say later. Furgol pushed himself harshly, and at one point the 6-foot 1-inch golfer saw his usual weight of 180 dip beneath 150.

Like Hogan, he ultimately endured ten long years of hurt, disappointment, and obscurity before finally winning his first tournament, the 1954 Phoenix Open. Later that season he reached the summit—becoming the U.S. Open champion. Sportswriters pronounced the victory one man's inspiring triumph over a physical handicap, and truly it was. With his struggles seemingly behind him, he told the *Saturday Evening Post* that September, "It's not the money that has brought me the greatest satisfaction. It's the feeling that I'm no longer a nobody. I belong."

His first round at the 1960 Open had him wondering whether he didn't still belong, even at age 43. He started his day at Cherry Hills dramatically, chipping in at the 1st hole for a birdie. From that point on, he one-putted 11 holes and two-putted all the rest. "Boy, if I could have putted [in 1957] like I putted today I'd still be playing regularly," he said. "And I missed a 15-incher on 16!"

Ted Kroll, who was grouped with Furgol, shot a sound 72. At almost 41 years old he was scaling back a successful playing career while holding a club position in Florida. He still entered 15 tournaments or so a year, and he almost always played well enough to earn a sizable check. Occasionally, as his recent fourth-place showing at Colonial demonstrated—he could still produce the kind of golf that made him the top money winner in 1956. That season Kroll won three tournaments, had his best-ever finish in the Open (a tie for fourth), reached the finals in the PGA Championship, and earned $72,835.

This startling amount, the record for single-season prize money—and the sum Palmer drew a bead on in 1960—was spurious since $50,000 of the total came from one tournament victory, George S. May's defunct "World Championship." None of his fellow pros begrudged him the distinction, though. Ted, wounded three times in the war and awarded the Purple Heart, didn't begin his playing career until 1948, when he was 29. (Similarly, Jay Hebert, wounded seriously at Iwo Jima, joined the tour at age 33.) His peers took to him immediately, and later he became one they sought when they needed a swing checkup.

When the first marquee group of the tournament—the 9:04 a.m. threesome of Gene Littler, Bob Rosburg, and Mike Souchak— completed their day's work some four hours later, the man everyone was talking about wasn't Littler, one of the favorites, or Rosburg, the 1959 Open runner-up who had attracted a fair amount of pretournament backing himself. It was Souchak, the barrel-chested, 33-year-old former college football player.

Souchak, using his driver judiciously and wielding a hot putter, took full advantage of Cherry Hills's exceptional birdie opportunities on the front nine. At 1, he holed an uphill 25-foot birdie putt from just off the back edge of the green and followed it with a 13-footer on number 2, a 12-footer on 6, and a 6-footer on 7, all for birdies. Souchak one-putted eight of the first nine holes and made the turn in four-under 31.

Hardly a word had been exchanged between the player and his assigned caddie, Babe Aranjo. But things were going so well that when he finally two-putted a green, Mike, an easygoing fellow, deadpanned, "I'm not putting very well today." At another point during the round, feeling relaxed, he struck up a conversation with *Cleveland Press* reporter Jack Clowser. "Say, do you ever see that little crippled boy named Mike who was trailing me around at the Carling Open last summer?" he inquired. Souchak had made eye contact with the boy, a polio survivor using crutches, at the 3rd hole and persuaded the marshals to allow the child to accompany him inside the gallery ropes the rest of the way. The husky golfer chatted with the small spectator during the round and called him Little Pal.

On Cherry Hills's back nine, Souchak's performance was less of an artistic success, yet his three best shots occurred there: the putt he was proudest of, a curling, downhill eight-footer that saved par on the 10th; a six-iron tee shot at the par-three 15th; and a pitch that covered the flag at the long 17th. He had to scramble on holes 11 through 14 and took his only two bogeys after hooking his tee shots at the 13th and 14th. He offset one of them at the 16th with a 20-foot birdie putt, but he squandered a 5- or 6-footer for birdie at 17.

Before the start of his round, Souchak had received from one of the reporters a copy of a Jesuit prayer for good luck. Now spotting the writer while striding up the 18th fairway, Mike took out his money clip and pointed to the prayer. "I've got it right here with me," he said, smiling. It seems to have worked. Although he finished the back nine in one-over 37, his round of 68 affirmed that all parts of his game were sharp.

Most encouraging of all for Souchak was his putting. He used only 26 strokes on the carpet, his best effort since the previous year's Ryder Cup series.

"I haven't putted well all year until today," he said afterward in the press tent, crediting a 30-minute lesson he received from Jack Burke, Jr., in Oklahoma City, with improving his putting mechanics. "I have the feeling that this time the whole game is together at one time." As his colleagues had witnessed from time to time in his six years on tour, when that happened, he could go off on a scoring rampage. In the 1956 St. Paul Open, Souchak birdied the last six holes to edge Jerry Barber by one shot. More amazing, Mike's first professional victory, the 1955 Texas Open, featured the most phenomenal scoring in tour history.

In the tournament's first round he shot a 60, tying the tour's existing 18-hole scoring record and setting a 9-hole record of 27. Souchak's amazing second nine started nicely with a birdie on the 10th hole, hinted of something special with an eagle three on the 13th, and concluded gloriously with five straight birdies. With subsequent rounds of 68, 64, and 65—the latter brought off in high winds and freezing temperatures—he set a 72-hole scoring record of 257. The tournament's runner-up, Freddie Haas, lagged seven strokes behind. Even on San Antonio's short, easy Brackenridge Park Golf Course, Souchak's performance was monumental.

One of ten children in a Berwick, Pennsylvania, family, Mike witnessed topflight football as well as golf close to home. His older brother Frank played football for the University of Pittsburgh and was skilled enough at golf to finish tied for ninth—the low amateur—in the 1953 U.S. Open. Mike pursued a similar path. Following a stint in the Navy he entered Duke University on a football scholarship and ultimately was named an all-conference tight end. He also made the school's golf team, which was coached by his football line coach. Mike roomed one year with Art Wall, a Duke golfer who was three years ahead of him.

After college, in the summer of 1952, Souchak went to work at Valley Forge Golf Club, outside Philadelphia, where the pro was a Duke teammate's father. Then, in April 1953, he got the break of his life: he was hired as an assistant pro to Claude Harmon at the Winged Foot Golf Club.

Harmon, the 1948 Masters champion, was renowned as a great teacher and role model for young golfers on the rise. Harmon's assistants always did well. Jack Burke, Jr., Dick Mayer, Shelly Mayfield, and, subsequently, Dave Marr numbered among the graduates of "Harmon University."

If having Harmon as mentor wasn't enough, Souchak also could turn to Tommy Armour, the Scottish golf champion of the twenties and thirties and one of the day's elite golf instructors in the United States. The "Silver Scot" was a Winged Foot member, and when he returned north in 1953 from his winter lair at Boca Raton, Florida, he took great interest in the new assistant pro. That summer, 26-year-old Souchak and 58-year-old Armour played golf together a couple of times a week on one or the other of A. W. Tillinghast's two incomparable Winged Foot courses. Soaking up the wisdom and style of Har-

mon and Armour at one of the country's golfing landmarks—
could an up-and-coming golfer even fantasize a better apprenticeship? "I had the best summer that anybody could ever
have," Souchak would comment many years later.

Mike entered several tournaments that year, finishing
once in the top ten. He resigned his post at Winged Foot to join
the 1954 tour full-time and flirted with victory twice before
finishing in second and third. Then in 1955 Souchak burst into
stardom. The week after his record-breaking Texas Open victory he picked up his second tour win at the Houston Open,
and right up until the Masters, six weeks later, he did not
shoot a single round above par. He tied for fourth at the Masters, tied for tenth at the U.S. Open, and took second in six
other tournaments.

When Souchak finished 1955 fourth on the money list,
and 25-year-old Gene Littler, a four-time winner, finished
fifth, golf fans wondered whether successors to Snead and Hogan had arrived. The two Young Lions—or "Trailer Kids," as
Gene Sarazen referred to the group of clean-cut, college-
educated pros who traveled the tour with their families by
trailer—became the first of their peer group to crack the top
ten. In 1956 Souchak had an even better season, capturing
four tournaments, the most wins on tour. A third golfer under
the age of 30, Dow Finsterwald, a lean Ohio University gradu-
ate, joined him and Littler in the top ten.

Surprisingly, Souchak's game headed south the next season. He produced 15 top-ten finishes but no victories. Then in
1958 he recorded one tour win, the St. Paul (Minnesota)
Open, but he finished in the top ten in only seven other tournaments. Now 31, an age when golfers expect to be in their
prime, Souchak was overtaken by the other Young Lions, who
were breaking through on tour one by one. Storming 1957's
top-ten money list were Dow Finsterwald (third place), Arnold
Palmer (fifth), Paul Harney (sixth), Billy Casper (ninth), and
Ken Venturi (tenth), each of whom was under age 30.

Souchak and Littler, who was suffering through his own slump in 1957 and 1958, dropped off the list. By the time they each finally regained their edge in 1959, they no longer were the leading candidates to become the game's next great players.

A stocky 5 feet 10 inches and 220 pounds, with the fore-arms of Popeye, Souchak's build in 1958 was more appropriate for the Southern Conference football season than for the PGA circuit. His broad shoulders and powerful arms helped him drive the ball farther than all tour players except Bayer (him-self a former football player—a tackle for the University of Washington), but his weight was becoming a problem. Ac-knowledging that he frequently felt tired, which led to less time on the practice range, he put himself on a strenuous diet early in 1959. In the season's first few months, Souchak fin-ished in the top ten in several tournaments; then in April, at a relatively svelte 199, he won the Tournament of Champions, leading all the way.

In June Souchak returned to Winged Foot for the U.S. Open, and he almost captured the first major title of his career. Needing a birdie three at the final hole to tie Billy Casper, he struck his second shot poorly and then chipped short of the hole with his third. He finished tied for third with his former boss, Claude Harmon, the host professional. Four weeks later he won the Western Open, overtaking Palmer, whom he trailed by five strokes after 54 holes, with a final-round 65. In mid-August, at the Motor City Open, it was Souchak against the field. Mike's margin of victory was a prodigious nine strokes. He was back now—*all* the way back—to where he was in 1956.

During his career, the rap against Souchak had been that he lacked ambition, that he wouldn't make the sacrifices needed to be the best. Indeed, every few weeks, whether he was winning or losing, he'd pack up and head home to be with his family. Though admirable, these reunions, many believed, flattened his rise on the tour. Following the Motor City triumph, perched atop the 1959 money list with three victories, he did it again.

Harmon phoned him at home in Durham, North Carolina, and urged him to get back out there, to feed off of his hot streak, but the call fell on deaf ears. Except for competing on the American Ryder Cup team, Mike stayed put at home with his wife, Nancy—the couple was expecting their third child—and not just for a week or two but for the rest of the year. His peers could not believe him. By season's end, he had slipped to sixth on the money list.

Despite the hiatus it looked as though 1960 would continue where 1959 had ended when Souchak won the San Diego Open in late January, closing with a five-under-par 67 for a tournament record 269. But his play over the next two months turned flabby, epitomized by a mediocre Masters (a tie for 16th place). Two strong outings in the five tournaments preceding the Open, however—a tie for fifth at Colonial and the fifth at Oklahoma City—gave him reason to hope that his game was shaping up.

After posting his 68 in the championship's first round, Mike noted that he had not forgotten his failure a year earlier to capitalize on the best opportunity he'd ever had to win the Open. Many times since he had replayed mentally the crucial holes at Winged Foot. "It's been a long year thinking about that. This time we throw the whole ball of wax at 'em."

To the press, he appeared more than merely hopeful; he sounded ready to take on the world. "They told me when I came here that this course wasn't built for long hitters like me," he said, his raspy, little-boy voice incongruous coming from such a burly man. "Well, let me tell you something: I was hitting them long, I was getting them close, and they were going in the cup. Give me a better formula."

It was a model that eluded one of his fellow competitors, Gene Littler. The hottest player on tour and one of its top three or four putters, the Machine was malfunctioning on the Cherry Hills greens. Souchak took nine fewer putts on the front nine than he did, Littler told reporters after shooting a woeful 76. At the 5th hole one of Littler's shots hit a fore-caddie and bounced into a creek, and at least twice during the round he used the wrong club. If a United Press International newspaper account is to be trusted, his round reached its comic depths far out on the back nine when a donkey in an adjacent field brayed while he was teeing off, leading him to yank his drive off line.

"Played terrible," he mumbled afterward. When the scribes pressed him for explanations he answered, "All I know is the winner won't have a 76 on his card." A gracious man with an impish sense of humor, Littler shrugged his shoulders, smiled, and said, "Well, back to the pit," and started off for the practice area.

The third member of the group, Bob Rosburg, a chunky, balding man who wore eyeglasses, looked like a high school teacher, not a professional athlete. But Rosburg was a lot tougher than he looked and a marvelous natural talent. When he was 15, he defeated Ty Cobb, the legendary baseball thug, 7 and 6 in the club championship at San Francisco's Olympic Club.

At Cherry Hills, the 33-year-old veteran with five career wins shot a one-over-par 72, despite finishing bogey-bogey. This was quite an accomplishment for a man who'd sat out much of the 1960 schedule because of a couple of ailments. But, having knocked the ball all over the yard, Rosburg, a free-speaker, didn't try to kid anyone; his score was much better than he deserved.

"Littler and I looked like we'd never played the game before," he stated. He attributed his creditable results to Cherry Hills's relatively soft conditions. "If we hit some of those wild shots we did today at Tulsa [Southern Hills] or Winged Foot we'd have been in the 80s," he said. At one point, he actually got to two under par, and it really irked him that he failed to turn in a low score on a day in which the course played so easily. Besides, only the day before he had curtailed his final Open preparations at nine holes following a razor-sharp 31.

Two groups back, Doug Sanders was rolling along at four under par after 15 holes. The handsome young Georgian in his fourth year on tour bogeyed the 16th, but after parring the 17th he needed only another par on the final hole to join Souchak as the early leader. The tee markers on the 18th hole were situated only some 20 feet from the hole's outstanding architectural feature, a large pond. The tee shot had to carry over the water at least 210 yards to reach the safety of the fairway on the other side.

Sanders set himself in the splay-legged stance that was his alone and began the take-away that also was his alone—so short, was the quip, he could swing in a phone booth. Just at that moment, a bass leaped out of the pond not more than 30 feet away and splashed noisily back in. Sanders discontinued his swing and set up again as the spectators, chuckling, watched the pond's agitated surface bubble where the fish had disappeared.

The golfer's concentration was gone now and presently so was his tee shot—hooked into the drink. He finished with a double-bogey six and came home with a disappointing 70. But Sanders, a reputed party man, accepted his fate good-naturedly and reveled in recounting the incident. "That fish looked like a whale," he said later in the locker room. "It made such a splash, I thought somebody was throwing old beer cans away."

Sanders's fish story marked only the first of several unusual occurrences at Cherry Hills's southeast corner, where the 17th hole's island green and the 18th tee huddle at one end of the pond. Sam Snead arrived at the 548-yard 17th hole one stroke over par. Lying two in the rough, he dug his ball out with a nine-iron and watched as it skipped across the moat fronting the green, rolled onto the green, and died some 12 feet from the flag. The Slammer capitalized on his good fortune and holed the putt for a birdie.

"It was the most amazing thing I've ever seen," said his fellow competitor, Gary Player. Amazing or just plain lucky, the shot kept Snead free of the double-bogey that might have prematurely dashed his hopes for the long-sought title. Of course, he then three-putted the 18th for a bogey and a 72, but it easily might have been a 75. Afterward he seemed in surprisingly good humor, though at one point a shard of sarcasm poked through. "How'd you find the course?" a writer asked. "From the looks of it, I *couldn't* find it," he answered. Although Sam had showboated for the crowd on the 1st hole, feigning terror over an easy wedge to the green, one thing seemed certain: regardless of what he said, this was not just another tournament for him.

At the 17th hole, as Snead and Player tried to break par for the day, a jittery Jack Ellis tried to avoid the ignominy of an 80. Ellis was one of the tournament's three alternates (he replaced two-time U.S. Amateur champion Charlie Coe, who withdrew at the 11th hour because of business demands). A former Oklahoma State golfer, he was treating himself to a year on tour before entering the ministry. The 22-year-old was as green as they come, with season's earnings that barely topped $200. Yet there he was, accompanying the golf legend and the defending British Open champion before a large gallery in the National Open.

Badly needing a birdie, he skied his tee shot (stroke number 1), sliced a four-wood into a fairway bunker (2), hit his ball out of the sand but into the rough (3), landed his next shot in the moat (4), lifted out (5), poked his ball back into the water (6), took another drop (7), reached the green (8), and two-putted (9 and 10). When the round mercifully ended, Ellis's scorecard added up to an 86. "I just choked," he said later, grinning.

As for Player, his prolonged acquaintance with Cherry Hills seemed to pay off. He turned in a confidence-building round of 70. Afterward, while enjoying a buffet meal in the club's main dining room with his wife, Vivienne, he rhapsodized over what it would mean for him to win the championship. "Do you realize that only eight players in history have won both the American and British Opens?" he asked Johnny Hendrix, of the *Augusta Chronicle*. "And it's been something like 40 years since a foreigner has won this tournament." On both scores, he was exactly right. Clearly, the South African still aimed to be the greatest golfer in the world.

Bob Verwey, who once lay awake listening to Gary's dreams, walked over to his brother-in-law's table. Although he had shot a 75, he, too, was upbeat. "If I qualify for the last 36 holes, I'm going out there and have myself quite a time Saturday," he vowed. "I'm just going to charge everything. If I get to play the 36 holes, I'll have won about $350."

"That's all he thinks about is money," Gary said with a grin.

A moment later Player glanced up at a closed-circuit television monitor in the dining room as Ben Hogan three-putted at the 9th green. "You have to feel sorry for a fellow who plays as well as he does—just better than anybody else—and can't putt anymore. Geez, if I could just concentrate like he does."

It was about two o'clock now, and most of the threesomes had made their way onto the course. The day's final big-name group—Arnold Palmer and former champions Cary Middlecoff and Jack Fleck—had just gone off, accompanied by an expansive gallery; probably only Snead's and Hogan's were larger.

The day had warmed up to 80 degrees and light breezes had arrived, keeping conditions comfortable for the players and spectators. The crowd, swarming happily over the beautiful course, seemed huge. The occasion felt almost like a summer fair. Rip Arnold's kids and other children from the neighborhood adjacent to the club set up lemonade stands beneath the cottonwoods and Chinese elms (five cents for a small glass, ten cents for a large). Ladies in straw bonnets strolled or sprawled on the grass while the true golf fans strained for a view of their favorites.

Wearing a ten-gallon cowboy hat, Ralph Hutchison, a club pro from Saucon Valley outside Philadelphia, announced scores at the 18th green, as he did regularly at the Open and the Masters. Ed (Porky) Oliver, one of the tour's most popular pros of the past 20 years and now a Denver resident, was introduced. Porky, who was recovering from recent lung cancer surgery, received a heartwarming ovation.

Souchak's 68 still was the low score, but with two thirds of the field yet to complete their round, it was questionable how long it would hold up. Matching Sanders and Player with scores of 70 were Dick Stranahan (no relation to Frank), a tour novice with 1960 earnings of $294 and a portfolio that included a job as a model in a West Coast beer company's billboard ad campaign; West Virginia club pro Joe Taylor, whose career highlight was a victory over Sam Snead in the 1954 West Virginia PGA; and the well-known amateur Don Cherry.

Cherry was a talented golfer with an impressive amateur record. Apart from winning dozens of amateur tournaments across his native Texas, he was a semifinalist in the 1952 U.S. Amateur, defeating Frank Stranahan and Gene Littler to reach that point; he won the 1953 Canadian Amateur; and he played undefeated on two U.S. Walker Cup teams. But he was best known for singing and had had several hits to his credit in the fifties, including "Band of Gold," "Ghost Town," and "Namely You"; he had appeared on the Ed Sullivan and Arthur Godfrey television shows; and in 1959 he was the voice on the Mr. Clean commercial. He also was married to the 1956 Miss America, Sharon Kay Ritchie, Colorado's representative in the beauty pageant.

After his round of 36-34—70, Cherry informed the press that for only the second time in almost four years of marriage he had allowed his wife to watch him compete. Three-putts at Cherry Hills's 2nd and 3rd holes had jeopardized her visitation rights. "I almost sent her in," he confessed. He didn't explain the usual prohibition, but he didn't have to; everyone knew he owned a volcanic temper.

Rip Arnold, a member of Cherry's threesome, shot an embarrassing 84. Cherry Hills's popular 42-year-old head pro scuffed two shots on the 1st hole and never righted his game. A sympathetic member of his gallery whispered, "He's no kid, you know. He played in the 1938 Open here." Cherry Hills's other representative, amateur Claude Wright, also competed in the '38 Open, but he managed to come in with a 74.

It seemed that the next likely threat to Souchak's lead would come from an intriguing trio of fortyish golfers who were just finishing their round. Going into the championship, Art Wall, Julius Boros, and Jerry Barber all were near the top of their game. On this day Wall went out in a shaky three-over-par 38 but recovered with a two-under 34 on the tougher back nine for a hearty 72. Julius, or "Moose" as he was called, shot an indifferent 36-37—73, and received little attention.

Barber drove wildly, landing in the rough more often than in the fairway, and missed several greens, but he putted bull's-eyes. When his work was done, his card carried six birdies, which turned out to be the most of the day, four bogeys (including a damage-controlling one-putt at the 2nd hole), and the fine score of 69. Barber knew that you couldn't play each round as sloppily from tee to green as he had and contend for the U.S. Open. On the other hand, he knew that it was not uncommon for Open champions to struggle in one round and still manage to bring home a score that didn't knock them out of the competition.

"I can't say that I played well," he told the press in his articulate, staccato fashion. "But the secret of winning golf is to score well when you're playing well and score well when you're playing badly, as I was today. I'm certainly happy to get the round out of my system."

Barber, wearing a golf cap with the bill turned up, making him look a bit like a jockey, parred the 1st hole, bogeyed the 2nd after driving into the rough, then holed a 12-footer for birdie at 3. After pushing his tee shot into the rough, he saved par with a nine-footer on the 4th green. He birdied the par-five 5th hole with a ten-foot putt, but then at the 6th he left short a par putt of less than four feet. After six holes: two pars, two birdies, and two bogeys. Three pars followed for an even-par 35 going out.

The roller-coaster ride continued on the back nine. After parring the 10th hole he dropped a birdie putt at the 11th and again alternated par and birdie at the 12th and 13th. On the next two holes he missed the green with his approaches and took bogeys. As he did on the front nine, he played the first six holes in pairs of par, birdie, and bogey, but this side he finished off brilliantly—holing an eight-footer for birdie at 16, parring the long 17th, and rolling home a winding, 16-foot putt for birdie at 18.

After showering and changing, Barber passed Wall at his locker and took the unusual step of apologizing for his play. "Art, I'm sorry I played so badly today and probably loused up your game, and Moose's, too," he said. Wall knew that Barber, a stern critic of himself when he fell short of his standards, was completely sincere. He urged Jerry to focus on what went right—his clutch chipping and putting.

"You shot a great round today when things weren't going good," Art told him. "Tomorrow you'll get in stride, and think what could happen. It even scares me to think of it." It was typical of Wall to encourage and compliment a peer. In April he had been deeply disappointed when illness prevented him from defending his Masters title, but after Palmer's victory he remarked, "At least I can say that I gave the title back to a real champion."

Barber may not have realized it, but in the papers the next day he received further support from one of the game's shrewdest judges of a competitor's character, Walter Hagen. The Haig, now 68, was at the Open for a few days of kibitzing and elbow-bending before heading on to the Broadmoor and Aspen for some fishing. Arrayed in a linen jacket and yellow ascot, he watched the pint-sized golfer on a few holes and praised his coordination and the control he had over his swing. Barber might not have the supreme talent to seize the championship if he needed birdies on the final two holes, Hagen commented, but he had the guts to take it home. "If he wins the U.S. Open," he told Larry Robinson of the *New York World Telegram and Sun*, "he'll never realize it until he sees his name on the trophy. He plays for keeps."

FOR THE FIRST 11 holes Tommy Bolt was just another of the 150 U.S. Open contestants, fighting it out with "Old Man Par"— Bobby Jones's personification of his abstract opponent. Then at the par-three 12th hole, he reverted to "Thunder Bolt."

Earlier, at the 1st tee, he appeared to be in no better shape than the day before. Ever the clotheshorse, he was dressed in a flashy black and green outfit but he had his shirt collar pulled high and his sweater buttoned up even though it was still and balmy. He told his new caddie, Dick Lehms, that he had a cold, he was dizzy, and his hands were puffy. "It was obvious when he went to the practice range before teeing off that he wasn't feeling well," Lehms, a 15-year Army veteran, confirmed later.

Out on the course his notorious temper got the best of him after a few unsatisfactory shots, the first instance coming on the 2nd hole when he slammed down his club and buried the blade in the ground. But overall he plugged away and managed to play the front nine in even-par 35. Another par followed at 10, and then at the par-five 11th hole he produced an impressive par in spite of hitting a ball out-of-bounds.

The 12th hole is a picturesque par three, 212 yards long. From an elevated tee, golfers look out over a narrow lake that covers practically the entire distance to an elevated green before curving left. A bunker and trees guard the right side of the green; trees and the lake the left. The tee shot, usually a long iron, must carry all the way to the green.

Bolt's ball, however, did not carry quite far enough and ended up in the water. Tommy, claiming that it landed on the bank between the lake and putting green and trickled back into the water, argued that he should be able to take a drop on the side of the lake nearest the green. The USGA official on the scene disagreed. He directed Tommy to take a drop on the near side of the lake, but also to drop a provisional ball on the far side; they would obtain a final ruling later. Tommy took a four with the provisional ball, but a six with the ball dropped where the official instructed. "He didn't seem to care after that," Lehms said.

Bolt's fellow competitors, Claude Harmon and Ken Venturi, saw Tommy grow angrier and angrier as he bogeyed number 13, squandered a short birdie putt at 14, bogeyed 15, and missed makeable birdie putts at 16 and 17. On the 18th tee, now five strokes over par, he hit a low screamer into the large pond recently visited by Sanders. Seething, he teed up a second ball, which splashed into the water as well.

His third attempt cleared the pond, but Bolt still had one more use for his driver. He raised the offending club and flung it into the pond, clearing Harmon's head by somewhere between a few inches and a few yards. Photos taken by *Sports Illustrated* cameraman John G. Zimmerman suggest that Claude was in flinching range, but never in harm's way. (According to his caddie, the club slipped out of his hand; nobody else gave such a charitable interpretation.) At that point a young boy ran out from the gallery, dove into the pond, and fished out the club. Reports of what followed conflict wildly.

One account, which appeared in some newspapers the next day, has it that the boy darted through the crowd, hopped a fence, and fled with his trophy. Most eyewitnesses, however, say the boy was caught and Bolt got back his driver. According to one report, the boy tried to run away with the club but was chased and coaxed back by Bolt, who tipped him ten dollars for his service. As the boy was eluding capture, some spectators reportedly suggested that he throw the club back in.

"A small boy did not run away with the club," Thurston H. Jenkins of Columbine Valley, Colorado, stated more than 30 years later in a letter published in *Golf Digest*. "My son, David, got the club out of the lake and received a ten-dollar tip from Tommy's caddie." Responding to the letter, Bolt said a Rochester, New York, reporter named Bruce Koch chased down the boy and returned the club to the owner. Koch confirmed this, asserting that the boy resisted giving up the driver but finally did so for a reward. Koch says that he gave the boy 5 dollars, and, no, Tommy didn't reimburse him; Bolt claims that he tipped the kid 15 dollars.

In any event, Bolt took an eight on the hole and stormed off the last green, practically trampling a youngster who, not appreciating the risk he was taking, requested Tommy's autograph. Bolt turned in his scorecard with the 12th hole left blank. His marker, Claude Harmon, subsequently described to the USGA's Joe Dey what happened and the score of six was verified. Tommy's lopsided 35-45—80, however, soon became irrelevant.

Bolt found Dey and informed him he was withdrawing due to illness. Fending off reporters, he hurriedly collected his belongings in the locker room (but not before lending Ed Furgol a couple dozen golf balls) and made a run for his car. There his wife, Mary Lou, sat crying. Cornered by a member of the press, he complained, "I'm sick, man. Don't bother me." It was a scene at once bizarre, hilarious, and very sad.

Ken Venturi, like most people, found the club-throwing incident a hoot. He said he had visions of playing a "onesome" the next day. "With Bolt gone and Harmon dead, I thought I was going to get lonesome," he joked. Harmon was not amused. He held his hands about a foot and a half apart and said indignantly that the airborne driver had missed his head by that much. "If that club would have hit me," he announced, "I would have had the best of it from then on because his club was in the water and I still had one in my hands."

Harmon and Venturi somehow managed to weather Thunder's storm with minimal damage, bringing in scores of 73 and 71 respectively. Venturi's even-par total, like the 72 of fellow Bay Area native Rosburg, was much better than it might have been. The normally superb iron player—many rated him the tour's best—hit only ten greens in regulation. But on this day, his putter was his best club. It saved him from going over par on the front nine, it carried him below par for the first time with a nine-footer at the 11th hole, and it worked magic for him on the last two holes.

After bogeying the 16th to go one over par, he put his tee shot at the long 17th hole under the bough of a blue spruce. Ken punched his second shot out into the fairway and then played up safe, short of the moat fronting the island green. Pitching his fourth shot to the green, he watched in dismay as his ball carried 25 feet past the hole. But he collected himself and canned the long par putt coming back. Amid the furor on the last hole, Venturi stepped up to a 20- to 25-foot birdie putt and tapped it gently on the slick green. It was right on target, but would it have enough steam? Yes! It fell into the cup, exhausted. It was the best putt made at the undulating, front-sloping 18th green all day.

"I feel pretty good," Venturi said later to Phil Norman of

the *San Francisco Examiner.* "No reason why I can't go on from here." But, no doubt, he easily could have imagined several reasons why producing a comeback was doubtful. In the ten tournaments since the Masters, Ken had cooled down substantially from his early-season brilliance. Leading up to and including the Masters, he had one win and five top-five finishes; since then, a tie for fifth at Colonial and a fifth at the "500" Festival Open.

Then there was his top rival for Hogan's throne, Arnold Palmer. He'd lost head-to-head to Arnold back in the 1953 U.S. Amateur, and twice Ken had been burned by him in the Masters.

Above all, Venturi had been fighting silently against the effects of his third agonizing Masters defeat and what he later called a "mania" that year to win a major tournament. Two loyalists who wrestled with him over his growing fatalism about winning a major championship walked in his gallery at Cherry Hills: his wife, Conni, who normally stayed at home with their two young sons, and Ed Lowery, a wealthy San Francisco auto dealer who had sponsored him when he was starting out. (This was the same Ed Lowery who played hooky to caddie for Francis Ouimet in the 1913 Open; he also was the man who introduced him to Byron Nelson.) They shared his doubts.

The next day, a story written by George Franco in the *Denver Post,* headlined "Bolt Tough on Caddies," reported that caddie Dick Lehms and his predecessor, Fuzzy Seyfried, each had been reassigned. Lehms was now one of the crew updating the big scoreboard near the first tee—more than 20 people were required to operate it—and Seyfried had to content himself with working the leader board in the press tent—both duller, but steadier positions, Franco noted.

The PGA fined Tommy Bolt $100 for "conduct unbecoming a professional," and another tale was added to the legend of the Terrible-Tempered Mister Bolt.

*   *   *

Henry Ransom remembered Cherry Hills well. There, in his first-round match at the 1941 PGA Championship, he shot a 66—and didn't win. Nineteen years later he wasn't quite up to that day's form, but in the stroke-play Open his two-under-par 69 placed him in a far better position—a tie for second place with Jerry Barber.

What a day for a 49-year-old who balanced three jobs and was playing in only his fourth tournament of the year. One of many well-known Texas golfers who got their start in the 1920s (as a boy he caddied a bit for Rice University student Howard Hughes), Ransom was a club pro at St. Andrews Golf Club, in St. Andrews, Illinois; he was the golf coach at Texas A & M University in College Station; and he was a rancher with 350 head of cattle in nearby Bryan. Of the last-named occupation he quipped, "I bought the cattle to make a living, but it turned out I had to make a living for them." Lately, his tournament play was of little help on that score. He had banked less than $2,400 in prize winnings in 1960.

Before the start of the Open Rip Arnold had stressed that players would have to bear down hard when they reached the final four holes. Ransom's performance confirmed the host pro's analysis. After 14 holes, Henry stood four under for the round, poised to overtake Souchak. But at the par-three 15th, he missed the green with his tee shot and couldn't hole a six-foot par-saving putt. And at 17 he reached the green in regulation figures, only to three-putt from 35 feet.

Still, Ransom, the day's biggest surprise, had much to be proud of—pitching to three feet for a birdie at the 1st hole, rolling in 25- and 30-foot birdie putts at numbers 5 and 6 respectively, and being the only contestant all day to birdie the 14th hole, a 470-yard, dogleg left, par four. There his long approach shot soared off his three-iron to within 12 feet of the pin, and he rapped home the putt. All in all, the veteran of 11 previous National Opens dating back to 1939 played exceptionally well, especially considering his physical state. He had a sore right wrist, which he wrapped tightly with tape to minimize the pain; he walked with a limp, the result of stubbing his toe recently against an iron television stand in a motel room; and he had hay fever.

Johnny Bulla, another graybeard who happened to be grouped with Ransom, couldn't make any magic of his own—with one small exception. Trapped near a tree on the 17th fairway with only a left-handed swing possible, he pulled the putter out of his bag and advanced the ball 160 yards. Johnny was a hard-luck player in major championships during his prime, finishing second twice in the British Open (including once to Sam Snead, whom he persuaded to enter) and once in the Masters. He fared no better in semiretirement: 36-39—75.

A COUPLE DAYS BEFORE his 12:24 P.M. tee time, Dow Finsterwald informed the press that he had made a point of checking the back side of the Cherry Hills scorecard. Having received a two-stroke penalty for taking a practice putt during the Masters, he wasn't going to commit the same faux pas again. Cherry Hills had no such rule, but as it turned out he didn't need any extra putting. He produced a rock-solid, even-par 71 that did nothing to shake the confidence many forecasters had shown in him before the start of the championship.

Bruce Crampton, a 24-year-old Aussie who had seen scant success playing portions of the three previous years on tour, did even better—36-34—70. This was particularly surprising because Crampton, weak and shaky from a ten-day stomach malady, had entered the tournament under the care of a doctor. A couple days earlier he had joked, "What a way to treat a visitor! Here I am a stranger, I've got a stomach ailment, and now I learn I'm playing the first two rounds with Ben Hogan and Dow Finsterwald. It is enough to make even a healthy man shake." Actually, he was not that green. This was his third U.S. Open; in his first, in 1958, he finished more than respectably, tied for 19th.

En route to his one-under-par round, the Sydney, Australia, native made one of the day's four eagles, knocking down to size the 563-yard, par-five 11th hole. Crampton, a rather grim, intense young man, followed his long, well-positioned drive with a three-wood that stopped 15 feet beyond the hole. He then nursed in the tricky, downhill putt. The brilliant fairway wood was just the kind of long approach shot the large gallery had anticipated—but not from Crampton.

Ben Hogan, the group's third member, had been executing shots like that for 20 years with no erosion in skill. But by the time he reached the 11th tee, he was desperate for a par, never mind an eagle. He was riding on successive bogeys at holes 7, 8, 9, and 10. (When Hogan had last suffered through a lapse of four straight bogeys was anyone's guess, but if it in fact ever happened it was *years* ago.) At 9, his tee shot had hooked into the crowd, hitting a man in the stomach, which seemed to upset Hogan. Down came the Hawk's name from the leader board, and up went the name of an amateur—Jack Nicklaus.

After the 10th hole, Hogan did steady his game and reached the 18th tee at two over par. There, the Old Guard's leader sailed his four-iron second shot over the green and into the crowd, and he stumbled home, like a commoner, with a six. The double-bogey left him with a 75, the same score 19-year-old Bob Verwey brought in several hours earlier.

For once, though, putting was not his bugaboo. Ben three-putted only one green, the last, and he took 34 putts for the round—not a brilliant performance certainly, but adequate. Afterward, the threesome's scorekeeper, Mrs. Garland Valentine, uttered what diehard Hogan fans knew only too well but would hesitate to say themselves. "He stands over the ball too long. I never saw anyone freeze like he did on so many putts." Strangely, the golfer himself professed he "wasn't too unhappy" with his round. The pin placements, he said, were difficult, but fair; no, he had no complaints about the course.

In Friday's papers, some members of the press questioned whether Hogan could make the cut, never mind make a run for the championship.

THE 1:20 P.M. GROUP comprised a fascinating trio at different career stages: 41-year-old Walter Burkemo, 28-year-old Billy Casper, and 20-year-old Jack Nicklaus.

Burkemo, one of the great match-play golfers of the 1950s, had advanced to the finals of the PGA Championship three times in four years, winning the title in 1953. He also held the distinction of having shot the lowest fourth-round score in U.S. Open history—a 65 in 1957. But he had won only one tournament other than the PGA in 13 years as a pro. A rugged, powerfully built man, the onetime Army sergeant carried shrapnel in his back, the remnants of wounds sustained in Europe during the war.

"Sarge" had attracted some rare attention in April when he finished tied for sixth at the Masters. He wasn't expected to contend at Cherry Hills, though, and on the front nine he almost putted himself out of the tournament. After shooting a three-over-par 38, he parred the back nine for a 74, earning whatever little satisfaction a pro golfer obtains in fighting off a disastrous round.

Defending champion Casper, a consistent performer, had accumulated ten victories in five years on tour and a place among the top-ten money winners the past three seasons. Yet he failed to command the respect his record merited. The reasons were unclear, but they probably had to do with his unathletic appearance—he carried 215 pounds not very flatteringly on his 5-foot 11-inch frame—and his seeming lack of intensity. Billy shirked the practice range, preferring to occupy the nearest fishing hole.

In addition, he played a conservative brand of golf in which he concentrated on minimizing errors rather than pulling off high-risk shots. In winning the previous year's championship, he actually laid up each round on the 217-yard par-three 3rd hole, apparently figuring the single long bunker that cradled the green on either side and the out-of-bounds that backed it were too threatening to go for birdie; he parred the hole that way all four times.

Golfers who clout the ball great distances tend to receive the most attention—especially if they're fiery competitors—even if the rest of their game doesn't measure up. On the other hand great putters rarely win acclaim unless the rest of their game excels, too. At this point in his career, Billy displayed a dispassionate temperament while competing, and his tee-to-green skills, while superior to many tour players', paled beside his gifts on and around the putting green.

It was often noted that he shared a good deal in common with Gene Littler. Both were San Diego natives, both were graduates of the city's junior golf program, both were Navy veterans, and both were already master putters as tour rookies. But, unlike Littler, the 1953 U.S. Amateur champion, when Casper joined the tour in 1955 his overall game impressed few people.

Paul Runyan, the great golfer from the thirties and one of the country's top instructors, told him, "You'll never make it, kid." Ben Hogan, paired with him at the 1957 Palm Beach Round Robin, watched as Casper knocked the ball everywhere except the fairway but putted his way to a 66. Afterward Hogan, who shot a 71, gave him a less than sanguine critique. "If you couldn't putt," he said, "you'd be selling hot dogs on the 10th tee." Casper got the last laugh, though, winning the '59 Open, his first major championship. His game overall had improved considerably, but still it was putting that carried him.

He won the tournament because he took only 114 putts, a U.S. Open record.

Now at Cherry Hills, Billy opened with an even-par 71, the same first-round score he recorded at Winged Foot. Surprisingly, the only soft spot in his outing proved to be his putting. "I played wonderful golf but I putted terribly. I'm playing much better than when I won at Winged Foot last year," he said. Afterward he endeared himself to club and USGA officials when he observed to some Denver writers, "Maybe this is a tougher course than some people think." What may have been his truer feelings, however, showed up the next day in his hometown newspaper, the *San Diego Union*. "It's the easiest Open course I've played on, even if the scores don't show it," he told columnist Jack Murphy.

The defending champion's solid performance was overshadowed by that of Nicklaus, whose round of 71 attracted much more notice than his own. Nicklaus "played beautifully," Casper told the press, and added, "He's so strong." Indeed, according to one member of their gallery, Ohio State football coach Woody Hayes, Jack outdrove Billy on all but two holes.

Hayes was hardly a golf fan. Until he arrived in Colorado to conduct a football clinic in nearby Boulder, he didn't even know that the Open was being held or that Columbus's favorite son, Nicklaus, was competing. But, along with his wife and son, he followed Jack all 18 holes. He didn't spot in the gallery any of the Columbus sportswriters he knew, so he scribbled notes on his program, figuring the folks back home might enjoy getting some details. The next day the *Columbus Dispatch* quoted liberally from his jottings.

Nicklaus's character was as impressive as his golf, he noted, offering two incidents to illustrate. At the 8th hole Jack stood in line to use a drinking fountain, waiting his turn behind nine or ten spectators. Later, after he missed a two-foot putt to bogey the 17th hole, he stood his ground against a six-footer for par at 18.

Even Nicklaus, who tended to be his own worst critic, allowed, "I was pretty well satisfied with my play." He missed a few greens and he squandered a few strokes—the putt at 17, other three-putt greens at numbers 8 and 9—but, refusing to be undone by these lapses he also picked up three birdies. His 71 was not one of those isolated, lucky rounds that amateurs sometimes produce at the Open, Casper believed, and Billy stated confidently that the kid would "definitely be in contention all the way."

ALMOST SIX HOURS AFTER club pro Jack Koennecker kicked off the 60th National Open with an airtight birdie, Arnold Palmer butchered the same hole.

More than 120 of the world's best golfers had since followed Koennecker's path to the first tee, and virtually every one of them had opted for the control of a fairway wood or a long iron over the power of a driver. Not Palmer. "I figured I could drive the first green or get it close, and when you start with a birdie it gives you confidence," he explained afterward. But that was not what happened.

He pushed his drive into the creek, and the current carried the ball 30 yards or more before it stopped in shallow water near the green in an unplayable lie. No one, it seemed—not Palmer, not his fellow competitors Middlecoff or Fleck, and not the USGA official accompanying the threesome—saw where the ball had crossed the threshold of the hazard. As it turned out, a forecaddie had, and his judgment determined the point from which Palmer took a drop. Taking a one-stroke penalty (in 1960, players received only a distance penalty, not a stroke and distance penalty, for balls lost or out-of-bounds), Arnold hit a tree with his third shot, put his fourth over the green, chipped back five feet short of the hole with his fifth, and sank the putt for a six.

At the 2nd tee, Fleck noticed that Palmer and his caddie, Bob Blair, were bickering over something or other. The four-square Fleck ambled over and said, "Arnie, what the heck are you fighting with your caddie for? You've got a long way to go." Palmer promptly made up the two strokes to par with a birdie there and another one on the 5th hole. But at the tough 9th hole, an uphill 430-yard par four, he hooked his tee shot into some bushes, bogeyed the hole, and made the turn at one-over-par 36. At the 11th and 13th holes he collected two birdies, but bogeys on the 12th and home holes offset them. Still, overcoming an infamous start, Palmer had struggled on for a one-over-par 72, a tolerable Open score that placed him only four strokes behind Souchak.

Middlecoff viewed Palmer's efforts with admiration. In an article that he wrote for his hometown newspaper, the *Memphis Commercial Appeal,* he characterized Palmer's round as "wobbly and scrambling." But, he noted, Palmer "was able to hold his round together and make enough birdies to stay well within striking distance of the leaders on a day when he was clearly not at his best."

Neither was Middlecoff. Playing in Memphis two weeks earlier, he seemed to have brought his game to just the right pitch in preparation for the Open. There, he tied for eighth place with rounds of 70-69-66-71, finishing only three strokes out of the three-man play-off—an encouraging showing for a veteran who had been playing infrequently. But in his first day at Cherry Hills he had a miserable six-over-par round—38-39—77.

His downfall started on the 5th green, where he blundered away a birdie chance and ended up taking a bogey. Facing an eight-footer that would have brought him back to even par, he accidentally moved the ball with his putter, costing him a stroke, and then missed the putt. The next day in his newspaper column, he said of the effect the gaffe had on his subsequent poor play, "Such things are hard on a set of nerves that are not what they were, and which were always inclined to jumpiness."

Middlecoff was a precursor to the next generation of golfers who came from well-to-do families and played golf in college. After filling several thousand teeth as an Army dentist in 1945 and 1946, he shunned his father's sensible advice to join his dental practice and became a professional golfer. Soon after winning the North and South Open while still an amateur in 1945, he was hailed as the next big star.

For nine seasons, 1947 through 1955, "Doc" Middlecoff won more tournaments than anyone else—34, including two Opens and a Masters. Wanting to win desperately, however, the high-strung, fidgety player often was afflicted by nerves. Above all, he was an excruciatingly slow player. A joke on tour had it that Cary gave up dentistry because no patient could possibly hold his mouth open that long.

Earlier in the year, Middlecoff had left his club job at the posh Diplomat Hotel Golf Club, in Hollywood, Florida, a post whose duties had limited his tournament schedule for the last couple of years. The tall, handsome Tennessean with a certain resemblance to Ted Williams was hoping, at age 38, to squeeze a few top seasons out of his playing career. In April he missed the cut at the Masters—a humbling experience for the 1955 champion—but for the past month he'd worked hard on his game, and coming into the tournament he liked his chances. Yet now one of the game's biggest all-time winners was at serious risk of elimination from the Open. He had competed in the national championship for 13 consecutive years, and the only time he'd ever missed the cut was the 1947 championship, his first one.

Fleck shot a fine, steady round in 36-34 to join a group of eight at one-under-par 70, two strokes behind Souchak. For

14 holes he played the Open by the book—he had no three-putt holes, he missed only one green by any margin, and he recorded one par after another—the sole exception being the long par-three 8th hole, which he bogeyed. Finally, at 15, he broke through for a birdie on a 25-foot putt, and at 16 he duplicated that with the same results.

The few groups that came after the Palmer-Middlecoff-Fleck trio were less than pleased about the pace of play. Pat Schwab of Pensacola shot an 83, his worst score in four Opens, and he blamed it on the slowpokes in front of him. He claimed that his threesome had to wait at least five minutes before every shot and 35 minutes at the 8th tee. Joe Campbell, playing in the following group, told the press he thought his fellow competitor, Bob Goalby, would have shot a 66 or 67 "if he could have kept moving." Goalby, the tour's 1958 Rookie of the Year, shot a 73 without complaint.

As the final threesomes completed play, the players trudging up to the elevated 18th green more than 11 hours after the first group had started, speculation built about where the cut would fall after Friday. With the top 50 players having shot 74 or better, most guesses for the cutoff hovered around 147—a score that would set a new record for the lowest cutoff total in Open history; the existing record, set in 1948, was 148.

The cut, of course, was the furthest thing from Arnold Palmer's mind. In the press tent after his round, he, too, expressed some unhappiness over the slow pace of play—4 hours 45 minutes, in part thanks to the tortoiselike ex-champions, Middlecoff and Fleck—but his confidence seemed intact. Asked if he thought he was still in contention, he answered, "I hope I'm this close Saturday afternoon." And what will be your strategy on the 1st hole tomorrow? a reporter inquired. Palmer said he'd use his driver again. "You never can tell when you hit for a green," he said. "You might get a hole in one."

* * *

CONTRARY TO HOGAN'S AND others' predictions that Cherry Hills would be defenseless against the invading pros, Souchak's 68 held up all day long—probably a consequence of "Openitis," Bruce Crampton's term for players' excessive caution in the championship. On the other hand, 11 contestants broke par in the first round, one of the largest such contingents in U.S. Open history. In contrast, only four players beat par in the first round at Winged Foot in 1959, and no one did at Southern Hills in 1958.

Former hockey bad boy Bill Ezinicki never even flirted with par. In fact, he stumbled through the kind of round to which club pros are vulnerable when they play an Open course. His 39-44—83 was his highest score in a professional competition. "That was the toughest day I've ever spent," he told Gordon Campbell of the *Toronto Daily Star*. Like Tommy Bolt, Ezzie scattered not one but two tee shots into the pond on 18, and then he overshot the green, finishing with a nine. Despite his seven-bogey, one quintuple-bogey showing, the *Denver Post* ran a short profile on him the next day that no doubt introduced many readers to his colorful exploits on the ice.

Bill Spiller joined Gene Littler and more than a dozen other golfers at five-over-par 76. The outcome left the African American golfer with only a slight hope of making the cut. No mention whatsoever was made of him (or of fellow Angeleno Charlie Sifford, who shot a 74) in a *Los Angeles Times* article that focused on Jerry Barber's round and reported the results of Lloyd Mangrum, Paul Runyan, Dick Knight, and two minor southern California entrants.

Davis Love, Jr., shot a 74, a score that any first-time Open qualifier—particularly one with a damaged finger—could be proud of (in contrast, his boss, Wes Ellis, played a ragged 79). But the young golfer felt terribly let down because of the way his once tight round came helplessly undone. Through 13 holes, he was two under par. But then five holes consecutively he drove into the rough. "The ball never was in bad position," he said. "But without being able to put that finger on the shaft, I just couldn't get enough power to cut the ball out right." He bogeyed each of the last five holes.

Dutch Harrison and Deane Beman also shot rounds of 74. They, too, would have to do better in the second round, they knew, or there might not be a third and fourth.

The leaders after the first round:

Mike Souchak	31-37—68
Jerry Barber	35-34—69
Henry Ransom	32-37—69
Don Cherry (a)	32-38—70
Bruce Crampton	36-34—70
Jack Fleck	36-34—70
Huston LaClair, Jr.	34-36—70
Gary Player	33-37—70
Doug Sanders	32-38—70
Dick Stranahan	34-36—70
Joe Taylor	36-34—70
Billy Casper, Jr.	33-38—71
Stan Dudas	35-36—71
Dow Finsterwald	35-36—71
Ed Furgol	35-36—71
Jack Nicklaus (a)	36-35—71
Dave Ragan	36-35—71
Ken Venturi	35-36—71

CHAPTER 6

JOE DEY, THE U.S. GOLF ASSOCIATION'S FASTIDIOUS EXECUTIVE DIRECtor, was hardly one to cut loose into the wee hours, particularly during the draining Open week. Having run this and other USGA national championships for a quarter century, he had little enthusiasm for that sort of thing now, if he ever did.

Every year, the first round was long and worrisome. There was no telling the extent to which the players might complain to the USGA—the holes are cut in impossible-to-reach locations, the greens are mowed so short and the grass is so parched it's on the verge of dying. But, during the first round, Dey heard little, if any, of this, and none of his on-course officials made any critical blunders with which he'd be confronted by the players or press.

Apart from addressing the unpleasantness with Tommy Bolt, the Open champion he had praised highly only two years earlier for his self-mastery, Dey had to inform Chuck Kocsis, a well-known Michigan amateur, that his 32-year-old wedge was illegal because the clubface markings were too close together. All in all, not a bad day. When it was over, he enjoyed a quiet meal and hit the sack early. He wanted to be sharp for another extended day, the second, and last, round involving the entire field, down to 149 after Tommy Bolt's extravagant exit. Joe needed to pace himself, because in 24 hours he'd be facing yet another marathon workday, Open Saturday, into which two 18-hole rounds would be packed.

At about the time Dey turned in for the night, Cherry Hills members began to arrive at the club for an evening's revelry. There was much to celebrate. The first day of the Open had been a smashing success, starting with the attendance. The turnout of 14,067 topped the record, set the previous year, for the first round of a U.S. Open.

That evening at the club, the tournament's general chairman, Potts Berglund, and his people were worn out, but too exhilarated to care. They'd labored for almost two years for this moment, and now they were going to have some fun.

WHY ANY GOLF CLUB would willingly host the U.S. Open will always be something of a mystery. But Cherry Hills Country Club, like previous host clubs, was filled with golf enthusiasts who wished to prove that their club, their golf course, and their town were as good as the best anywhere. Yet when the club began, in 1922, the members wanted nothing more than to be left alone.

The club was founded by a few male members of the upper-crust Denver Country Club who were fed up with their filled-to-capacity golf course. Golf fanatics all, they wanted a place where they could play anytime, free of crowded fairways, free of the distraction of dances and parties, and free of female golfers just learning the game.

The group found a fine piece of land—172 rolling acres one mile south of Denver, in Englewood, and one mile above sea level. Nearby, the eastern slope of the Rocky Mountains presented a breathtaking backdrop. The founders, described as the "bluest of Denver blue bloods," coughed up $1,000 each to purchase stock in a company set up to take title to the land,

and they lined up financing using their extensive business connections. Then they hired noted golf course architect William S. Flynn.

Give us a course, they instructed, worthy of hosting a major championship. Flynn was up to the task. He was then designing the wonderful mountain course where a young Sam Snead would caddie, the Cascades Course at The Homestead, in Hot Springs, Virginia. In the next few years Flynn would redesign two classic layouts, Shinnecock Hills in Southampton, New York, and Merion Golf Club outside Philadelphia.

Several club names were considered, and ironically, one suggested by a woman was picked. Alice Foster, wife of one of the group's prime movers and shakers, liked "Cherry Hills"—a cherry orchard occupied a knoll on the club's grounds—and so did the club members.

The Cherry Hills Club—"Country" was omitted from the name until 1945 to emphasize the golfing focus—thrived through the twenties and soon became *the* place to play golf in Denver. Then, in October 1929, the stock market crash jolted America, and Cherry Hills, reeling like most everything and everyone else, soon had to struggle for survival. It was a long road for the next ten years.

The picture brightened considerably when the USGA accepted club member Will Nicholson's petition and selected Cherry Hills for the 1938 U.S. Open. Shortly before the championship began, some pros questioned—as their successors did in 1960—whether Cherry Hills constituted a test befitting the National Open. Lawson Little, a dominant amateur golfer who turned pro in 1936, said nonchalantly that the pros would find the course easy pickings and predicted a winning score of 278, six under par.

Such a remark about an Open course was considered insulting, tantamount to comparing Cherry Hills to the local pitch and putt course. A 278 would shatter the Open scoring record, the 281 that Ralph Guldahl set winning the championship the year before. Open courses just don't play that easily, everyone knew.

Once the Open began, Cherry Hills proved to be more than many in the field could handle. Little shot 78-77—155, and made the cut without a stroke to spare. He and second-year touring pro Sam Snead finished tied for 38th place with a score of 25-over-par 309. Sam, blazing the fantastically profitable season his peers thought never again would be approached, surprised many with his inept showing. What an immense comedown after almost winning his first Open the year before!

Although Ben Hogan was still seeking his first tour victory nine years after turning pro, finally he had gained the upper hand in his long battle to stay out on tour. Having qualified for his third Open, he hoped to advance to the final 36 holes for the first time. But the hard-bitten Texan sustained another in a long line of bitter disappointments: he missed the cut by one stroke. So did 25-year-old Jim Turnesa, a member of the well-known New York golfing family. His brother Mike, another of Vitale Turnesa's seven golfing sons, fared better. He took 31st place with a 307, but he finished out of the money; a 306 would have earned him a princely $50.

Mike Souchak's older brother, Frank, qualified for the Open, but missed the cut. Ralph "Rip" Arnold, an assistant pro at the nearby Denver Country Club, made the cut but then shot a dismal 86 and withdrew. He'd have other cracks at Cherry Hills, however. The next year he was appointed the club's head pro.

Of the more than 100 entrants who failed to complete the four rounds, no one attracted more attention than little-known Ray Ainsley, a pro from Ojai, California. Ainsley opened with a respectable 76 and after 15 holes on day two appeared headed for a 77; a 153 would have qualified him to play the final day's double round.

At the par-four 16th Ainsley pushed his approach shot

into rocky Little Dry Creek, which at the time belied its name. Rather than take a drop, for some reason he decided to try to hit out of the creek. He swung once at his submerged ball and barely advanced it. A second swing produced a bit more success; helped by the current, the ball floated a few yards downstream. Third, fourth, and fifth swipes followed. Still his ball rested in the creek.

By this time, as the soggy golfer continued to slash away, rules official Red Anderson was laughing so hard he had to ask Ainsley's fellow competitor to help keep score. When Ainsley finally got his ball onto *terra firma*, he lay 15, and a little girl was overheard telling her mother, "Mummy, it must be dead now, because the man has quit hitting at it."

Ainsley took a 19 on the hole, setting a dubious U.S. Open record that still stands. He finished the round in 96 and missed the cut by 17 strokes. Asked why he didn't simply take a drop for a one-stroke penalty, a common procedure, Ainsley replied, "I thought I had to play the ball as it lay at all times."

Even the championship's top finishers were no match for Cherry Hills's par 71. Two-time Open winner Gene Sarazen finished in tenth place at 296, 12 strokes over par. Paul Runyan, a short-hitting veteran who embarrassed Snead later that year in the most lopsided PGA Championship final ever (8 and 7), was one stroke better at 295. Byron Nelson, the 1937 Masters champion, continued to outshine his boyhood caddie mate, Hogan; he finished tied for fifth at 294.

Only the victor, defending champion Ralph Guldahl, was the equal of par. As he approached the last green and a cluster of photographers, he stopped, pulled a comb out of his pocket, and arranged his dark, wavy hair. Now he could proceed. His 284 placed him six strokes ahead of his closest competitor, Dick Metz. In the entire tournament, only 15 rounds were completed under par.

After all was said and done, the first U.S. Open held in the West was an unqualified success. For Denver, the 1938 Open injected an estimated $200,000 into the city's moribund economy and raised its profile among American cities. For the struggling Cherry Hills Club, it generated a timely $23,000 profit and gained a national reputation for William Flynn's golf course.

So impressed was the Professional Golfers Association with the course that, only three years later, it brought the PGA Championship to the club. Unlike Henry Ransom, who departed in the first round despite shooting a 66, Byron Nelson advanced all the way to the finals, defeating in daunting succession Guldahl, Hogan, and Sarazen. Nelson's contest with Hogan was thrilling. All even after 34 holes, they traded approach shots to the island green. Hogan's ball splashed into the moat, sinking his hopes for the title. Nelson ultimately succumbed to Vic Ghezzi in an equally gripping final that was not settled until the 38th hole.

In the summer of 1958, the USGA awarded the club, and the city of Denver, its second National Open, the 1960 championship. Cherry Hills's first task was to recruit a tournament chairman. The board asked member Harold R. Berglund, a business executive, to take on the job. Berglund said he'd need some time to decide, and he proceeded to speak with the general chairman of each of the past five Opens. They each warned him in turn, Look out! If they had known beforehand how much work it would take, they *never* would have accepted the position.

Berglund, undeterred, told the board he'd serve as general chairman, but only under two conditions: he must have autonomy as boss, including independent check-writing authority, and the board must agree to refrain from criticizing his actions. The board complied.

Twenty-one months of tireless work later, as tournament week drew near, the Cherry Hills–USGA treasury overflowed. Even though ads in the classy 230-page program were rele-

JULIAN I. GRAUBART

gated to a narrow band of space along the bottom of each page, sales totaled $215,000, $40,000 more than any Open program had ever raised. And thanks largely to a successful sales campaign at Christmastime, ticket revenues totaled $155,000, pointing to a strong turnout. Daily tickets cost only two dollars for each of three days of practice rounds, five dollars for each of the first two championship rounds, and six dollars for the final day's 36-hole competition. A "season pass," good for admission all six days, cost only $16 ($26 if you wished to have access to the clubhouse). Approximately 9,000 season badges were sold, topping by more than 1,300 the high set at the 1956 championship.

It looked as though Denver's boosters had a chance to top the record three-day attendance of 43,821 set the year before by New Yorkers at Winged Foot (because of rain, the final round was postponed one day for the first time in U.S. Open history, raising the turnout to 56,000). Berglund, known as an unflinching wagerer on the golf course, went so far as to predict more than 60,000 in attendance and crowed impulsively to the local press, "I'm delighted that Denver is outdoing these other people." To his committee chairmen and vice chairmen, he announced, more soberly, "We have—financially—the nut cracked. Now it is up to all of us to put on a good show."

As a result of the robust financial news, on the Saturday before the tournament's start Berglund and the USGA's Dey announced an increase in the prize money from $50,000 to $60,000. The winner would now receive $14,400 instead of $12,000. Dey reportedly was reluctant to fatten the purse, fearful that revenues at future Opens might be insufficient to match the higher sum, but he gave in. On Sunday, June 12, a banner headline in the Denver Post sports section read, "Denver to Present Richest of All U.S. Opens Thursday." On Monday, a relieved Potts Berglund turned over the tournament reins to Joe Dey's 12-person USGA Championship Committee.

120

*   *   *

BERGLUND AND HIS TROOPS had paid the utmost attention to every detail involved in making the Open pleasant for the competitors, spectators, and press and profitable for the club and city. And the members of Cherry Hills Country Club and the people of Denver had pitched in like neighbors to make the 60th National Open a shining success.

The first day had been all one could hope it would be, and for some, at least, so had the first night. From the half-timbered, neo-Tudor clubhouse, the sound of clinking glasses, laughing voices, and the popular Murray Arnold band wafted out across the dark golf course, carrying farther than the first round's booming drives. Inside, the dance floor bustled for hours and the club's bar did land-office business. Of the last guests, who departed around 2:00 A.M., more than a few realized that the sun would soon be rising, the golfers and crowds returning to start the second round of the Open.

CHAPTER 7

DAVIS LOVE, JR., GOT A LUCKY BREAK. HIS THREESOME HAPPENED TO be scheduled to go off first in round two. This would minimize the time he'd be waiting around the club getting nervous or pounding out balls on the practice range, which could further aggravate his finger injury.

Rising for the 8:00 A.M. tee off certainly had caused no problem; Davis had barely slept a wink all night. In any case, not having to putt on greens scarred by players' spikes gave him a marked advantage. His long game severely hampered by his injured index finger, he needed to have a strong putting round if he hoped to make the cut.

Love dug himself into a deep hole in no time flat. On the shorter, easier front nine, he bogeyed the 2nd, 4th, 6th, and 7th holes and failed to collect a single birdie. His 39 made his situation extremely grim. But then Love steadied himself remarkably well. He ran off six consecutive pars, birdied the difficult par-four 16th (scene of woebegone Ray Ainsley's infamous 19), and parred in for a hard-fought, second straight 74.

It was just before noontime, and the early tee time didn't seem so favorable after all. Now the waiting began, along with the rehashing of all his mistakes and lost opportunities over

Cherry Hills's 18 holes. More than 50 golfers hadn't even started play yet, so in a sense his day was just beginning. It would be hours before he would know whether he had made the cut.

Davis's chances seemed modest at best. Playing conditions on Friday, June 17, 1960, were still unusually benign for a U.S. Open. The USGA had watered the greens the night before, so although they were standard fast Open greens they were not unreasonably slick. The mercury was rising fast toward 94 degrees, making it the hottest day of the year in Denver; but the pros in the field were accustomed to playing in sweltering heat, having just come from Memphis and Oklahoma City. So unless the wind suddenly kicked up or rain clouds rolled in—unlikely, because the day was clear, with practically endless visibility—Cherry Hills was likely to be docile, and Love's 148, historically a fine 36-hole score, might not earn safe passage to the championship's final day.

That Davis was in trouble was confirmed a half hour after he finished, when a threesome headed by Paul Harney and Rex Baxter, Jr., completed play. Harney, a 30-year-old tour regular with four victories to his credit, followed up his first-round 73 with a 70. The Massachusetts native with the accent like the Democratic presidential candidate, John Kennedy, was safely home for the final 36 holes.

Baxter, a 24-year-old private first class stationed at Fort Sam Houston, outside San Antonio, improved by 12 strokes over day one. After shooting a nervous opening-round 79— what one might expect of an untested pro still seven months away from his Army discharge—he breezed around the course in 67 strokes. What turned around his game was a sharp-shooter's approach shots that led to eight one-putt greens. Five of these were unimposing birdie putts—at the 1st hole, a 3-footer; at the 3rd, a 12-footer; at the 11th, a 15-footer; at the 13th, a 2-footer; and at the 17th, a 4-footer.

The U.S. Junior champion in 1953 and the 1957 NCAA

individual champion while part of the winning Houston University team, Baxter did not three-putt a single green. His only bogey came at the watery par-three 12th—a hole that was to give others fits this day—where he landed in the bunker that hugs the front right of the green.

Even with the splendid four-under-par round, his halfway mark, a 146, would get him nowhere in the 1960 Open. Nonetheless, the 67 stacked on top of his sterling amateur record—in 1957 he also won the Trans-Mississippi championship and played well on the winning U.S. Walker Cup team—made one wonder what he might do playing the tour full-time.

An early tee time did little to help Henry Ransom, one of the first-round leaders. After birdieing the first hole with a seven-foot putt, the part-time cattle rancher saw his game reverse course like a spooked herd. One day after his surprising 69, he sagged to a 76, the result of poor club selection and errant short putts. His 145 almost certainly would take him out of contention, he knew, but like Baxter, the veteran would still get to enjoy the whole championship and maybe make a few bucks, too—something few would have predicted.

His fellow competitor, Johnny Bulla, was not so fortunate. The medalist in the Open's sectional qualifying tournament in Denver duplicated his uninspired first-round score of 75. No need for him to wait around glued to the scoreboard; his pleasant, extended stay in Denver was over.

SPECTATORS STARTED TO POUR onto the club's grounds around 9:00 A.M., and the 9:04 trio of Crampton, Finsterwald, and Hogan became the first group to attract a substantial gallery in the second round.

Young Crampton, the unknown 1956 Australian Open winner at age 20, continued to dazzle as he had rarely done before American galleries. Bunkered on number 12 and unable to see the pin, he punched out and his ball traveled dead straight into the hole for a birdie. His par 71 gave him a two-round tally of 141, a score that would have given him the early tournament lead were it not for the unflappable Dow Finsterwald.

Dow collected seven pars and two birdies for a front-nine 33 that featured consecutive chip-ins. At the par-four 7th hole he landed in a bunker and needed two shots to dig out; the second one, though, found the bottom of the cup. The next hole he chipped in again, leading Hogan to tell the press afterward, "That Finsterwald is a magician around the greens." On the back nine, his game lost some of its precision, starting with a bogey at the 10th hole.

Few spectators noticed, but Finsterwald and his caddie had been squabbling over club selection during the round. In golf protocol, particularly in high-level professional golf, caddies offer advice only when asked, and they're expected to acquiesce to whatever is the player's decision. Some pros who use the same caddie for months or years at a time may condone, or even encourage, the caddie's opinions. Finsterwald's Open caddie, Tony Altomare, was not his tour caddie, yet the man still dug in his heels.

At the long, difficult 470-yard 14th, Finsterwald asked Altomare what club he should use to the green. The caddie, in a snit, replied, "Why should I tell you? You've asked me twice already today and didn't use my advice." Finsterwald, a distinguished-looking attorney's son from Athens, Ohio, blinked this aside. Just as he was about to hit away, Altomare said, "You don't have enough club." When the shot came up short, he added, "I told you it wasn't enough." Dow bogeyed the hole, and the two men bickered all the way to the next green, where Tony was invited to quit if he was unhappy. The caddie put down his man's bag and stalked off the course, leaving Finsterwald no better off than the weekend hacker who lugs his own clubs.

Altomare had been caddying at Cherry Hills since April,

but before that he had been a fixture on tour for years. His abandonment of Finsterwald surprised few tour players familiar with him. The man could be as stubborn as Open rough, especially when his pride was involved. Years later, Finsterwald recalled with amusement an incident from 1959 involving the caddie, Doug Ford, and himself.

Tony had been Ford's caddie for some time when, at the end of the Pensacola Open, Ford told him, "I don't want you next week." Abrupt player-caddie falling-outs like this, though commonplace, often produce hard feelings. In a downpour Finsterwald and Ford hopped in their car bound for St. Petersburg and the next tournament. Just outside the Pensacola club's entrance, off to the side of the road, stood Tony Altomare, drenched, one hand holding a suitcase, the other hitchhiking. Ford could hardly have relished the thought of Altomare's company all the way to St. Pete, but he and Finsterwald pulled over. Someone rolled down a window and said, "Get in. We'll give you a lift." The caddie, with a look of disdain, replied, "I wouldn't ride around the block with you guys."

At Cherry Hills, Finsterwald soon had a replacement for Tony. Charles LaFranchise, a Hogan diehard, stepped forward from the gallery and asked the golfer if he could be of service. Twenty-five years earlier he had done a fair amount of caddying, including for the well-known pro Abe Espinosa in Chicago. LaFranchise, 47, was now a television personality in Oregon, reportedly working for a Portland station in which Hogan had an interest. Among other duties he was the star of the *Uncle Charley Show*, in which he played saxophone and sang "Happy Birthday" greetings to his young viewers between Mickey Mouse cartoons.

With peace restored and his temporary caddie standing quietly off to the side, Finsterwald went on to birdie both the 16th and 17th holes and to par the 18th. The strong finish gave him a 69, lifting him temporarily to the 36-hole lead with a two-under-par 140. "Dow didn't ask my opinion on what clubs to use, but we did talk over playing short at the 17th," LaFranchise explained afterward. Meanwhile, Altomare was claiming that out on the course he had felt sick to his stomach from the heat. But he acknowledged that he had jeopardized a nice setup. "I'm sorry this happened. I like this club but I'm afraid this could cost me my job here. I'd like to go back and caddie for him."

Finsterwald was amazingly gracious, calling Altomare "a good caddie," but officials at the club were not sympathetic. Caddie chairman Fred Newton said, "He's a veteran. He should know better. I'm sorry this happened, too, but Finsterwald is right. He's under great pressure and shouldn't have to put up with this." Dick Johnson, a Colorado State University golfer who had caddied at Cherry Hills to pay for his tuition, was assigned to Finsterwald for Saturday. LaFranchise returned to the gallery, his momentary career as a tour caddie history; but "Uncle Charley" carried home to Portland an improbable story he could dine out on for years to come.

More immediately a story circulated about the third member of the threesome, Ben Hogan. It was said that the Hawk, known for powers of concentration that verged on trance, played two holes before he realized that Finsterwald had switched caddies. The tale was probably apocryphal but it might not have been, so strenuously was Hogan struggling to redeem a round free of three-putts and get back into the championship picture.

Despite his opening-round 75, Hogan hadn't given up for a minute on his fifth Open crown. Before teeing off he told some friends, "I've got to go today. I don't think I can win in that Midwest heat"—a reference to the 1961 Open site, Oakland Hills, outside Detroit. He wasted little time staking his claim, birdieing four of the first seven holes. Following a morale-lifting 12-foot birdie putt at number 1, he tapped in a three-footer and a gimme at numbers 4 and 5 respectively, then canned one more of 12 feet at the 7th hole. Even with a bogey at the 9th hole he was out in 32, three strokes below par. So much for the pundits who warned he might miss the cut.

Ben's approach shots to the green were impeccable, easing the task he faced once he was handed his putter. Finsterwald later called it the "finest exhibition of iron play" he had ever seen. At the same time Hogan's driving was unusually erratic and his putting was painful to watch. On the greens the old pro stood bent over even the three-footers for up to 30 seconds before finally starting back his putter.

At one point the scorekeeper accompanying the next threesome, watching the immobile figure from the fairway, jotted down in her notebook, "This waiting is killing us." It also had to be draining for Hogan's large, fervent gallery, particularly when, on three straight holes on the back nine, he missed birdie putts of six, five, and four feet. He also two-putted from 12 and 15 feet on the back nine. In the middle of a tense moment as he was preparing to putt on the 12th green, a spectator emitted a resounding burp, to which another fan quipped, "Nice out." The gallery roared, and even the dour Hogan had to chuckle.

A ten-foot birdie putt at 13 was canceled out when he misfired his tee shot at the 15th, a deceptively difficult 196-yard hole with a creek menacing an elevated green on its left and rear flanks. Coming to the demanding final hole, the scene of his double-bogey of 24 hours earlier, he was still three under par. He would have to work hard to preserve his 68.

Word of the Hawk's dramatic turnaround had attracted to the scenic 18th hole an enormous crowd (the *Denver Post* estimated Hogan's gallery at 6,000). Many spectators, unable to see over taller fans lining the fairway, had resorted to carrying the day's best-selling concession stand item, a one-dollar cardboard periscope. Others, anticipating the hottest day of the year, had come wearing sensible hats for protection against the sun. Some of the ladies in the crowd successfully combined whimsy and practicality in the hats they wore. The most clever one was worn by Mrs. Robert M. Siegfried, reported *Rocky Mountain News* society editor Dorothy Jane Burke (in 1960 newspapers' "society pages" usually dispensed with married women's first names). The large white straw hat, underpinning a miniature of the clubhouse and the lake, was a replica of the 18th hole, topped by a large golf ball.

Hogan, wearing his standard white billed cap, uncorked a long drive safely over the lake and onto the tilted fairway, leaving himself well positioned for the long uphill approach shot. When he reached his ball, his caddie, Chuck Marshall, had the temerity to suggest, "For gosh sake, let's make sure we don't do what we did yesterday." Ben answered, "We have to shoot for it and see what happens." He selected his three-iron and with surprisingly little wasted motion he got set in his stance and sent his ball soaring through the air. As the crowd followed its flight, silence gave way to hopeful murmurs that quickly built to a roar as the ball landed on the front of the green and rolled up two feet from the hole.

Ben started up the steep incline to the green, seemingly oblivious to the wild cheering. Shouts of "Atta boy, Ben!" and "Go get 'em, Ben!" greeted him. One spectator, knowing Hogan's reputation for aloofness, said, "It doesn't make any difference what the crowd does; he won't acknowledge the applause." But at that moment Hogan broke into a smile and tipped his cap. When he got ready to putt out, he froze over the little putt for a full 20 seconds and then, to everyone's relief, holed it. His 67 was his lowest round in the U.S. Open since he last won the championship in 1953 (he shot a 67 at Oakmont in the first round in which no other player in the field broke 70).

Hogan's round electrified Cherry Hills. Few expected such a clutch comeback at this stage of his career. Even if his day turned out to be a fluke, it had given thousands a taste of the

Open the way it used to be when it belonged to Hogan, when the Hawk's cold perfectionism dominated the proceedings. As he moved through the crowd, his arm curled behind his wife Valerie, he smiled as many well-wishers patted him on the back and shook his hand.

Since Hogan wouldn't come to the press tent, the press went looking for Hogan. The writers found him and all but encircled him in the locker room as he mopped his brow and answered their questions quietly, thoughtfully. A broad smile returned to his face when he recounted, hole by hole, a round completed without a single three-putt. He had seven one-putt greens and, in all, needed only 28 putts, though many were short ones. He also reported happily that although he had carried oxygen in his bag he didn't use any during his round. His headaches, apparently, had been chased away by his fine play.

But all was not perfect, he confessed. For one thing, he still did not feel comfortable judging distances—an unexpected admission from a man with an uncanny sense of distance. Years later Harvey Penick recalled in his *Little Red Book* the time Hogan was playing in a televised match on *Shell's Wonderful World of Golf.* Ben disagreed with the yardage listed for a par three. It wasn't 152 yards, he said; it was 148. Later the hole was measured. He was right—precisely; the scorecard was wrong.

That kind of instinct eluded him at Cherry Hills. "I hit some good shots today but I don't think I'm real sharp. I can't get the feel of this course. And I think in order to play a course real well you have to feel it." These cautionary remarks aside, Hogan was upbeat and eager for the next day's challenge. Where once he rarely recognized other players' skills, he praised Finsterwald's. And where once he was often plain rude to reporters, he bantered with the newsmen pressed around him. Asked if he still concentrated well, he joked, "I don't think I'm as mean as I used to be." He smiled and added, "Getting too old and can't fight anymore."

Was he too old to stand up to the championship's arduous 36-hole conclusion? someone asked. No, that would be no problem; he was in good physical condition, he answered. "Age doesn't affect the way you hit the ball; age just frays the nerves," he added. This led to a question about his habit of freezing over his putts.

"What I need is someone to put a rubber band on my putter. I cannot, for the life of me, bring the putter back. And I don't know why. Short putts or long putts—it doesn't matter. I can't bring the putter back." Then he recounted an incident from the late 1930s when he was paired with "Wild Bill" Mehlhorn, a PGA tour pioneer who won 20 tournaments in the 1920s. Mehlhorn, one of the finest golfers ever from tee to green but by then past his prime, left an approach shot a foot and a half from the hole. "You know where he played his next shot from?" Hogan asked. "A sand trap. That's the sort of thing that can happen to you."

Even in this rare, triumphant moment at Cherry Hills, a remote, surreal recollection emerged from Hogan's subconscious, accentuating his own excruciating case of the yips. None of the writers whom Hogan had eating out of his hands made much of the anecdote; none drew the obvious comparison between the Mehlhorn of the story and the Hogan of 1960. All they—or anyone else—cared about was that Ben Hogan was off life support.

As EVEN THE MOST casual sports fan in 1960 knew, Hogan had risen from the dead before—and much more profoundly than a single round of golf could ever represent. After colliding with his own mediocrity throughout the 1930s attempting to be a winner in professional golf, he finally broke through in 1940. The nadir and, at the same time, the turning point in this long, humbling period arrived at the start of 1938.

The morning of the first round of the Oakland (California)

Open, practically broke and on the verge of having to return home to Fort Worth yet again—now with his young wife, Valerie, in tow—he discovered that the tires had been stolen off his car. It hit him like a sucker punch to the solar plexus. Sam Snead spied the stoic Texan pounding his fists against a wall outside the Sequoyah Country Club. "I can't go another inch," he muttered, as close to tears as anyone had ever seen him. "I'm finished. Some son of a bitch stole the tires off my car."

Near desperation, he played for his golfing life that tournament as one possessed. In the final round he shot a 67, finished in second place, and earned $285, enough money to stay out on the tour. Many days of struggle would still lie ahead before he would become a somebody on tour, but he never again came close to forfeiting his career. "I played harder that day than I ever played before or ever will again," he would say later.

He won his first individual title in March 1940 at the prestigious North and South Open, played in North Carolina on the famous Pinehurst No. 2 course. Within two weeks, he owned two more tournament victories. Hogan finished the year the top money winner (with $10,655) and received the Vardon Trophy, named in honor of British golf champion Harry Vardon who had died three years earlier. In 1941 he won five events and repeated as top money winner and recipient of the Vardon Trophy, then awarded to the player with the year's finest tournament record.

Despite his long-delayed burst into stardom, Hogan's thirst for improvement was stronger than ever. It wasn't only that he demanded fuller payback for his many years of toil, including his painful childhood, though that was part of it. Nor was it only that he craved above all else in his career a major title, an accomplishment enjoyed by his childhood rival, Byron Nelson, though that, too, was part of it. Above all it was that he lived for the challenge of playing golf *well*. His pursuit of excellence in this immensely difficult game absorbed every bit of his considerable intellect and physical force.

He drove himself in practice, often working for hours before *and* after tournament rounds, sometimes with his callused hands so sore and split he could scarcely hold the club. In this sense, Hogan at practice was performing manual labor, which anticipated his later advice on how to become a great golfer: "Dig it out of the ground."

Observers noted that seeing Hogan on the range after he had completed a round, you couldn't tell whether he was ten strokes ahead or ten strokes behind. What many failed to realize was that he not only was trying to perfect his technique— his swing, his control over the ball's flight, the contact his clubface made with the ball—but he was also trying to master his concentration on each swing, training himself to avoid even one mental lapse during competition. Hardworking golfers who followed in his path sometimes compared favorably their own practicing habits with Hogan's. They may have hit as many balls as Hogan, as they claimed, but probably nobody ever brought as much rumination to each shot.

Early in 1942 he told sportswriter Grantland Rice, "I still believe that golf is largely a matter of forcing yourself to keep your mind on every stroke you play. I keep in fine physical shape, but too often when I finish a round I am dead tired— not physically, but mentally—and nerve-worn." That year he won six tournaments, including the Hale America National Open, a wartime substitute for the U.S. Open, which had been canceled and didn't resume until 1946. Hogan believed the event, sponsored by the USGA, along with the PGA of America and the Chicago District Golf Association, should have counted as a major championship, but hardly anybody else did. In any case, for the third consecutive season he topped the money list and received the Vardon Trophy.

Although he failed again in 1942 to win a bona fide "major," at the Masters he demonstrated conclusively that he had the reserves to excel when it meant the most. Over the final two rounds he clawed back from eight strokes behind to tie the leader, Byron Nelson, at the end of 72 holes. The next day, in an 18-hole play-off, Nelson erased Hogan's early three-shot margin, but only by playing the greatest golf of his career, to win by a single stroke, 69 to 70. Although the former caddie-mates and their wives had formed a two-car convoy on the tour, the men never were particularly close. During the play-off they barely exchanged a word (not so their wives, who stayed together chatting in the clubhouse). Remarkably, about 25 of their nomadic peers stuck around Augusta an extra day to watch the afternoon play-off.

By this time Hogan was already being described as a different kind of golf champion from his forebears, a hard-boiled competitor with ice in his veins. Grantland Rice characterized him in a May 1942 issue of *Collier's*—it was the first major national magazine article on the golfer—as "about as soft as a hydrant." Rice noted that Hogan "came up the hard way," but he provided no details that might have made Ben a sympathetic figure.

The details, like the player himself, were grim. He was born William Ben Hogan on August 13, 1912, in Stephenville, Texas, the third child of Clara (Williams) and Chester Hogan. The family lived in Dublin, about 80 miles southwest of Fort Worth, until Ben was nine and then moved to the big city. The father, a blacksmith who apparently suffered from depression, killed himself with a gun in the family's Fort Worth home in 1922. He was 37 and left behind a 32-year-old widow who had limited means to raise son Royal, 13; daughter Princess, 11; and Bennie, 9.

Bennie started selling newspapers around the Texas and Pacific Railroad Station, where he sometimes nodded off at night on a waiting-room bench. A small, skinny boy, he took up caddying at an unexceptional nine-hole course, Glen Garden Country Club. He was 11 years old and hardly taller than the bags he carried. Some of the caddies taunted him mercilessly until he whipped a couple of the bullies. On Saturday nights in the summer he would sometimes sleep in a sand trap so he would be first in line to caddie on Sunday. The best golfer among the caddies was a boy his age, rail-thin like himself but a foot taller, named John Byron Nelson, Jr. At Christmas, 1927, Ben surprised club members when he tied Byron in the annual nine-hole caddies' tournament before losing by a stroke in a nine-hole play-off.

Ben's mother, Clara, opposed his increasing involvement in golf, judging it a waste of time. Why couldn't he be more hardworking like Royal? Eventually she came to accept, grudgingly, Ben's absorption by the game, and when he was 16 she bought him a 40-dollar set of golf clubs—his first matched set. High school in his senior year took a backseat to traveling around Texas to play in amateur tournaments, and although Hogan was a fair student he dropped out before graduating. A brief, modestly successful amateur career ended miserably at a tournament in Shreveport, Louisiana. After a mediocre showing, he sold his wristwatch to pay his caddie and, hitchhiking, rode back to Fort Worth in an open touring car in the pouring rain. He was getting nowhere fast, so, with the questionable judgment of a 17-year-old, he entered the 1930 Texas Open as a pro, terminating his amateur status.

For the next eight years—Depression years—he found whatever work he could get in Fort Worth and practiced whenever he could. He felt ashamed to accept a job as a croupier in illegal dice games, but he found something else before long. In 1931 the Glen Garden pro, Ted Longworth, took him and Ralph Guldahl, a contemporary from Dallas, out on tour with him; Hogan ran out of money on the West Coast and needed to wire home for enough cash to get back to Fort Worth. In 1932, with $125 in his pocket, he tried his luck out on tour again, but soon broke, he shuffled back into town. A third foray in 1934 lasted somewhat longer. During this endless, discouraging period, there was one bright event. On April 14, 1935, Hogan married Valerie Fox, a local girl he first met in Sunday school when he was 12. She alone believed in his potential as a golfer.

At the end of 1936, with $1,450 in savings, the couple purchased a used Buick and set off for the 1937 tour. During the season, Hogan finished in the top ten in five tournaments, but Depression-era purses being what they were, the young couple anxiously watched their small nest egg dangerously shrink. Meanwhile, Byron Nelson won the Masters (then called the Augusta National Invitation)—and with it the nickname "Lord Byron," coined by O. B. Keeler of the *Atlanta Constitution*. And Ralph Guldahl captured his first U.S. Open. Hogan sat out both tournaments, having failed to qualify for either.

By January of 1938, Ben and Valerie's treasury hovered at $86 as they reached the Oakland Open, where Hogan courageously breathed life into his expiring golf career. Later that season he qualified for his first Masters and shared a team victory with Vic Ghezzi in the Hershey (Pennsylvania) Four-Ball. Placing in the top ten in 16 tournaments, he finished the year 15th on the money list. Nineteen thirty-nine offered more of the same—many high finishes, including three seconds, but still no victory. Then followed his three straight Vardon Trophy seasons. He had finally arrived.

In March 1943 Hogan was drafted and inducted into the Army Air Corps, becoming a second lieutenant following attendance at Officers' Candidate School in Miami. That year, the PGA tour was cancelled, but during the next two years Hogan smoldered as Nelson, exempt from the service because of a blood disorder, rose to become not only the tour's top star but the country's leading sports hero. Nelson won 8 tournaments in 1944 and a phenomenal 18 (including 11 consecutively!) in 1945, and both years he was named Athlete of the Year by the Associated Press.

Gene Sarazen, in a June 1955 *Saturday Evening Post* article, recalled sharing a ride with Hogan back to their hotel after the two tied for second place behind Nelson in the 1945 Tam O'Shanter Open. Sarazen took his check out of his pocket and said, "Ben, this is a lot of dough." Hogan, dressed in his officer's uniform, stared at him fiercely and replied, "When I take this uniform off, I'll make those guys retire."

Upon discharge in August 1945 he hit the fairways running, and the Nelson-Hogan rivalry became fierce instantly. One week, it was Nelson romping to victory in the Knoxville (Tennessee) Open, winning by ten strokes. The next week, it was Hogan's turn in Nashville—a four-stroke victory. The following two tournaments, in Dallas and Tulsa, Sam Snead won his fifth and sixth titles of the year. Then the earlier pattern resumed. Hogan shot an amazing 261 to win at Portland, Oregon, beating Nelson's 72-hole tour record by two strokes. Two weeks later, Nelson shot a 259 to win in Seattle and recover the record.

Hogan won five times in all during his abbreviated season, a bold statement to be sure, but 1945 belonged to Nelson. The final tournament of the year was played, fittingly, back where the two masters began their life in golf, Fort Worth's Glen Garden Country Club, now a much-improved 18-hole course. Hogan and 16 other golfers flew in from Miami on a cargo plane purchased from the Air Force by the pilot, Johnny Bulla. Ben finished tied for seventh. Lord Byron capped off his miracle season with an eight-stroke triumph.

By the end of 1946, Nelson had had enough of the grind. With six final tournament wins to his credit, he retired from regular competition with 51 career victories and moved on to ranching some land he bought in Roanoke, Texas, just north of Fort Worth. Hogan collected 13 wins that year, including his first major championship, the PGA. In the semifinals he skewered his regular partner in four-ball tournaments, Jimmy Demaret, 10 and 9, and paid for his roughshod victory with some unfavorable press. The always amusing Demaret, however, seemed to hold no grudge. Asked what Hogan had said during the match, he replied, "The only thing I ever heard him say was, 'You're away.' "

Nineteen forty-seven brought Ben seven more victories, followed by ten in 1948, including another PGA in May and his first U.S. Open title in June. His Open triumph, clinched with a score of 276, broke Ralph Guldahl's 1937 mark by five strokes and made him the first to capture both championships in the same year since Sarazen in 1922. Yet his historic season wasn't over. In August he won the Western Open, becoming the first man ever to win the then top-three professional events in the United States in a single season. When he was introduced at the presentation ceremony as the greatest golfer ever, he shrugged off the label. "I don't want to ever reach that pinnacle," he said. "Then there's only one place to go and that's down. I want to be a 'comer.' "

In little more than three seasons Hogan had won a phenomenal 35 tournaments, yet he still thought of himself—and he still *was*—a comer. In the midst of this greatest concentrated accumulation of tournament victories in the tour's 30-year history he was not satisfied with the quality of his play, and in 1947 he started working secretly on adjustments to his swing.

Why would the most prodigious winner in the game, and someone who had recently won his first major, change his swing? Hogan was utterly fascinated by the golf swing's complexity, and he continually examined its subtleties, experimenting first with one nuance, then another. What he was after in this period—and he succeeded in discovering—was the touch, a feel, that produced maximum control over the ball. He came to believe that the key to winning major victories, when pressure could wreak havoc with a swing, was to perfect a fade—a controlled left-to-right flight that tends to soften the ball's landing and thereby minimizes bad bounces.

Once a chronic hooker, he became so proficient at fading

the ball that in those days of caddies running around the practice range to retrieve their player's shots, he'd blast out one shot after another practically at his caddie's feet. After most shots, the caddie could open his shag bag and field the balls on one hop. Once, before the 1951 Ryder Cup matches at Pinehurst, Britain's Max Faulkner, venturing where angels fear to tread, approached Hogan at practice. "I say, Ben, I think I could help you with that fade."

The Hawk stared at him with those steely blue-gray eyes. "You don't see the caddie moving any, do you?"

And so 1949 began for Hogan like all the other recent years, traveling the tour with his one true friend, his wife, Valerie—only now in the comfort of an almost new Cadillac— and dominating golf tournaments. It seemed at last that he had captured the "feel" on the course that he had long been digging for. Following triumphs at both the season's second tournament, the Bing Crosby Pro-Am, and third, the Long Beach Open, he had won 11 of the last 16 tournaments in which he'd competed. Clearly the risk he had taken in fine-tuning his technique a couple of years earlier had yielded fabulous rewards.

The next week Hogan and Demaret finished the four rounds of the Phoenix Open tied for first place. In an 18-hole play-off Jimmy demonstrated that his adversary still was mortal and that he, with 22 tour victories, was much more than just a very funny man who wore technicolor outfits. Ben and Valerie, who were still settling into their first home, packed up their car and started the 1,200-mile journey east to Fort Worth.

On the morning of February 2, on a winding, foggy Highway 80 in West Texas, a Greyhound bus traveling west pulled out to pass a truck and veered directly into the path of the Hogans' car crossing a narrow bridge. Ben, realizing there was no way he could avoid a collision, let go of the steering wheel and threw himself protectively in front of his wife. Minutes later, Valerie, who was uninjured, pulled herself from the wreckage. With the help of two passersby she extricated Ben and laid him in the backseat. Ben's lunge to protect Valerie saved him from the steering column, which tore violently into the front seat. But he had a crushed left leg, a fractured pelvis, a broken left collarbone, a fractured left ankle, and a cracked right rib. Ninety minutes passed during which Hogan, in extreme pain, lost and regained consciousness. Finally an ambulance arrived, and he reached the Hotel Dieu Hospital in El Paso at 1:45 P.M.

Hogan was put in a cast up to his waist and started his recovery. In addition to Valerie, Ben had the constant companionship of his golf clubs, which leaned against a wall in his room. He also received a flood of get-well wishes that moved him to feel that in the future he must do better to reciprocate the public's warmth.

The good news was that it appeared he'd be able to play golf again. But then, on the verge of discharge, his condition suddenly took a turn for the worse; a small blood clot was discovered in his right lung. When a second blood clot formed in his left leg, the doctors feared that the pulmonary artery into the lung would soon be obstructed. His condition was critical. An obituary was composed by the Associated Press for its member newspapers and radio stations.

Alton S. Ochsner, a renowned vascular surgeon, was flown in from New Orleans to perform a rare procedure that involved tying off the inferior vena cava, a major vein in the lower body, so that no clots could travel to the heart or lungs. Hogan demanded to know if he'd be able to walk and play golf. The surgeon assured him he would. The operation lasted two hours and left Ben in a cast from his hips to his armpits and his left leg swollen and disfigured. The cast came off a week later.

Back home in Fort Worth in early April he was told that it would take five months for the swelling in his legs to go down and that walking a bit at a time would be the best therapy. Hogan, of course, overdid it, and sometimes Valerie had to get in their new car and cruise the neighborhood until she spotted him, sitting on the ground, unable to go farther.

Requesting the USGA's secrecy, Ben submitted an entry form for the U.S. Open, scheduled for June, just in case he should recover by then. But he wasn't close to being ready to walk a single round, never mind 36 holes in one day, and the up-and-coming Cary Middlecoff succeeded him as champion. It was not until August that he even took a full swing with a golf club again. In September he served as nonplaying captain of the U.S. Ryder Cup team, which traveled to Scarborough, England, and defeated Great Britain 7 to 5.

In November he took to the practice tee for the first time, but he still couldn't walk very well. To minimize swelling and leg cramps he wore athletic wrappings on both legs. His first round of golf came on December 10 at Colonial Country Club; he shot a 71 and followed it the next day with a 72, but he refused to credit the achievement as golf since he rode in a cart between shots. A week later he walked the entire eighteen holes, but it left him so spent that afterward he collapsed into bed.

Nonetheless, he sent off an entry to play in the Los Angeles Open, which would begin Friday, January 6. His plan was to play a few practice rounds in Los Angeles and then decide whether he was physically up to playing the tournament. He could hardly have picked a more hospitable place to start his comeback. Riviera Country Club was the site not only of his 1948 U.S. Open championship but of three L.A. Open titles.

In his first trial round, on Friday, December 30, he shot a two-under-par 69 that he called lucky. In each of the next four days, another practice round followed. He was rusty and in considerable pain, but he could get around. And as his practice-tee prowess and occasional dabs of on-course brilliance showed, he certainly hadn't forgotten the nuances of his craft. On Tuesday, January 3, he announced he would play.

Opening-day attendance hit 9,000, by far the highest total in the tournament's 24-year history. Hogan played creditably if erratically—he missed four fairways badly and three-putted three holes—and finished with a 73, five shots behind the leader, Ed Furgol. His legs and stamina seemed surprisingly resilient.

Sadly, the Hawk was not only the center of attention; he was also the center of controversy. Ben sparked a brouhaha when, distracted by a gauntlet of cameramen on the first fairway, he stepped back from his ball and said, "No pictures or no play." A sign to that effect was rushed out and then the photographers, who were just trying to do their job, hustled back to the clubhouse and protested. Their sentiments were shared by some of the Hawk's opponents, who noted that all golfers face the same distractions from cameramen every week.

Day two was an unblemished success. Ben kept his feelings about the photographers to himself and shot a 69 in front of another large gallery, including some of Hollywood's elite—Humphrey Bogart, Shirley Temple, and Danny Kaye, among others. Jerry Barber took the lead at 137 with a 68, trailed by Henry Ransom with a 139. Hogan was tied for third at 142 with former tennis champion Ellsworth Vines, followed by Furgol and Sam Snead at 143. The period's top black golfer, Teddy Rhodes, stood at 144. Bill Spiller, who shot a 78 the first day, withdrew from the tournament.

A downpour washed out Sunday's third round. Even though almost half the field had managed to complete play, the scores were thrown out. Hogan's group was on the 11th hole when the tournament committee canceled the round. The sun came out on Monday and helped return the drenched Santa Monica Canyon course to surprisingly good condition. Hogan shot his second consecutive 69 and trailed leader Barber, standing at 209, by only two strokes. Snead, tied for fifth at one-over-par 214, made up a stroke and remained a contender.

By Tuesday, Hogan was beat. Between most shots he rested briefly on a small folding golf seat. Even so, his shot-making remained strong and his putting steady. At the undulating 15th green, fate seemed to be backing him, as a putt of 60 feet found the bottom of the cup. When he completed play, exhausted, with his third straight 69, it looked as though he had penned a storybook comeback. All eyes turned now to the threesome of Jerry Barber, Jack Burke, Jr., and Sam Snead on the 14th hole.

The local favorite, Barber, had blown up with a 41 on the front nine and was out of it. Burke and Snead, each needing to make up two strokes to par over the last five holes to match Hogan's 280, parred numbers 14, 15, and 16. At the 17th tee, Sam drawled, "Looks like we need a couple of birdies," but Jack could only par the hole, which ended his bid. That left the Slammer, the 1949 Player of the Year, whose six victories included the Masters and the PGA Championship. As in the late 1930s, he was once again the game's biggest name. At the 17th green Sam canned the 14-foot birdie putt that he had to make. On to the par-four 18th hole, where two finely executed shots brought him to 15 feet of the hole.

As Snead approached the final green, the focal point of thousands of spectators packed tightly on the hillside that forms a natural amphitheater, a fan perched on a frail tree came tumbling down as a branch snapped under his weight. The crowd, and Snead, burst out laughing, breaking the tension. Then silence as Sam surveyed his putt, set his putter blade behind his ball, and rolled it into the heart of the hole. Relegated to a sidelight for most of the event, Snead had shot the round of the tournament, a stirring 66. Now an 18-hole play-off against his once and future antagonist waited. "Wish I didn't have to play tomorrow," the weary Hogan said. "I wish he'd won it out there today."

As it turned out, Ben did not play the next day. More rain fell and the play-off was postponed a full week until after the Bing Crosby tournament. By the time the two rivals finally returned to Riviera Sam won, rather easily, by four strokes, but many commented that Snead's heroics really hadn't spoiled Hogan's amazing comeback; nothing could diminish the gutsy courage of Hogan's return. Red Smith wrote in the January 12th *New York Herald Tribune*, "There is strong suspicion in this quarter that this was the most remarkable feat in the entire history of sports."

That June, the victory denied at Riviera was granted at Merion in the U.S. Open. It stands as the greatest triumph of Hogan's career, one that certainly would have made a memorable last chapter in the Hogan legend. (For Snead, a glorious 1950 season concluded bitterly. Although he had won 11 tournaments to Hogan's 2—the second being the unofficial Greenbrier Pro-Am—Hogan was voted the PGA's Player of the Year.) But more heroics lay ahead. In 1951 he entered only four tournaments and won three: at Augusta National, his first Masters title; at "the Monster," Oakland Hills, his third Open; and the "World Championship." The Hawk was subdued, though, in 1952. He played in only three tournaments: the Masters (seventh place), Colonial (first), and the Open (third).

He was 40 now—and a battered 40 at that. Surely his great days were over. But, no. In April of 1953 he won his second Masters, shooting a 14-under-par 274 that broke the tournament scoring record by five strokes. In June he won his fourth National Open, topping runner-up Snead by six strokes at Oakmont. And in July, playing in his first-ever British Open, the man the Scots called "the Wee Ice Mon" won by four shots at Carnoustie.

The Hogan legend, inscribed January 1950 in Los Angeles, was sealed July 1953 in Carnoustie.

And now in 1960 after a bad patch, Hogan had shot the

lights out at Cherry Hills in the second round. Yes, as they said, the last had not been heard from Ben Hogan.

JACK NICKLAUS HAD A relatively early tee time, 10:00 A.M., and that suited him just fine. After his self-possessed even-par 71, he was eager to get back out on the course. Like Arnold Palmer in the first round, he began his second round in the worst possible way: he drove into the creek bordering the right side of the hole. But unlike Arnold, he saved par with a brilliant recovery shot that finished four feet from the hole.

Through the first eight holes, Nicklaus held fast to par, only to see his efforts wasted at the uphill 9th where he flew his second shot, a five-iron, over the crowd and out-of-bounds, double-bogeyed the hole, and made the turn in 37. But the remarkably cool young man didn't crumble. At the 11th hole, after a poor pitch shot landed 18 feet above the hole, Jack confidently stroked home the slick downhill putt for a birdie. By the time he reached the final hole, his position to par was unchanged—still one over for the round. Here, too, he put his approach beyond the hole—about 16 feet—and here, too, he sank the sizable downhiller.

"I putted much better today," he said, but he couldn't understand why all the fuss about his second consecutive par 71. "After all, I've played in five of these." (Actually, it was his fourth U.S. Open.) Casper was less reserved about his fellow competitor's showing. "Jack is so long and straight off the tee, and he has a good stance like a real veteran. He has got to become one of the greatest if he continues to improve."

The defending champion Casper had a bewildering outing in which he dropped a few long putts, squandered many makeable ones, missed seven fairways and four greens, and scored one stroke lower than his opening-round 71. "It's crazy," he said, sounding perplexed. "I played at least five shots better in the first round than I did today, yet the score doesn't show it." The difference was his putting.

Poor chip shots on the front nine led to two Casper bogeys, but birdie putts of 15 and 30 feet offset them. On the incoming nine he birdied the par-three 15th hole with another 30-foot putt and scrambled to play par golf elsewhere. Although his putting improved from the day before, it was far from sharp. Billy failed to hole eight putts of eight feet or less. Nonetheless, when he completed his second round, he was tied with Crampton at 141, only one stroke behind the early leader, Finsterwald. Nicklaus was another stroke back at 142.

The third member of the threesome, Walter Burkemo, shot a 72 despite missing par putts of six feet at the 2nd hole and four feet at the 18th. Sarge made the cut with a 146, advancing to the final 36 holes along with one other player in the six-man Michigan contingent. Long-hitting Chick Harbert from Battle Creek, like Burkemo a former PGA champion who advanced to three PGA finals (in fact, he beat Burkemo in 1954), also landed at 146. In the spring, the veteran with seven tour wins had given up his club job and started training to get back into tournament play—at age 45. "I guess that six weeks of roadwork in Florida is paying off," he told John Walter of the *Detroit News*.

Four groups back, the next big-name threesome dragged along like retirees with nothing else to do. Arnold Palmer, Cary Middlecoff, and Jack Fleck had lost a bit of their luster—and gallery—from day one, even as they polished their golf. Middlecoff played beautifully for 16 holes. Poised at three under par, his streak of consecutive four-round Open appearances seemed certain despite his opening 77. But then at the 17th hole he three-putted from 12 feet for a bogey, and at 18 he left his approach shot 25 yards short of the green and needed three to get down. As it turned out, his 70 qualified him for the final 36 holes, but without a stroke to spare.

In his Memphis newspaper column the next day, the two-

In 1960, the confident tee-to-green play of 47-year-old Ben Hogan was still something to behold. But the hesitant putting of the familiar figure in the white linen cap was so appalling that it was hard to believe it was the same golfer. It was not unusual for Ben to agonize 20 seconds over the ball before he would putt.
(John Zimmerman/*Sports Illustrated*)

Even when Arnold Palmer was having a bad round, he was captivating to watch—grimacing over his ineptitude, struggling, trying to ignite a spark, pleading with the powers-that-be to intervene. This was the man the spectators saw during the first three rounds of the 1960 U.S. Open.
(John Zimmerman/*Sports Illustrated*)

At Cherry Hills, 20-year-old amateur Jack Nicklaus suddenly commanded national attention. Even allowing for added carry in Denver's thin air, Nicklaus's club selection was incredible. While most everyone laid up on the 548-yard, par five 17th hole with their second shot, Nicklaus cleared the moat fronting the green in two. One day in practice he reached the green using his 7-iron. (John Zimmerman/*Sports Illustrated*)

Gary Player curled in a difficult birdie putt on the 6th green enroute to a confidence-building 70 in the first round at Cherry Hills Country Club. Afterward, the 1959 British Open champion rhapsodized over what it would mean to him to win the U.S. Open. "Do you realize that only eight players in history have won both the American and British Opens? And it's been something like 40 years since a foreigner has won this tournament." The 24-year-old South African coveted a place in golf history. (UPI/Bettmann)

Tommy Bolt (*above*) drove his first two tee shots into the pond at the 18th hole in round one. His third attempt cleared the pond, but he still had one more use for his driver—he flung the offending club into the water. Accounts that the club cleared his partner Claude Harmon's head by inches seem greatly exaggerated. Bolt took an eight on the hole, shot 80 for the round, and withdrew from the tournament. (John Zimmerman/*Sports Illustrated*)

A par four on the 18th hole would have tied Doug Sanders with Mike Souchak for the first-round lead. Just as he was about to tee off, a bass leaped out of the pond 30 feet away and splashed noisily back in. Sanders discontinued his swing and set up again, but his concentration was gone and so was his tee shot—hooked into the drink. "That fish looked like a whale," he said later. Doug kept his fairway iron in play (*above*), but the damage had been done. He took a double-bogey six. (UPI/Bettmann)

Leader Mike Souchak was in complete command of his game during the second round. Here, on the 16th green, he coaxed in a ten-footer for birdie—the eighth three on his scorecard. Even with a disappointing bogey on the final hole, he shot a 67 to set a new U.S. Open scoring record of 135, breaking the 36-hole mark of 138. His lead going into "Open Saturday" was three strokes. (UPI/Bettmann)

Although Dow Finsterwald missed a makeable birdie putt at the 18th green in round two, his 69 lifted him temporarily to the 36-hole lead with a two-under-par 140. At 30, in his prime and having a typically strong year on tour, he seemed as capable of winning as anyone. (AP/Wide World Photos, Inc.)

When Arnold Palmer holed out for the 280 he'd predicted would win the Open, he took two quick steps forward, scooped his ball out of the cup, and without breaking stride pitched his red sun visor high in the air. On NBC's videotaped broadcast, an announcer cried, "Palmer has won! Palmer has won!" But it wasn't over. (John Zimmerman/*Sports Illustrated*)

Sam Snead, 48, the winner of every major golf title except the U.S. Open, went into the final day's double-round with high hopes. He might have remained a contender to the end but for one disastrous hole in round three—a triple-bogey seven at the par-four 9th. The experience was not as devastating as his infamous eight at the 1939 Open's final hole, but reporters drew the comparison in the next day's papers. The Slammer's diehard supporters needed no such reminder. (AP/Wide World Photos, Inc.)

Jack Fleck, the shocking upset winner over Ben Hogan in the 1955 U.S. Open, entered the final round only four shots from the top despite his putting woes. Then the hot putting round he'd been hoping for arrived just in time. He birdied the 1st hole, bogied the 2nd, and ran off birdies on each of the next four, including an 18-footer here at number 6. Four holes later, he was in a five-way tie for the lead— with Julius Boros, Mike Souchak, Jack Nicklaus, and Arnold Palmer. (AP/Wide World Photos, Inc.)

With six holes left in the championship, Jack Nicklaus had sole possession of the lead and he wasn't a bit nervous, he said afterward. But at the 13th green his poise finally flickered. Making a youthful error in judgment, he ran a 12-foot uphill birdie putt 18 inches above the hole and missed coming back. Another three-putt bogey followed at number 14, but he was still very much in contention.
(John Zimmerman/
Sports Illustrated)

The moat in front of the island green at the 71st hole where Ben Hogan's hopes for a record fifth U.S. Open title sank. Another foot or two and the climactic shot of the tournament, a 50-yard half wedge, would have hopped forward and crowded the pin at the front of the green. But the ball, bearing terrific backspin, landed at the top of the bank, trickled down, and settled at the edge of the channel. The Hawk splashed it out, but his high-risk gamble to go one up on Arnold Palmer had backfired. Palmer held sole possession of the lead for the first time. (UPI/Bettmann)

At the 9th hole in the last round, needing a birdie three for an unheard-of 29, Arnold Palmer knocked his approach shot into the gallery. His chip from in front of the scoreboard settled eight feet from the pin. But he saved par for a 30, tying the lowest nine in U.S. Open history and carrying him from seven strokes out of the lead to only two. Walking down the 10th fairway, he said, "I wanted that 29, damn it." (Denver Public Library)

Palmer, 30, seemed destined to win other U.S. Open titles when USGA President John G. Clock made the presentation on June 18, 1960, but Arnold never hoisted the championship trophies again. Three times in the next six years he would finish the Open's 72 holes tied for the lead only to lose in an 18-hole playoff the next day— to Jack Nicklaus in 1962, to Julius Boros in 1963, and to Billy Casper in 1966. (UPI/Bettmann)

time champion gave short shrift to his own standing ("For those kind enough to be interested in a man 12 shots off the pace . . ."), instead commenting on the players likely to compete for the title. One man not to be overlooked, he wrote, was his fellow competitor, Jack Fleck. "As on Thursday, Fleck played fine and steady golf. He was never in serious trouble, and a half-dozen putts that he missed came hairsbreadth close to falling."

Indeed, Fleck played doggedly consistent, totally unspectacular golf. He three-putted only once, at the 10th hole, and only one hole thwarted him in producing a round of machine-like proficiency. On the 4th hole, a 426-yard par four that bends sharply left around a stand of cottonwood trees, he hit into two different bunkers and had to play a third shot from under a spruce behind the green. Wielding his putter croquet style, the tall, likeable fellow knocked his ball to within 15 feet of the hole and salvaged a bogey.

In two rounds, Jack had 5 birdies, only 3 bogeys, and 28 pars, and when he came in with his second consecutive 70—a remarkable score considering 34 of those strokes occurred on the putting greens—the murmurs began. The unsung Bettendorf, Iowa, native wasn't going to do it again, was he?

Jack had been operating two municipal golf courses in Davenport, Iowa, for almost ten years when he decided to try the tour full-time in 1955. The tall, slender Iowan had won a few local tournaments over the years, but earlier forays on the national circuit had produced spotty results, to say the least. In 1950, when he and his bride, Lynn, drove to a number of tour stops, they spent eight dollars for every dollar he made.

At the '55 Open, with Fleck's season's earnings totaling a paltry $2,700, few noticed him until he arrived at the back nine of the Olympic Club, the only man standing between Ben Hogan and the record fifth title. Hogan had finished earlier with his best round of the tournament, a 70, and handed his ball to Joe Dey as a donation to the USGA's museum—that's how likely the outcome seemed. Fleck needed to go two under for the last five holes to tie Hogan's score, an extremely tall order given the course's merciless rough. To everyone's amazement, the unknown golfer made two birdies. In the play-off the next day, which he won 69 to 72, he never trailed.

As the American public made Jack Fleck's acquaintance, it learned that his victory was more than an athlete's Cinderella story; it represented the fulfillment of a deep-seated personal dream. For years, both on the road and at his pro shop in Davenport, the U.S. Open had been tied intimately with Fleck's existence. When he'd glimpse Lynn window-shopping, he'd tell her, "I'll buy you that when I win the Open." And when the couple was selecting a name for their first son, Jack wanted it to be the name of a U.S. Open champion. He favored Snead Hogan Fleck, Lynn revealed, but she wouldn't stand for it. Jack gave her a list of all the Open winners, and they settled on Craig Wood Fleck (after the first man to win the Masters and Open in the same year).

Hogan was a central figure in Fleck's golfing aspirations, making Jack's Open victory all the more powerful. Upon winning the play-off, the softspoken Fleck stated, simply, "I have idolized Ben since my caddie days." Ironically, the irons he used in the Open were manufactured by Hogan's young company; in fact, the owner personally delivered the two wedges needed to make the set complete.

The younger Fleck used to get so upset after making bad shots, Jack explained after his triumph, that he'd sometimes withdraw from a tournament on the spot. It had taken years to defeat this failing, and now he credited self-composure with his Open win. "He's in another world," Olympic general chairman Robert Roos, Jr., had observed during the play-off. "You could stick a six-inch needle in his back and he'd never know the difference." A week after his triumph, the champion told *Time* magazine, "Composure is the one thing I ever tried to copy from Ben Hogan."

*   *   *

ARNOLD PALMER IMPROVED BY one stroke over his first-round 72, but he was far less composed about his standing after 36 holes than he was after 18. He knew that with an even-par 71, he wasn't going to gain on the leaders; more likely he'd slip further behind. And what steamed him in midafternoon, as he received reports on Souchak and the other leaders, was that he felt he *should* have brought in a low number.

Once again, he went boldly with his driver off the 1st tee. Although he didn't reach the green he kept his ball in the fairway this time, and the results were a sight better than a double-bogey six; he birdied the hole. More representative of his day was an Associated Press photo that appeared in papers across the country showing him at the bottom of a steep bank slashing out of deep rough to the elevated 5th green. He parred the hole, though—his fourth consecutive par—and then birdied the 6th, a nonthreatening par three of 174 yards to a lightbulb-shaped green. He was now two under par.

But Arnold could only par the routine par-four 7th, and after parring the 8th the tournament favorite lost ground with his first bogey. He made the turn, disappointed, in one-under 34. After parring the 10th hole he told *Pittsburgh Press* sportswriter Bob Drum on the long, par-five 11th, "I've got to figure out some way to win this tournament." The rumination was reminiscent of his comment in the last round of the Masters. As he walked to the 17th tee, one stroke behind Venturi, he remarked, "Well, I've got to make two birdies." On this day at the Open he produced the spark he sought, birdieing the 11th, and he was back to two under par.

Then came the pivotal hole for Arnold, the par-three 12th. For the second straight day he bogeyed it and felt himself sag. Later he said he felt jinxed by the hole, not only because of the bogeys, but because of the hits his confidence was taking there. Following a par at 13, serious trouble returned.

The 14th, a long par four of 470 yards, was the only hole on the course with a "blind" tee shot (meaning players can't see the green from the tee). The fairway curves gracefully to the left; a deep creek flanks that side of the fairway and out-of-bounds clings to the right. To have a decent shot to the green, players needed a long, accurate drive. But Palmer drove out-of-bounds, and then, after putting his second drive in the fairway, he pulled his approach shot into the bank of the creek.

He pitched from there, but the best shot he could manufacture left him 30 feet from the pin, putting for a bogey five. Palmer did not fully realize it at the time, but this was his first crisis. He was the tour's boldest putter, but at this distance if he went after the putt too aggressively he risked a triple-bogey that could push him well out of reach of the leaders. If he lagged it up, a double-bogey was practically certain. Arnold bore down hard surveying the line and, with the luck of the extremely talented, holed the putt. Four consecutive pars concluded his round in 71. It was a score that Palmer thought should have been a good deal better. In fact, it could have turned out much worse.

About the best thing one could say about Palmer's position when his threesome came in 4½ dreary hours after teeing off was that he wouldn't be playing with either the slow Fleck or the slower Middlecoff the last day. Palmer didn't hesitate to attribute his failure to mount a charge to his sluggish companions. (American golfers were thicker-skinned then; later they yelped at even the hint of criticism.) "I figure it cost me four shots in the pairings. I could play three holes while those guys were playing one," he muttered in exasperation.

At 2:00 P.M., as San Diego-area pro Don Whitt turned in his scorecard, heat waves hovered over Cherry Hills's rolling fairways. The day's oppressive temperatures were reaching their most uncomfortable level. A thermometer mounted on a side of the clubhouse facing the sun read 107. Dripping wet with perspiration but feeling chipper (thanks to a 69), Whitt insisted to Jack Murphy of the *San Diego Union*, "I'm not sweating; it's just that my skin is leaking."

The golfers and the spectators weren't the only ones hot under the collar; in the air-conditioned comfort of the clubhouse, so were a delegation from Oakland Hills Country Club, site of the 1961 Open. Potts Berglund was entertaining the general chairmen and five cochairmen who were responsible for organizing the next championship. The group quickly grasped just how well planned the Denver event was and grilled Berglund anxiously with logistical questions. Potts fielded their inquiries with ease and agreed to turn over to the group all of Cherry Hills's plans and documents. Later he told the local press, "I think we made them a little nervous."

Berglund, who collapsed in bed happily in the wee hours of Friday morning, remained on top of the world throughout the day. Attendance reached 14,543—only slightly less than the Open's second-day record set at Winged Foot in 1959—and the two-day gate totaled 28,610. With 25,000 spectators hoped for on Saturday, a new three-day attendance record seemed certain.

MIKE SOUCHAK HAD PICKED UP where he left off in round one, and he made the turn in three-under-par 32. After parring the first three holes, he birdied the 4th with a ten-foot putt. At number 5, he chipped from a terrible lie to one foot of the hole to save par. A routine par followed at the par-three 6th. At the par-four 7th, he followed a well-positioned tee shot with a spectacular sand wedge that settled inches from the hole. Before the round was over, other marksmanlike sand wedges would follow. Arriving at the green wearing a grin, he tapped in for his birdie. Mike bunkered his next tee shot, a four-iron, at the

233-yard par-three 8th hole, but recovered impressively to save par.

Thus far, Souchak had faced a couple of sticky situations and resolved both skillfully. At the 9th hole luck came to his aid for the first time. Trying to avoid the large bunker that guards the right front of the green, he hit his seven-iron shot over everything. Mike chipped back too hard, but his ball clanked flush into the flagstick and stopped three inches away. It was a big break because his ball seemed likely to roll 10 to 12 feet below the hole.

Doug Sanders, playing two groups behind Souchak, knew where he stood in relation to the front-runner. What he didn't know was that, from tee to green, he was hitting the ball even better. Doug reached every green in regulation and gave himself a birdie opportunity on every hole; he converted on only two of them, however, both two-footers. Making the turn in 33, he remained where he had started the day, two strokes behind the leader.

About the time Sanders headed on to the back nine, a roar went up at the 5th green. Ken Venturi, having reached in two the 538-yard par five, holed his 18-foot, downhill putt for an eagle. As it turned out, though, the often streaky Venturi was unable to establish any momentum afterward. He shot a mediocre 73 that placed him at 144, amid the pack of qualifiers.

In Tommy Bolt's absence, his fellow competitor, Claude Harmon, enjoyed a safer, but not sounder, round. The well-known club pro could only match his opening score of 73 and had to content himself with merely making the cut. Although he'd played in only two tournaments since the 1959 Open—the 1960 Masters and Sam Snead Festival—he had hoped for so much more, having remained in contention throughout the 1959 tournament. Only a month before coming to Cherry Hills he had shot a record 61 at Winged Foot.

Of course, Cherry Hills's head pro, Ralph Arnold, gladly

would have walked in Harmon's wing tips. For the second day in a row, he failed to break 80. The *Denver Post* provided some charitable cover for Rip, noting that he had been tied up before the tournament with numerous details that deprived him of sufficient practice time.

Mike Souchak, on the back nine, needed sympathy from no one. He continued to overpower the course, bringing to mind criticisms of the tour heard during the 1950s. Golf writers such as Herbert Warren Wind had railed against certain tournament courses that allowed players to rely on mainly three clubs: the driver, wedge, and putter. Yet this was the National Open. Wasn't an Open course supposed to test players' skills with all 14 clubs? Long-hitting Souchak had been playing many of Cherry Hills's holes fairway wood-wedge-putter.

On the 444-yard 10th hole, he went with his driver—one of only six times he used the one-wood all day—and he needed only a wedge to reach the green. Two putts and he had his par. At the 563-yard 11th, a strong birdie prospect, he pulled his second shot, a four-wood, and lay just behind a bunker that was stationed on the left side of the green. From there he made his best shot of the day—a sand wedge that he deliberately chipped against the face of the bunker, glancing his ball off the sand and rolling it to within four feet of the hole—and then canned his putt for a well-deserved birdie. He parred the troublesome 12th, using a five-iron from the tee. Mike's sand wedge came through for him again at the 13th hole, leaving him with a short birdie putt that he made.

The 14th hole featured the day's most talked-about shot and his second big, lucky break. Lying in the rough, 15 feet to the right of the green and 70 feet from the flag, Souchak saw that Bob Rosburg's ball on the green might be in a position to help him, and he asked Rossie to leave it be rather than mark it. His chip ricocheted off Rosburg's ball and landed inches from the cup. "I didn't have quite enough English," he joked in the press tent afterward. Souch estimated his ball would have run at least six feet beyond the hole if the two balls hadn't collided. But they had, and he strode to the next hole five up on the field. Things could hardly have been better.

At 15, a 196-yard par three to a slightly elevated green, Souchak's tee shot found a bunker, but he saved par with an eight-foot putt. He played the 402-yard 16th hole shrewdly. Using his power to his advantage, he went with his three-iron off the tee and pitched a nine-iron to ten feet of the hole. Souchak's body English, mirroring the intensity of his effort, had grown more animated during his round. Up around the green, which slopes from back to front, several photographers prepared to capture the moment. After carefully studying the line, the leader tapped the ball with his putter, and as it rolled toward the hole his eyes narrowed and his jaw clenched resolutely. He bent at the knees and raised his putter skyward as the ball fell into the cup. This was the eighth three on his scorecard. He was completely in command now.

After his first practice round at Cherry Hills, Souch vowed not to go for the 17th green in two. Let the others try, he'd said; if they do, it will work in my favor. After a strong drive left him only a four- or five-iron away, he was tempted to overrule his better judgment and go with the flow. He resisted, however, and choked up on his seven-iron and punched the ball forward to set up his approach shot. When he landed his sand wedge on the green, a tremendous cheer went up, making Souchak wonder what had happened because there was nothing especially difficult about the shot. He soon learned that his ball had just barely cleared the moat. He missed an 8- to 10-footer for birdie, but he moved on to 18 knowing he had made the right decision. One more par now and he'd have a 66, a rare and wonderful U.S. Open score.

At the final hole, Mike reached the fairway safely with a three-wood off the tee, and then went with a four-iron. Having an uphill lie, he played the approach shot to hook but it went straight right, landing in the rough amid the spectators ringing the green, 70 feet from the pin. When he arrived at his ball, he saw that paper cups and candy wrappers were scattered about and his ball was resting on a crushed cup. He received permission to move the cup, and he did some housekeeping around his ball, all the while appearing unfazed by his predicament.

As he prepared to chip onto the green, he patiently asked the spectators to back away a bit more, and then he paused again and requested a Cherry Hills official to move out of his field of vision. "I see those red pants out of the corner of my eye," he said pleasantly. Mike's chip came up eight feet short. He missed the putt by an inch and tapped in for a five, his only bogey of the round.

Souchak was disappointed over the loosely played hole, but it dampened his spirits only temporarily. Caddie Babe Aranjo smiled broadly as he accompanied his man off the course. Souchak's 67, following his first-round 68, set a new U.S. Open scoring record of 135, breaking the 36-hole mark of 138 set by Snead in 1948 and matched by Hogan in 1952 and Billy Joe Patton and Dick Mayer in 1957.

Although he was hardly a new face in golf, in the press tent he was asked to say a bit about himself. Feeling exhilarated, he summarized his biography with amusing brevity: "Call me Mike or Michael, I have no middle initial, and I'm one of ten children." Turning to his game, but remaining lighthearted, he credited George Bayer with having contributed to his development as a golfer. Before Bayer, Souchak explained, *he* was considered the game's longest driver. But when he lost that distinction, he figured he might as well cut down on length and go for accuracy. (George, who had come in a half hour earlier with his second straight 72, trailed Mike by nine shots.)

As for his just-completed round, his ball-striking had been much better than in the first round, he observed. Although he had taken only 26 putts, including 10 one-putt greens, he added, "If I had putted as well today as I did yesterday, I would have really had a score." As it was, nobody could remember Souchak missing a five- or six-footer in the six rounds he'd played since receiving the putting lesson from Jack Burke in Oklahoma City. What exactly did Burke teach you? he was asked. "Trade secret," he replied, winking. Then he added, in all sincerity, "Jackie has restored my confidence and straightened out my putting stance. He's been working with me as long as I've been a pro."

Oklahoma City, the site of the previous tournament, must have seemed long ago and far away to Souchak's fellow competitor, Gene Littler. Less than a week after receiving the winner's check there and arriving in Denver one of the Open favorites, the soft-spoken golfer departed quietly, having shot a 76-74—150 and missed the cut by three strokes.

Bob Rosburg also left, though less quietly. Whether it was over the glacial pace of play and the heat, as was reported, or simply his dismal four-over-par 75, the temperamental golfer stalked off the course, beside himself. With putting prowess that approached Billy Casper's and Jerry Barber's, he had the capability to come from way behind. That's the way he'd won the 1959 PGA Championship, charging back from six strokes in the last round to defeat Barber. But this time the gap appeared far too wide. According to one report, Bob said he assumed his 147 wouldn't make the cut (it's more likely he *hoped* it wouldn't). So he packed up his satchel, stowed his clubs in his car trunk, and drove off, apparently not intending to return.

Souchak's nearest pursuer, Doug Sanders, was living dangerously on the second nine. At number 10, he came up just short of the green—it was the only hole on which he missed a green in regulation, as it turned out—but he chipped close and one-putted for his par. Another par followed at the 11th hole, but then he three-putted the par-three 12th for a bogey. After parring 13, he sank a 12-footer for birdie at the 14th hole. Then at the side's second par three, the 15th, he three-putted once again. So despite 15 holes of exceptional ball-striking, Sanders languished at one under par for the day and five strokes behind Souchak for the tournament with the three difficult holes ahead.

Doug parred the dogleg 16th and came to the 17th determined to make something happen. The 5-foot 11-inch, 160-pound Sanders was a relatively short hitter, so when he decided to go for the small island green in two, he was taking a considerable gamble. An hour earlier, Souchak had spurned a four-iron or five-iron shot there as too risky; Sanders went for the green with his three-wood. He caught the ball crisply but watched with increasing concern as it soared well over the moat and appeared to bound off the green and into the lake—the same water hole he'd visited the day before from the 18th tee.

Sanders hustled up the fairway, wondering whether he had sacrificed a solid round for one ill-advised shot. When he crossed over the moat, though, he discovered to his relief that some iron pipes behind the green had stopped his ball from entering the water. The ball leaned against the pipes, an obstruction that could be removed without penalty. Doug replaced the ball where the pipes had been, chipped to five feet of the hole, and walked away with an extremely lucky birdie four.

Buoyed by this unexpected turn of events, at 18 he fired his approach right at the flag, came up eight feet from the cup, and holed his birdie putt. His sixth one-putt green and dramatic birdie-birdie finish on the back nine gave him a 68 and a new lease on life. Just like that he pulled within three strokes of Souchak. "Yes, sir, that old fish was back, but he jumped this time *after* I had driven," the jocular Sanders told a crowd of eager notetakers in the press tent.

Lost in the silliness surrounding Thursday's leaping-fish

incident was the realization that the 26-year-old Sanders now was good enough to contend for the National Open. A fun-loving country boy from Cedartown, Georgia, he had good looks and a swaggering, masculine style that made him appealing to male and female golf fans alike. Even though he had not yet taken to sporting the technicolor wardrobe for which he'd later be known, Sanders's on-course image as a breezy entertainer overshadowed his developing talent. As a result, few had noticed that as a golfer he was on the threshold of stardom.

His second round at Cherry Hills surprised those who might have expected just another diverting yarn from the good ol' boy who often stuck his golf tee over one ear. If television cameras had been present to record the field's shots over the entire course, no one could have avoided the fact that from tee to green, Sanders had played better than anyone, including Hogan and Souchak. His only soft spot had been his putting: the leader had taken 52 putts in the two rounds; the runner-up, 60.

Doug joined the tour in 1957, following three years of polishing his game on a golf scholarship at the University of Florida and a couple more seasons of entering, and often winning, amateur tournaments. He decided to turn pro after he won the 1956 Canadian Open, becoming the first simon-pure (a term the era's golf writers liked to use for amateurs) to do so. Defeating Dow Finsterwald in a play-off, he pulled off what *Golf Digest* called the "most surprising victory of 1956." Dow walked off with the first-prize money of $2,400; Doug took home the winner's trophy. Heading into the 1960 Open, he was winless for the year but riding on the longest in-the-money streak on tour—a record that meant something then, because only the top 30 or so players in each tournament left with any prize money.

Sam Snead, no doubt aware of the great round of his rival Ben Hogan, kept himself in contention, at 141, with a two-under-par 69. When he completed his round 15 minutes behind Sanders, he said he had a hunch that Sanders, not Souchak, was the player to beat—not that Sam had given up on his own chances. "Give me a good start tomorrow and I might sneak in there," he remarked nonchalantly.

Raising his hopes was an up-and-down round that helped him gain on the field even while it lost ground to Souchak. The Slammer took advantage of the course's benign welcoming holes. He birdied three of the first four, but felt that he should have opened with five in a row. Although his round boasted six birdies in all, it was undermined by almost as many mistakes.

Nonetheless, the showman in Snead came out on the 17th tee, a likely sign that he felt positive about his round and his position. During the day, several players had complained about horses that members of the Arapahoe County Sheriff's Posse rode outside the course perimeter to control pedestrian and motor traffic. It seems the horses whinnied whenever they spotted one another, distracting some golfers as they played holes that bordered the property line, such as 17. While Sam was teeing off there, a palomino neighed loudly. Sam, unfazed, crushed his drive, turned toward the creature, and said, "Well, horse, can you do any better?"

By the time the Snead group completed play, the only threesome of consequence still out on the course was that of Jerry Barber, Julius Boros, and Art Wall. Barber repeated the unusual pattern he had set the day before—wobbly golf, solid score. The little man came in with five birdies, five bogeys, and an even-par 71, placing him among the leaders at 140.

As expected, Julius Boros was heard from after all, thanks to the best back nine of the championship. On the front side, he took 36 strokes, continuing the indifferent golf he'd exhibited on Thursday. But then the stocky, placid fellow got hot and snuck in with a three-under-par 33. He was back in the picture at 142. (Another Boros played in the tournament—

Julius's brother, Ernie. A professional playing out of Julius's home, Southern Pines, North Carolina, he missed the cut in 76-77—153.)

Art Wall, failing to make the move many expected, shot a 73 for a 36-hole score of 145, which landed him far down the list of qualifiers. Could he make up ten strokes and climb over more than two dozen players in two rounds? It would take a miracle—or at least a repeat of his phenomenal comeback at the 1959 Masters.

It was 6:00 P.M. when the veteran trio completed play. Although eight threesomes and the Venturi-Harmon twosome still were finishing their second tour of Cherry Hills, the leader board going into the Open's double round had taken final shape. Souchak led at 135, followed by Sanders at 138, and Barber, Finsterwald, and Fleck at 140. The surprising amateur from round one, Don Cherry, having set down a 71 alongside Thursday's 70, was tied at 141 with Sam Snead, defending champion Billy Casper, unsung Aussie Bruce Crampton, and veteran Ted Kroll, who improved upon his first-round 72 with a fine 69. Snead's fellow competitor, Gary Player, had shot a disappointing 72 and was tied at 142 with Ben Hogan, Julius Boros, and Jack Nicklaus. The field's 22-man amateur ranks had shrunk to only two: Cherry and Nicklaus.

Bob Goalby, stranded two groups behind the plodding Palmer-Middlecoff-Fleck threesome, didn't let slow play disturb him. The former college football quarterback improved by three strokes over his first-round 73 and stood tied with Palmer at 143. They were joined at one over par by Johnny Pott, who shot one of the day's best rounds, a 68; by Paul Harney, and by three others.

Dutch Harrison, the sly old hustler, scrambled successfully to save his skin and became the oldest entrant to make the cut. His one-under-par 70 featured a bogey on the 4th hole, where his tee shot nestled against a tree; a par at 9 on a 40-foot chip-in; and two medium-length birdie putts at 11 and 17. Not that

he needed luck to score well; as a 50-year-old club professional Dutch still had a highly competitive game and wasn't to
be counted out just yet.

Early in 1958, at age 47, he finished second in the Los
Angeles Open, and two weeks later he won the Tijuana Open
Invitational. In 1959 he recorded three top-ten finishes, including a third to Sam Snead and Mike Souchak at the Greenbrier tournament in which the Slammer shot his 59. "I just
shot 68-68-68-69, and still Sam was 14 strokes better," he said
with a chuckle. And on the 1960 winter tour, he boasted a
third-place tie at Tucson.

Dave Marr, who played both Cherry Hills rounds with
Dutch, had figured the Arkansas Traveler somehow would
manage to make the cut. He'd seen Harrison up close before.
As Marr, a droll, charming fellow, recalled in the April 1992
Golf magazine, he was grouped with him early in the 1960
season at the Bing Crosby tournament. When Dutch tried to
mislead him on club selection by playing an easy five-iron on a
par-three hole that called for an eight-iron, Dave was ready.

"Man, I really hit that one!" Dutch exclaimed.

"Dutch, I've been had before," Dave replied, laughing.

At Cherry Hills, Marr was had, but not by Dutch. On the
last green in the first round, as he was addressing a curling,
downhill 25-footer, a spectator peering into binoculars blared
over the hush, "Casper's even par."

"So was I until then," Marr said later, finally able to smile.
"I jabbed that son of a gun way past and missed the putt coming back." With the resulting 72 followed by a 73, he still made
the cut comfortably by two strokes.

The third member of the Harrison-Marr group, amateur
Wallace Rose, was not up to their caliber as a golfer—he exited
the Open with an 80-79—159—but his spirit seemed every bit
as refreshing as theirs. A pint-sized letter carrier from Lexington, Kentucky, he tried for his first Open because he figured
the ten-dollar entry fee was a bargain for two rounds at the

excellent qualifying site. After completing the local qualifying stage as the first alternate, he advanced when a qualifier withdrew. In the 36-hole sectional competition, he finished again as the first alternate, and on the Sunday night before the Open he was notified that he was in. Just before the tournament, he told Larry Robinson of the *New York World Telegram and Sun,* "This golf is way over my head, of course, but what a thrill to play in the biggest championship."

Charlie Sifford matched Harrison's 74-70 start, and the two were paired for the final two rounds. Sifford, who qualified for his first Open in 1959, had improved upon his 36-hole score at Winged Foot by six strokes and made the cut for the second straight year. But, as usual, one had to look hard at the stoic golfer chomping on the customary cigar for signs that he was pleased.

Ed Furgol lost the putting touch in the second round, and he soon dove from the list of leaders. Standing on the final tee, he was disappointed with his four-over-par effort, but resigned about his play. What could he expect, being a full-time club professional? Making the cut, at least, appeared secure. A par four would give him a 75 and a two-round score of 146; even if he were to make a bogey he looked like a pretty good bet.

Furgol, steering clear of the lake, promptly pushed his drive out-of-bounds. Rattled but determined not to flirt with the water hazard, he duplicated the mistake on his second tee shot. Because of the USGA's benign one-stroke penalty for hitting out-of-bounds, it wasn't too late to salvage the hole with a six, maybe even a five. But this time it was the lake that got the best of him. Furgol staggered home with an eight, the accursed "snowman," and just like that the subject of one of the first round's happier stories dropped out of the competition. The 1954 Open champion finished three over the cut at 150.

Davis Love, Jr., at 148, missed the cut by one stroke. All afternoon he had suffered a slow death, fully conscious that on this muggy summer day William Flynn's layout was presenting few problems the field couldn't solve. Just his luck—the halfway cut, 147, was the lowest in U.S. Open history. Fifty-five players shot that score or better, and when the pillaging was surveyed at day's end the number who broke par in round two totaled 18 (7 more than the day before), an Open record for a single day. Davis, who accepted his fate stoically, wasn't one of them; nor was Deane Beman.

The U.S. Open already had produced considerable anguish for young Beman. In 1958 the cut at Southern Hills was 154, reflecting the course's severe conditions. Deane, after opening with a more-than-respectable 75, collapsed to an 83. In his other three appearances, he never even came close to making the cut, but this Friday at Cherry Hills would prove to be the most heartbreaking day of his young golf career.

To make the cut Beman needed a 72 or 73 following his first-round 74; and without costly errors on two holes, he would have succeeded. The University of Maryland junior got off to a great start. He reached two under for the round when he holed a 10-foot birdie putt on the 5th hole followed by a 30-footer at the 6th. He gave back one stroke with a bogey on the 8th, the course's longest par three and first truly difficult hole, but still he made the turn with an encouraging 34.

Trouble arrived at the 444-yard 10th, where Deane drove into the hole's single large fairway bunker and, in getting out, half shanked his ball. His double-bogey six dropped him to one over par and suddenly he had little margin for error. Disaster struck two holes later when he hit his three-iron tee shot into the pond that snakes in front of the 12th green. Tight as a drum now, he took a drop and, trusting the normally friendly eight-iron, pitched a second ball into the water. A quadruple-bogey seven there ended his chances—or *should* have. Refusing to quit, he birdied the 15th and 17th and brought home another respectable 74. He, too, fell one shot short of the cut.

* * *

AFTER BILL EZINICKI'S EMBARRASSING first-round 83, the former hockey brawler had nothing to play for except pride and the desire to acquit himself well for his peers and club members back home in Massachusetts. Ezzie came out quietly resolute on Friday. The 1st hole he birdied, sinking an eight-foot putt. The 2nd hole: ditto on a six-footer. Bogeys followed, however, at 7, where his approach bounded off the green, and at 9, where he drove into the left rough behind a tree. At 11 he almost holed a 40-foot chip for an eagle and he just missed birdie putts on 15, 16, and 17. In any case, his second-round score, a 72, was much more like the real Ezinicki. "I guess I was a little anxious yesterday," he said softly, trying to explain his ill-timed rash of hooked tee shots. He returned home to Boston to prepare for the start of the Vermont Open on Monday.

Bill Spiller, needing to break par to have a chance to make the cut, fell victim to some early mistakes and never gave himself a chance. His 76-82—158 was not the winning score he'd playfully predicted for himself before the tournament, but he certainly had nothing to be ashamed of. Pros with far more experience and success in big tournaments also missed the cut—both stars from the past such as Paul Runyan and native Aussie Jim Ferrier and current-day "names" such as Billy Maxwell, Fred Hawkins, and Jay Hebert (not his younger brother, Lionel, who squeaked by with two strokes to spare). Future tour notables Mason Rudolph and amateur Charlie Coody also came in just over the cut.

Middlecoff and Wall were not the only well-known players among the 55 survivors who'd be returning to Cherry Hills Country Club with virtually no chance to win. At 145 were 45-year-old Lloyd Mangrum, once Hogan's premier adversary and the winner of a phenomenal 36 tournaments in his career (a total that would have been greater if he hadn't served in the infantry during the war); Doug Ford, a 15-time victor whose scrambling style always compromised his chances at an Open course; and Frank Stranahan, the muscle-bound, temperamental former amateur standout.

Twenty-two years after missing the cut by one stroke at the 1938 Open, Jim Turnesa returned to Cherry Hills as a 47-year-old and hit the magic number, 147, right on the nose. South Africa's young Bob Verwey continued his charmed existence. Following his first-round 75 with a 72, he, too, came in right at the cut.

Few of these players would be well compensated for their extra day's efforts. Although the Open (unlike the regular weekly tournaments) paid prize money to all who made the cut, only the top dozen professional finishers would take away more than $1,000—the standard for a good payday at the time. The bottom half of the field would receive a small reward ranging between $240 and $400. Not that the purse distribution squelched the also-rans' incentive. Two strong rounds could produce a top-ten finish that would make them eligible automatically for the next year's Open. Besides, this being their occupation's preeminent annual competition, all but the most dejected would fight to the end with their best effort against the course, against their opponents, and against themselves.

Unlike the field as a whole, the "locals" were treated rudely by Cherry Hills. None of the half-dozen Colorado entrants survived the cut, including Jim English, the low amateur at Winged Foot, and Jack Koennecker, the player who struck the championship's first shot.

Although the second round lacked the hijinks that colored the first, neighing horses were not the only diversion from the parade of stone-faced golfers. Bob Hill, a Webster, New York, pro, reached the 17th hole knowing he had no hope to make the cut. So, when his ball dropped into the moat fronting the green, he decided to splash his way out. To the applause of the spectators, Hill rolled up the right leg of his white trousers, took off his shoe and stocking, and blasted away. The ball stayed put. Perhaps recalling the legendary Ray Ainsley's woes, Hill reconsidered his plan, took a drop, and finished with an eight.

Bob Goetz, a pro from Tulsa, Oklahoma, did the unthinkable—he missed the ball entirely on his tee shot at the 18th hole. It was only the beginning to a thoroughly embarrassing seven, but much to his relief he made the cut at 147. Frank Harned—a Cleveland, Ohio, assistant pro who three-putted from *six inches* on Thursday (he stubbed the blade while putting and double-hit the ball, advancing it only two inches)—incurred a two-stroke penalty when he arrived for his tee time five minutes late on Friday. It hardly mattered, though; he came in 13 shots over the cut.

Wes Ellis's tee shot at the 8th hole landed in the left hip pocket of spectator Everett Pond. Ellis received a free lift and went on to shoot 73, but it wasn't enough to offset his opening 79. The members of Mountain Ridge Country Club in West Caldwell, New Jersey, were getting back their pro and assistant pro (Davis Love, Jr.) earlier than they would have liked.

Never in the Open's history had a left-hander won the title, not surprising considering how few southpaws had competed in the previous 59 tournaments. Thorne Wood, a 30-year-old pro whose presence on tour was being underwritten by a group called the Carolinas' Left-handed Golfers Association, was the only hope for lefties in 1960. Playing in his first Open, the Asheboro, North Carolina, resident matched the day's worst round, an 85, and missed the cut by 14 strokes.

Cherry Hills member Claude Wright endeared himself to all who looked on as he played the watery, par-three 12th hole. There his tee shot plunked into a muddy bank at the edge of the pond. Rather than take a drop, he chose to try to chop his ball out, even though it meant he, too, had to take off a shoe and sock, roll up his trouser leg, and plant one bare foot in water rising above his ankle. Wright's hard but off-balance swing produced a hollow thud that only managed to bury the ball deeper in the bank. Smiling philosophically, he then took a drop, only to be assessed a two-stroke penalty for doing so at the wrong place. He left the hole with an eight but his humor intact.

So MUCH FOR COMEDY. There would be few amusing sideshows on Saturday. And at the end of the exhausting 36 holes of golf, only one man would rejoice.

If Mike Souchak was that man, many golfers and fans would be delighted. He was a down-to-earth, warmhearted bear, and he was a very good golfer—a huge hitter with a feathery touch around the green. He wasn't obsessed with winning a major championship, but he deserved to own one. Not surprisingly, he approached the tournament's climactic final day with the same strategy as most any golfer with a chance to win most any tournament.

"I'm just going out there and shoot the best I know how," he said after his second round. "I'm not going to play safe or shoot for a certain score"—possibly a reference to Ben Hogan's calculating tactics. Nor was he thinking about beating Hogan's scoring record of 276, even though back-to-back 70s would accomplish the job.

That evening, Souchak dined out with a good friend, Father George Feeney, a Phoenix priest who was an ardent golfer. Later that night, speaking by phone with a *Greensboro Daily News* reporter, the Durham, North Carolina, resident sounded more determined than earlier. "I'm going out there with just one thing in mind. That is to bring that big trophy back home to North Carolina."

Ken Venturi, nine shots behind the leader, tried to persuade himself that he still was in contention. Objectively, though a long shot, he *was*. Yes, he'd been thwarted three

167

times at the Masters; but in winning nine times in little more than three seasons on the tour, he had blazed his own thrilling comeback victories.

In the 1959 Los Angeles Open he charged back from *eight* shots behind Art Wall after three rounds to win with a closing 63. "Ever seen anything like it?" a reporter asked him afterward. "Yeah, same thing happened to me in the 1956 Masters," he answered ruefully. The victory meant the world to him. He told the press at the time, "The Los Angeles Open gave me back a piece of my pride." And now, if he could set astir that pride and capture his first major championship, there was no telling how far he might go.

Jack Fleck departed Cherry Hills in much better shape than Venturi did, but he was frustrated that he couldn't get more putts to fall. He took eight more putts in the round than Souchak. All the same, only five strokes separated the two men in the tournament. As in 1955, Jack was tied for third place at the halfway point. That year he got hot on the second circuit of San Francisco's Olympic Club, and moved from nine strokes out of the lead after 18 holes to only one behind after 36. This time he was hoping such a hot round, or two, lay ahead.

Dow Finsterwald, tied with Fleck at 140, was optimistic even though the Open had not been kind to him in a decade of appearances. A consistent winner on tour with nine victories since 1955, he had never finished in the top ten in golf's most significant event. After sharing the lead at the 1959 championship with an opening round of 69 and trailing by only three strokes at the halfway mark, he dropped nine strokes behind leader Casper with a third-round 75 and finished tied for 11th.

With that sobering experience and his recent near-miss in the Masters—not to mention his resilient response to a mutinous caddie—he had reason to feel confident. And if he needed a little added motivation, all he had to do was recall how he had been critiqued in a May 2nd *Time* cover story on his friend Arnold Palmer. In contrast to Palmer's boldness, *Time* wrote, Finsterwald "too often plays golf like an old maid: a top hole-by-hole tactician, his cautious strategy is simply to finish well up in the money." Yes, it would be extra sweet to win at Cherry Hills.

Likewise for Jerry Barber, who also stood at 140. Although he was having a wonderful golf season, no one believed that a diminutive 44-year-old with only four career victories could stay up with the big names over the Open's 36-hole grind—except Barber himself.

In relation to par, Billy Casper stood precisely where he was at Winged Foot after 36 holes, one under par. But in 1959 that put him on top of the scoreboard; in 1960 it left him six strokes behind leader Souchak. "Nobody can ever guess what's going to happen in a golf tournament," Casper told the press after his round. "I think I've still got a chance to win this thing, but that's just a theory. I'll just do what I've always done—hit one shot at a time and play the game the only way I know how." He knew how to putt exceptionally well, and that's what he would have to do on Saturday to be the first U.S. Open champion to repeat since Hogan in 1951.

As for Hogan, seven strokes behind Souchak, he was in a position similar to his standing in 1951 when he trailed leader Bobby Locke by five strokes after 36 holes. But that Open was played on the fiendishly punishing Oakland Hills, which was more than all but a few in the field could cope with; this one was on the much more forgiving Cherry Hills, which encouraged any number of capable golfers to attack par. Hogan badly needed to hole some putts, and he needed Souchak to come back to the pack as so many early-round Open leaders had done over the years. In the 59 championships, only three men had won wire to wire: Walter Hagen in 1914, Englishman Long Jim Barnes in 1921, and the Hawk himself in 1953.

Hogan had to know this could well be his last real hope to win a record-breaking fifth U.S. Open title. How many more chances would a golfer approaching age 50 get? Since his miraculous 1953 season, his tenacity had been rewarded only with near-misses—a tie for sixth in 1954; the play-off loss to Jack Fleck, the most bitter defeat of his career, in 1955; and a tie for second in 1956, when he missed a 30-inch putt on the 71st hole.

In 1957 Ben withdrew just before the first round because of illness. In 1958 he was never a threat for the title; but it being the fifth year after his last Open championship, he needed a top-ten finish to secure an exemption from having to qualify in 1959. He got it—he tied for tenth place—thanks to a clutch final round of 71. In 1959, starting the final round only three strokes out of the lead, he finished poorly with a 76 for an eighth-place tie.

Jack Nicklaus examined the scoreboard before leaving Cherry Hills Friday afternoon. He saw that he was tied with Hogan at 142, meaning the two golfers might be paired for the final 36 holes, when twosomes would replace the threesomes of the first two days. When he learned later that indeed he would be playing with the golfing legend for the first time, he was awestruck but not overwhelmed. Hogan-Nicklaus would be a fascinating pairing to say the least, one that was reminiscent of a twosome from the famous 1920 Open at Inverness—that of 18-year-old Bobby Jones and the 50-year-old Vardon.

Two golfers in a National Open could not be more different than Jack Nicklaus and Ben Hogan. One was the 20-year-old son of a prosperous, devoted Columbus, Ohio, pharmacist; the other was the 47-year-old product of the Depression and a father who took his own life when his son was just nine. One had the good fortune to enjoy the advantages of a well-to-do family, including the run of Scioto Country Club; the other had to endure the rough-and-tumble caddie yard at Glen Garden Country Club to break into the game he loved. One was a fun-loving college fraternity member; the other, a high school dropout but the driven owner of a fledgling golf equipment company. Nicklaus was the robust young athlete with prodigious natural skills at the threshold of greatness; while Hogan, a middle-aged athlete with the finest self-made golfing skills ever, struggled to demonstrate his greatness one last time.

Arnold Palmer, the heir apparent to Hogan and Snead, was hardly mentioned in second-round newspaper accounts. In a few articles, writers declared matter-of-factly that the pretournament favorite was out of the running for his second major championship of the year.

Perhaps they had forgotten Palmer's closing 65 to win the Desert Classic, his birdie putts at the 71st and 72nd greens to seize the Pensacola tournament, and his stout-hearted shot-making at the Masters. Yes, he would need help from Souchak as Hogan and others would, but making up eight strokes over two rounds surely was not beyond him.

The morning round would tell the tale. Although Palmer hadn't yet figured out a way to win the tournament, he knew that if he could get hot in the morning and close the gap to four or five strokes anything could happen in the afternoon of Open Saturday.

The leaders after 36 holes:

Mike Souchak	68-67—135
Doug Sanders	70-68—138
Jerry Barber	69-71—140
Dow Finsterwald	71-69—140
Jack Fleck	70-70—140
Billy Casper	71-70—141
Don Cherry (a)	70-71—141
Bruce Crampton	70-71—141
Ted Kroll	72-69—141
Sam Snead	72-69—141
Julius Boros	73-69—142
Ben Hogan	75-67—142
Jack Nicklaus (a)	71-71—142

Gary Player   70-72—142
Arnold Palmer   72-71—143
(6 others at 143: Bob Goalby, Paul Harney, Johnny Pott, Dave Ragan, Bob Shave, and Dick Stranahan.)

CHAPTER 8

No one—no one other than the usga's policy makers, that is—
liked the Open's double-round conclusion—not the tournament officials and not the volunteers, not the spectators and
not the press, not the caddies and certainly not the players.
But few argued to change it.

Holding the championship's final 36 holes on the same
day was the way it had been done since 1898, when the Open
expanded from a 36- to a 72-hole competition. Besides, playing two rounds in a single day was not unique to the U.S.
Open. The British Open concluded with a double round at the
time; the U.S. Amateur decided its champion in a 36-hole
match (as it still did many years later); and until the PGA
Championship changed its format from medal to stroke play in
1958, it scheduled 36-hole contests for each of the final few
rounds. Those tournaments, requiring play for up to an entire
week, were much more grueling than the three-day U.S.
Open. After Hogan won the 1948 PGA, in which he played an
exhausting 213 holes of golf, he avoided the tournament until
1960.

The critics of the Open's 36-hole finish argued that golf is,
or should be, a game of skill, not endurance. Young contes-

tants receive an unfair advantage when golfers are required to play two rounds in one day, they said. But the USGA believed that an Open champion should exhibit not only consummate shotmaking skill but physical and mental stamina over an extended period; players worthy of the title, they said, should have a swing that withstands the grinding weight of Open pressure.

The double round tested these attributes and, as the USGA saw it, produced a better champion than the typical four-day, single-round-per-day tournament could do. This was a debatable point, to be sure, but, undeniably, Open Saturday was integral to the USGA's presentation of the national championship as, in every respect, the game's ultimate test.

Bobby Jones, who had such refreshing insight about all facets of the game, found a single 18-hole round wanting as the standard for settling a major competition. In the 1966 collection, *Bobby Jones on Golf*, he wrote, "I admit, as some have urged, that 18 holes constitute a round of golf. But since this came about by accident rather than design, the fact supplies no reason why 18 holes should be accepted as an adequate test in important competition."

As for the contention that younger golfers have an advantage in a 36-hole windup, the record book did indicate otherwise. Go back to the 1920s and one discovers that the winner's average age was just under 30. In the 14 Opens held since World War II, it was 34; only three of the victors in this period had yet to see their 30th birthday: Lew Worsham, who was 29 when he won in 1947; Cary Middlecoff, 28 in 1949; and Billy Casper, just shy of 28 in 1959. Clearly experience and the mental control that it cultivated outweighed youth as a factor in winning the Open. If golfers in the 30- to 35-year-old age range were not as physically resilient as they were in their 20s, apparently they still were sufficiently fit to complete 36 holes of golf without having their skills compromised.

To hold two rounds in the last day, the USGA had to expedite play, which meant that the scheduling was tight and the pairings often anticlimactic. Successive pairings were poised to embark at six-minute intervals—the same speedy pace Jerry Barber complained about at his sectional qualifying round. The composition and order of the twosomes stayed the same for both rounds on Saturday, regardless of third-round scores.

To change the location of the holes, USGA officials walked onto the putting green after the morning round's last group completed each hole, replaced the cup, and cut a new hole in exactly the predetermined location. Four and a half hours after starting the morning round, players were due back on the first tee for their afternoon round. This allowed contestants about an hour to freshen up and have a quick snack.

In the years before 1960 golfers with the same scores did not necessarily play together on Saturday morning. In 1958, for example, Tommy Bolt, the leader at the halfway point at 142, was paired with Bruce Crampton, whose score was 148; a year later, the 36-hole leader, Billy Casper, at 139, was paired with Lionel Hebert, at 145. The leaders often were scattered widely across the golf course, depriving the tournament of the drama provided when leaders battle head-to-head or in adjacent pairings.

The Cherry Hills 1960 Open marked the first time the tournament's two halfway leaders were paired on Saturday. All the top scorers were clustered so they would have similar playing conditions and they were scheduled to go off consecutively, though not last in the field—a practice that began in 1961 and has continued at all subsequent championships. The USGA organized the day's pairings in three groupings. First came players whose scores placed them in the middle of the field, next came the contenders, and last came those who barely made the cut.

Almost all the golfers in the first ten pairings were out of the title picture going into the third round, with scores ranging from the first pair's 146 to the tenth pair's 144 (Don Whitt) and 143 (Dave Ragan). At 8:00 A.M. the "dew sweepers," Chick Harbert and Rex Baxter, launched Open Saturday, another spectacular, sunny day. It was cooler than Friday but still warm for Denver, with the temperature already touching 70 degrees.

Harbert jumped off to a weird, but wonderful, beginning. After the first three holes, he had taken only one putt, the 18-footer he sank on the 1st green. Two less conventional birdies followed—one a holed 80-foot sand shot at 2, the other a chip-in from 50 feet at 3. With this invigorating trio of threes, he went on to shoot a 69 for a respectable 54-hole score of 215. His two-under round was only the first of 11 below-par rounds in the morning, 6 of them under 70. Baxter, the second-round wunderkind whose 67 attracted national attention, relapsed to a more characteristic 76.

Art Wall, playing in the day's second pairing with Lloyd Mangrum, had no tricks up his sleeve after all. By the time he reached the lovely but by now infamous 12th hole, his situation was dismal, and there his hopes expired. After his tee shot landed near the pond's edge, he had to take his next shot with a bare foot planted in the pond. The result: a double-bogey five that led to his eventual 78 for the round. The 1960 Open was all but over for the gentleman from Pennsylvania.

Ken Venturi followed five groups behind. When he came into view shortly before noon on the 18th fairway, his peculiar splay-footed walk identifying him from far down the fairway, his body language confirmed the story on the giant scoreboard. He, too, was out of it, bound for a 74, and only his two most loyal galleryites, wife Connie and friend Ed Lowery, paid him much attention. So another pretournament favorite's hopes of climbing back into contention had evaporated, and Venturi's wait for that first major victory continued.

Only three early starters played up to Harbert's level. Dave Marr and Doug Ford both shot one-under 70s for three-round aggregates of 215. And most noteworthy, the ageless wonder, Dutch Harrison, shot his second consecutive 70 and actually held the early three-round lead at 214. Not that the Arkansas Traveler was composing his victory speech during lunch (nor was his fellow competitor Charlie Sifford, who blew to a 77). At the start of his round, 20 players stood between Harrison and Mike Souchak, nine shots ahead.

THE FIELD'S SECOND GROUPING, ten twosomes' worth of contenders and would-be contenders, teed off between 9:00 and 9:54 A.M. Leading the way was that most intriguing pairing of Ben Hogan and Jack Nicklaus, deadlocked at 142. Following them, in order, were Gary Player and Julius Boros (both at 142 as well), Arnold Palmer and Paul Harney (143), Bob Goalby and Richard Stranahan (143), and Johnny Pott and Bob Shave (143).

Next in the procession to Cherry Hills's 1st tee at 9:30 A.M. came the leaders Mike Souchak (135) and Doug Sanders (138), followed by Dow Finsterwald and Jack Fleck (140), Jerry Barber (140) and Bruce Crampton (141), Billy Casper and Ted Kroll (141), and Sam Snead and Don Cherry (141).

Nicklaus felt some unease about his day-long playing companion. He had heard all the comments about the aloof Hawk: "Don't expect him to utter two words to you all day." "Careful what you say to him; if he thinks it's stupid, prepare for that contemptuous glare." Years later, Fred Hawkins characterized Hogan as a Jekyll-and-Hyde figure with his fellow golfers. He might act considerately toward you, or he might snub you as though you didn't exist, Hawkins said. But on Saturday, June 18, 1960, playing for the first time with the legendary champion, Jack found him an ideal fellow-competitor—nonintrusive and gentlemanly. And, as he said time and again between the two rounds, he couldn't get over the way the man struck the ball.

Nicklaus was not exaggerating; Hogan's shotmaking was near-incredible. The Hawk hit all 18 greens in regulation—a rare performance in the Open—and he made two birdie putts for a 69. Only his putting prevented him from repeating his 67 or going lower still.

If ever Nicklaus were going to crumple, this would have been the time. There he was, the chubby, pink-faced man-child playing on the game's greatest stage, accompanying arguably the greatest player in history. For 18 holes, he observed the master firsthand as he launched on target one well-tempered shot after another and marched down the fairway in a cocoon of concentration, wearing that ambiguous grin that wasn't a smile.

How could the kid possibly hold a club without trembling, never mind play his own game? But Nicklaus did play his own game—that overpowering, awesome game. It was less perfect golf than Hogan's, but the young man registered his own two-under-par 69. Their matinee round over, the duo was tied at two-under-par 211.

VERY FEW PLAYERS HAVE both the game and the unflappable nature to thrive on U.S. Open golf courses. Julius Boros was one of them. He drove the ball straight and he extricated himself from bunkers and thick greenside rough as well as anyone in the game. Once on the green he could be erratic, but in the big-money events he was known to wield his putter like a magician's wand.

Known as Moose because of his stocky 6-foot, 215-pound build and his plodding gait down the fairway, Boros took forever to reach his ball, but hardly any time at all before hitting it. The swing, a syrupy arc with a metronome's tempo, approached Snead's in gracefulness. But he never played to the crowd and he never lost his composure as Sam did on occasion. Julius traveled from one shot to the next, from one hole to the next, showing the same unsmiling expression, keeping his feelings to himself. Right from the start, he seemed utterly relaxed, even on Open courses.

Like Tommy Bolt and others who had served during World War II, Boros turned pro later than his successors. In the spring of 1950, at age 30, the son of Hungarian immigrants gave up his accountant's job in his native Connecticut and became assistant pro to Johnny Bulla at Mid-Pines Country Club in Southern Pines, North Carolina. In his first Open that summer he finished ninth; in 1951, a year in which he finished the tour 34th on the money list with only $4,697, he came in tied for fourth; and in 1952 he overcame Ben Hogan to capture the title at Dallas's Northwood Club.

Which highlighted another characteristic Boros shared with Bolt—he never feared the Hawk. Going into the third round four strokes behind him, Boros attracted little notice and few spectators. But then, on the back nine, he cooly took only 11 putts for a 68 and pulled ahead dramatically by two strokes as the Hawk, wilting in 98-degree heat, slipped to a 74. Chomping nonchalantly on blades of grass and swinging with a cigarette dangling from his lips, he scrambled in the fourth round for a 71 and a four-stroke win. It was his first victory on the tour. Afterward, Hogan said to Boros, "You're a magician" and called him Mandrake. The victory was a balm for Boros, whose wife had died in September of 1951 giving birth to the couple's first child.

Over the next eight years Boros averaged only one win a year, but he had a wonderful knack for saving his best for those tournaments with the largest purses—the so-called World Championship of Golf, for instance, which he won twice. And nowhere did he play so consistently well each year as at the Open. Apart from his fourth-place tie in 1951 and the title in 1952, Julius had top-five finishes in the 1955, 1956, 1957, and 1958 championships.

At Cherry Hills, though one of the pretournament favorites, he received hardly any ink, even after his second-round

69. His mediocre 73 on Thursday, of course, had much to do with it, as did his pairing with Wall, whose name was on many prognosticators' lips, and Barber, whose opening 69 attracted widespread attention. The Connecticut newspapers pretty much ignored Boros, perhaps because he had been living in North Carolina for the past decade; and the North Carolina papers, which covered the former Duke football player Mike Souchak as one of their own, barely mentioned him.

But when Boros and Gary Player came in moments after Hogan and Nicklaus, the reaction was not unlike that of the spectators at the 1952 Open: Where'd Boros come from? He had a terrific round and posted a 68 for an aggregate 210 that startled everyone, including the leaders out on the course. Player, desperate to reduce his seven-stroke deficit to Souchak, could do no better than an even-par 71 for a 213 total. He knew from glancing at the scoreboard near the first tee that he would be lucky to make up more than a stroke or two. Through 15 holes, Mike Souchak was one over par.

For leader Souchak, most of those 15 holes had been a struggle, and he was lucky indeed to be so close to par. At the beginning he took few chances and routinely parred each of the first four holes. On the par-five 5th he hit his tee shot into the creek bordering the fairway's right side, but he offset the penalty stroke by planting a wedge two feet from the pin.

By now, with the course's easy stretch winding down, Souchak was anxious to make something positive happen. And it did on the 6th green, where he sank a 25-footer for birdie. The large gallery trailing him and Doug Sanders exploded as Souch pumped his fist, his eyes bright with excitement. But soon the electricity fizzled. After parring the 7th hole, he gave back first one, then a second stroke at numbers 8 and 9 and made the turn in 36.

Even with the two consecutive bogeys, he had extended his lead to five shots over Sanders, who double-bogeyed the long, trying 8th hole and finished the outward nine in three-over 38. But Sanders wasn't his only pursuer. Up ahead, Boros, rumbling along like a freight train toward his 68, had cut deeply into his own seven-stroke shortfall; and playing in the following two pairings, Finsterwald and Barber were stirring. Finsterwald fired back-to-back birdies on the 6th and 7th holes. Moments later, at 9, he examined a four-foot birdie putt that would send him out in 32. He missed it but still he had gained three shots on Souchak and trailed by only three strokes in the tournament. Jerry Barber, who got to two under par through eight holes, also had whittled away at his five-stroke deficit.

Souchak's trials continued on number 10, where he faced a 33-foot putt to save par. For the second time in four holes he canned a long one. Perhaps this *was* his day. The unexpected par could not have come at a better time. He went on to birdie the 11th hole to get back to even par for the round, and then he almost aced number 12. Settling for his second straight birdie, the leader was back to one under par. His position looked better than it had at any time during the round. Then, abruptly, the pendulum swang back again. He played the next three holes unsteadily, as dozens of nervous Open frontrunners of the past, and when he exited the 15th green he was back to one over par.

Arnold Palmer, now at the 18th hole, had suffered as well. That morning he woke up telling himself that if he was going to lose the Open he would at least go down fighting. And fight he did over the first 17 holes—not that many golf fans were present to witness the battle, what with the Hogan-Nicklaus and Boros-Player pairings preceding him and Paul Harney and the twosomes featuring Souchak, Finsterwald, Barber, Casper, and Snead following him. But each time Palmer appeared ready to sustain an attack he made a mistake that gave back his gain.

Again he let rip with his driver on the 1st hole. As in round two, he drove the ball long and in the fairway, but it got tangled in the ring of rough fronting the green and he needed four more shots to get down. Bogey. After parring the 2nd hole, a brilliant explosion at the well-bunkered 3rd rewarded him with a tap-in for birdie. The round's second birdie at the par-five 5th hole, following a par at the 4th, mitigated any lingering annoyance he felt about his opening-hole bogey.

In the first two rounds, Palmer had parred and birdied hole number 6, the course's shortest and easiest par three; on this day he bogeyed it. Disgusted, he immediately fought back with a birdie three on the 7th hole and parred the rugged par-three 8th. One under par, he turned to the uphill par-four 9th hole, which had surrendered precious few birdies throughout the tournament. Palmer had yet to *par* it—his cards read five-five—but it wasn't his style to play cautiously for par. He teed off thinking birdie but immediately got himself in a fix. After chipping too strongly from the greenside rough, he ripped off his glove and holed out with a double-bogey six.

Although he had fired three birdies going out, Arnold Palmer was headed for the back nine with a mediocre one-over-par 36. He badly needed to make more birdies, and fast, but just as badly he needed to avert any more bogeys—or double-bogeys.

At the 10th hole the pressure continued to mount when he landed his approach shot in the bunker to the right of the green and barely escaped the sand, leaving himself with a 20-foot downhiller for par. Now he faced a similar predicament to that at the 14th hole in the second round, where he holed the 30-footer for bogey. Only now he had 14 fewer holes with which to catch Souchak.

Palmer, needing to clean up this mess right after his six at the previous hole, was one very upset golfer, but he had to control his anger and think—*think*. A too aggressive putt here, he knew, and a second consecutive double-bogey was not beyond imagining. Arnold curled over his ball in that increasingly familiar putting posture of his that resembled a question

182

mark. Bringing his body to total stillness, he tapped the ball and kept his head down and steady. He looked up in time to see the ball dive into the hole—a strong, gutsy par.

Palmer pulled back to even par with a birdie at 11 and then, for the first time, parred the watery par-three 12th, where his confidence had taken such a beating in each of the first two rounds. His fifth birdie of the round followed on number 13, pushing him under par for the first time since the 5th hole.

He had pulled off a remarkable comeback.

Five holes remained in which only the 17th offered a reasonable birdie opportunity. Palmer parred the next two holes, numbers 14 and 15, and suddenly he had only three holes on which to go to work. A 70, he knew, wouldn't carry him very far. Figuring he needed another stroke or two against par to stand any chance of gaining on Souchak, he went for broke. The results were: a bogey at the 16th, a par at 17, and another bogey at the home hole.

Palmer had turned in five birdies for the round, yet he shot a one-over-par 72. His position looked bleak, indeed. Souchak, with three holes to play, also was one over par. At the moment, Palmer was the same eight strokes behind the leader as he had been 18 holes earlier. And meanwhile, he had fallen further behind all four of the players in the two pairings directly in front of him, losing four strokes to Boros, three to the still dangerous Hogan and the kid Nicklaus, and one to Player. Palmer stormed off to the locker room.

Souchak, now on the 16th hole, seemed destined to turn some suspect golf into an acceptable round. He birdied the testy par four to get back to even par, then parred number 17. Another par and he would be in reasonable shape—substantially ahead of Sanders, who was having a terrible time, and a still comfortable four strokes in front of Boros, five in front of Hogan and Nicklaus, and six in front of the surprising Johnny

Pott, who was completing his second consecutive sub-70 round in the twosome just ahead.

Souchak had settled into his stance on the 18th tee with a final waggle, had brought back the club over his right shoulder and started to uncoil into his downswing when a spectator pressed the shutter on his box-style camera. The shutter's grinding noise startled the golfer, but it was too late for him to abort his swing. As his clubhead tore into the ball, Souchak told himself to just get it across the lake. He skied it to the right and called out in the perpetrator's direction, "You've ruined my shot!" as the ball traveled out-of-bounds.

Spectators were prohibited from bringing a camera onto the course, and as the player and gallery turned toward the guilty party he tried to escape with the camera wrapped in his shirt. Officials quickly collared the man and escorted him off the premises—small consolation for Souchak. He took a double-bogey six for a 73 and a three-round score of 208.

"It's over and done with," he told reporters back in the locker room. Trying to put the best face on the incident, he added, "There's nothing I can do about it now, and this afternoon is a new day." As true as the latter remark (albeit a malapropism) was for Souchak, it was truer still for his opponents. Boros suddenly was only two shots out of the lead; Hogan and Nicklaus, three; and Pott, four. And Souchak's terrible misfortune brought new life, as well, to a handful of competitors still out on the course.

Dow Finsterwald, after his front-nine 33, came home with a disappointing 37, but he had made up three vital strokes. Jerry Barber matched Finsterwald's 70 and the two joined Boros at 210, only two shots out of the lead. Jack Fleck faded a bit to 72 after his steady 70-70 start; he still couldn't get putts to fall but nonetheless gained a stroke on Souchak. And professional singer–amateur golfer Don Cherry clung to the top of the scoreboard with a 71, his third straight round at par or better. Nothing in his U.S. Open record—three missed cuts and a 49th place at Winged Foot the year before—foretold such a sterling effort. He now joined Fleck and Pott at 212, only four strokes off the lead.

Souchak had left the door ajar, but not all the leading scorers going into Open Saturday stepped into the championship picture. Sanders finished with one of the morning's worst scores, a 77, which landed him at 215, seven strokes behind his fellow competitor. (More surprising, he came back with an 82 in the afternoon.) Bruce Crampton contracted his own case of Openitis, the major symptom being a 75 that knocked him out of contention at 216. Ted Kroll, who went into the morning round tied with Crampton, shot the same untimely 75. And defending champion Billy Casper, Kroll's fellow competitor, only managed to match Souchak with a disappointing 73 and was still six shots behind the leader at 214.

Before his 9:54 A.M. tee time, Sam Snead seemed in fine fettle. A father and son watched him take a few putts at the practice green and the elder fan said abruptly, "OK, let's go. You've seen the great Snead." Sam looked up at the boy and observed, "And I am great, son."

He likely would have remained in good humor—and in the thick of the competition—except for one disastrous hole. On the par-four 9th, his drive landed very close to a bush. All he could do was pitch out, and to do so he practically had to sit on the shrub. Not surprisingly, he struck the ball too firmly and it skipped across the fairway and settled in the opposite-side rough. From there Sam hit into the large bunker guarding the green and then scuffed his explosion shot. On the green in five, he holed out in two for a *triple*-bogey seven. It wasn't as devastating as his infamous eight at the '39 Open's final hole, but some of the reporters present drew the comparison in the next day's papers. Snead's diehard supporters needed no such reminder.

Still, the Slammer regained his sense of humor in time for some entertainment at the 18th tee. There he interrupted his swing preparation, produced a piece of string with a hook on it, stepped toward the bank of the pond and cast the line. Then he stepped back and hit his tee shot. He finished with a 73 that left him all but out of it, six shots behind Souchak.

TRAILING BEHIND THE SNEAD-CHERRY twosome were the field's final seven pairings, composed of players on the cusp of the cut with scores of 146 or 147. Only veteran Jackson Bradley, a club pro at the River Oaks Club in Houston, broke par—a 69 that gave him a creditable three-round total of 215. Two-time champion Cary Middlecoff consolidated his return to respectability with a 72, but Bob Verwey shot the morning's worst round, a 79. Al Feminelli, a New York City pro, shot a hole in one of sorts on the 12th hole. After his first tee shot splashed into the water, he tried again, and this one dove into the cup for a par three.

Bringing up the rear in the day's only threesome were Howie Johnson, Bill Johnston, and Bob Rosburg. Rosburg still was not a happy camper, but he had cooled off and calmed down after his second-round 75 and returned to Cherry Hills to complete his work. He shot the kind of round expected of him all along, a par 71.

By the time Snead and Cherry came in from their morning round the field's first grouping of ten twosomes had already teed off for their afternoon and final round, and the vanguard of the contenders, Hogan and Nicklaus, were minutes away from doing the same. Only now could anyone get a meaningful perspective on the championship going into the final 18 holes. This is how it looked:

Mike Souchak	68-67-73—208
Jerry Barber	69-71-70—210
Julius Boros	73-69-68—210
Dow Finsterwald	71-69-70—210

Ben Hogan	75-67-69—211
Jack Nicklaus (a)	71-71-69—211
Don Cherry (a)	70-71-71—212
Jack Fleck	70-70-72—212
Johnny Pott	75-68-69—212
Gary Player	70-72-71—213
Billy Casper	71-70-73—214
Dutch Harrison	74-70-70—214
Bob Shave	72-71-71—214
Sam Snead	72-69-73—214
Arnold Palmer	72-71-72—215

(8 others tied at 215: Jackson Bradley, Doug Ford, Bob Goalby, Chick Harbert, Paul Harney, Bob Harris, Dave Marr, and Doug Sanders)

Like runners in the third quarter of a mile race jostling to stay within striking distance of the pacesetter, nine golfers had positioned themselves to get within five strokes of Souchak. If 65 years of U.S. Open history counted for anything, the bid for the crown was effectively a ten-man race.

In the 56 U.S. Opens held over 72 holes dating back to 1898, no man trailing by more than five strokes after 54 holes had ever won the championship. Three golfers had overcome a five-stroke deficit to capture the title: Walter Hagen in 1919, Johnny Farrell in 1928, and Byron Nelson in 1939.

Judging from more recent history, one was tempted to discount the chances of all but Souchak and his top five pursuers. In the 14 championships conducted since the end of World War II the most strokes made up in the final round by the eventual winner was three. Jack Fleck, three shots behind Hogan after 54 holes in the '55 Open, caught him at the 72nd green and beat him in the 18-hole play-off the next day.

Souchak looked and sounded shaky following the conclusion of his round. And who could blame him? There he was, on the verge of redeeming a round that threatened on and off to blow up in his face, and a malignant hand seemed to descend and sabotage all his good work. Between rounds he told a few reporters, "I don't know what's the matter with me. I'm in a fog. I can't figure out what I'm trying to think about. Maybe that six on 18 will wake me up."

Mike's nine nearest pursuers included three long shots—Pott and the amateurs Nicklaus and Cherry; three mavericks—Fleck, Barber, and Player; and three very strong challengers—Finsterwald, Boros, and Hogan.

Johnny Pott, still looking for his first win on the professional tour, seemed likely to break through soon but probably not at the National Open. Not that he wasn't playing well; only Hogan and Boros had joined him in breaking 70 in each of the second and third rounds. For the season as a whole, his fourth on tour, he was enjoying his best year. At San Diego in late January he had defended his 54-hole lead impressively with a closing 69; it took a 67 by Souchak to edge him by one stroke for the win. Pott, a member of the 1955 NCAA championship Louisiana State University golf team, also had to his credit a third-place tie at New Orleans in April, a sixth-place tie at the "500" Festival Open in late May, and a fourth-place finish just a week earlier in Oklahoma City.

That said, Pott still looked extremely vulnerable. True, his game was sharp and he had performed well in his two previous Opens—a 41st-place finish in 1957 and a tie for 19th in 1959. But he was a golfer with limited experience in coping with championship heat. Could he shoot the third-straight below-70 round he'd probably need to win?

For three rounds, the amateur Jack Nicklaus had proven that he belonged alongside the likes of his fellow competitors Hogan and Casper in this, golf's greatest championship. One day he would intimidate opponents down the stretch with his reputation for flourishing under pressure while others collapsed. He didn't have that reputation in 1960, but he did have enough raw, precocious talent to render his age and amateur status all but irrelevant.

In ten years—half his life—Jack had mastered advanced training in the activity he loved best. He'd been tested thoroughly along the way, and he'd handled brilliantly each successively greater trial, the last being the 1959 U.S. Amateur final against Charlie Coe. But was he up to the game's ultimate test, the afternoon round of Open Saturday? Was he ready to manage his game and himself when he made that first mistake or encountered that first inevitable patch of bad luck?

Don Cherry's performance was a shock. Only four players in the field had shot par or better in each of the first three rounds: Barber, Finsterwald, Nicklaus, and Donald Ross Cherry. Seeing the 36-year-old amateur post a single good round, maybe even two, would not have been surprising—he plainly could play the game—but not three. Not with his Open record; not with his disposition.

"The worst temper the world has ever seen" was the way he later characterized his self-control as a golfer. "I made Tommy Bolt look like Little Red Riding Hood," he would tell writer Curt Sampson in an August 1992 *Golf Journal* piece. But at the 1960 Open he seemed ready and able to let his game do his talking.

In the week before the Cherry Hills Open Cherry had dreamed on three different nights that he was winning the championship. Now, in daytime's improbable reality, that dream was within reach. And even wildly improbable dreams sometimes did come true in the U.S. Open—Francis Ouimet knew this; so did Jack Fleck.

In the five years since his miracle Open win against Hogan, Fleck had rarely lived up to the promise of his transcendent effort; but he surely was not the one-shot chump some made him out to be. In the year after the '55 Open, a period in which his flowering game, and confidence, would have benefited from intensive tour competition, he let himself be tied up with endorsements and exhibitions and missed the cut as the defending champion. He then got involved in a golf course enterprise in Rochester, Michigan, as a professional manager. Only in 1959 did he start to rebuild his tournament career. He took a club job at the El Caballero Country Club near Los Angeles but still won a decent $12,500 in 24 tour starts that included a tie for 19th in the Open and two second-place finishes late in the season. The end to his long victory drought finally came in the Arizona desert in February, 1960.

Golf fans and most everyone connected with the tour were delighted that Jack, now 37 and as unpretentious as ever, had persevered and triumphed in Phoenix. But in Denver he was not a candidate for the hearts of the fans or the press. There seemed to exist a belief that he had had his brush with immortality; if a Hogan or Snead couldn't win, let it be one of the tour's younger stars.

Whatever, Fleck's chances going into the final round looked dubious. His established composure—*that* he knew he could count on. But his putting? At four shots out of the lead he could wait no longer for his putts to start to fall. He needed a speedy, dramatic shift in fortune on the greens.

Jerry Barber, on the other hand, was the best putter of the ten contenders. Using a beat-up, taped-together blade putter and employing his peculiar grip in which his left wrist pointed straight up, Jerry had wonderful feel for long putts and rarely three-putted. It wasn't his putting that was the problem; it was, in contrast to Fleck, his composure.

Even in the midst of his best year in golf—two wins, fourth on the money list—he had suffered lapses that raised doubt about his ability to win a big one. At both the DeSoto and the "500" Festival tournaments, he gave up a 54-hole lead and had to settle for second place. Apparently he plain choked in his best chance for a major title. The three-round leader at the 1959 PGA Championship, he needed a par on each of the last two holes for victory. On both holes he hit good drives and faced routine approach shots to the green; both times he hit into a bunker and bogeyed.

Some golfers cave in many times before they are sufficiently resilient to seize the day on the next big opportunity; others accumulate too much psychological baggage along the way to withstand the strain. Which was Jerry Barber?

Gary Player was even more unpredictable. He believed that winning the U.S. Open and the other major American championships was somehow his manifest destiny. This was a theory nobody on tour, except maybe Bob Verwey, subscribed to. But Player had the kind of cockeyed optimism, as well as deeply held faith, that made him a threat even though he was the furthest from the lead of the legitimate contenders. But, one wondered, did he have the game?

Dow Finsterwald, who had one major title to his credit, the 1958 PGA Championship, seemed as capable of winning as anyone, Boros and Hogan included. At 30 he was in his prime and was having a typically strong year on tour with wins at Los Angeles and New Orleans and the near-miss at the Masters. He was striking his irons with greater authority than ever and using a draw, rather than a fade, with good result.

Given his solid overall game, a believable scenario would have the other contestants fall by the wayside one by one, with Finsterwald the only golfer left standing at the end. And Finsterwald, with his pleasing dry sense of humor would somehow top his delightful statement to the press after he won the PGA: "Gentlemen, you've got yourselves a colorless champion." A second, equally believable scenario was: Dow would play well but finish runner-up, as he had done 23 times in his first five seasons on tour.

Boros and Hogan, no question, both knew how to win the Open. And both had demonstrated in memorable fashion that they knew how to win coming from behind—Boros in 1952 and Hogan in 1950 and 1951, years in which he started the final round two strokes behind.

Boros, whose 68 was the best score of the morning, was in an enviable position for the climactic fourth round. Playing several twosomes ahead of Souchak, Finsterwald, Fleck, and Barber, he could put pressure on his opponents by posting a few timely birdies in the relatively easy opening holes. The Hawk was less likely to succumb to such pressure, so it mattered little that he was playing ahead of Boros. It might even be an advantage playing directly behind Hogan; he would know exactly where his—and Souchak's—chief rival stood.

Hogan had come a long way since that dreadful first-round 75, and Cherry Hills was abuzz at the prospect of the great champion finally capturing the record fifth Open title. As always, Hogan's main concern was not his opponents but himself. How much longer could he continue to hit one green after another in regulation figures? Could he shoot another 69 without holing any more putts than he did in the morning? And if he did shoot another 69, would his total of 280 be good enough to win?

No way, of course, to know the answers. What Hogan did know was that it was hard as hell to shoot below par when you couldn't sink a damn putt to save your life. All he could do was to play 18 more holes one at a time, bringing to each shot every ounce of judgment and skill he'd accumulated in his 30 years as a professional golfer. Continue to avoid bogeys and give himself chances to hole a few birdie putts. He, too, could use some luck on the greens.

ARNOLD PALMER JUST DIDN'T seem to get it: he was out of it. He was seven strokes behind leader Mike Souchak. Nobody—*nobody* came from seven strokes behind in the last round to win the Open. Nobody—*nobody* leapfrogged 14 golfers in one round to win the Open, especially when four of them were past champions, Ben Hogan among them.

When Palmer walked off the course headed for the locker

room he seemed more obsessed with breaking the course—the proud cowboy pitted against the indomitable bronco—than winning the National Open. Bumping into Jack Clowser of the *Cleveland Press*, he said, "I've thought right along I could lick this course. It isn't too late to do it." But he still seemed at a loss about what he needed to do, where he was going wrong.

During lunch he said to the *Chicago Tribune*'s Charles Bartlett, "How do you figure it? Here I have 13 birdies [actually it was 12] for 54 holes and I'm two over par. It doesn't add up." What Palmer was not including in his computation, of course, was his painful bogey count: ten bogeys and two double-bogeys. Never mind; his situation had finally become clear to him and he was starting to formulate a plan: "Gotta get some more birdies or this Grand Slam I'm going for gets shut off right here," he told Bartlett.

It was drawing near to his 1:42 P.M. tee time. Palmer picked out a fresh shirt from his locker. Chatting with a couple of reporters and players, he still was trying to figure a way he could win the tournament, a proposition his companions deemed near-ridiculous. Various accounts of the scene exist, but all seem to hinge on Arnold's floating out a trial balloon: "Wonder what a 65 would bring this afternoon?" Bob Drum of the *Pittsburgh Press*, Dan Jenkins of the *Fort Worth Press*, and a couple of golfers lounging in the area grinned. (The Jenkins account of this scene includes Venturi and Rosburg. Rosburg did not remember being present and, indeed, could not have been; he had started his morning round 1 hour 20 minutes after Palmer and was still out on the course.)

Drum, a big, garrulous fellow who had followed Palmer's career since Palmer was 15, instructed him simply to drive the 1st green, ram home his eagle putt, and take it from there. Palmer, who was finishing off a hamburger, laughed along with the others. Then Drum gave a more serious answer to Arnold's question about the effect of a 65. He stated bluntly: "That won't be good enough." Which apparently struck a raw nerve, and Arnold snapped back, "Oh, yes it will. It'll put me at 280, and that's a play-off figure."

Arnold Palmer then stormed off, banged out a dozen balls or so on the practice range, and headed to the 1st tee.

CHAPTER 9

BACK IN HIS DAYS ON THE ROAD WHEN HE WAS THE TOUR'S BIGGEST name, Ben Hogan was as demanding about the food he was served as he was about his golf. Steaks and other staples had to be prepared just so or they were returned forthwith. But on this Open Saturday, as on all others, lunch was little more than a necessary refueling stop. Less than an hour after signing his third-round scorecard, he was back on the 1st tee for the final round of the 1960 U.S. Open.

It was 1:30 P.M. By 5:45, when the championship was decided, he would have figured dramatically in the wildest final 18 holes in U.S. Open history. But that was four unforeseeable, unimagined hours away.

Back on the course, Hogan pushed on methodically, exactly as in the morning, reaching every green in regulation, stamping out one par after another. Only a helicopter could disturb his heightened concentration, and then only momentarily. One hovered overhead on the 4th hole until Hogan instructed officials to shoo away the curious pilot. And so, with pars at each of the first five holes, the Hawk remained two under par for the championship, searching for that elusive first birdie.

Jack Nicklaus, his fellow competitor, found his own immediately at Cherry Hills's easy 1st hole. Jack gave himself a good chance to birdie the next two holes as well, but he missed putts of eight and six feet respectively. The young man's fuzzy putting continued at 4, where he three-putted for a bogey. But he redeemed himself at once at the 538-yard 5th hole. After a long drive, he let fly a breathtaking one-iron that stopped 20 feet from the hole, and then rolled home the putt for an eagle three. Nicklaus was now four under par and shadowing leader Souchak, who was then about to start play.

Playing in the twosome just behind Hogan and Nicklaus, Julius Boros got off to the kind of solid start he wanted, too. After pars at 1 and 2, he birdied the 3rd hole to join Nicklaus at four under par.

It surprised no one that Arnold Palmer, playing directly behind Boros and Gary Player, selected his one-wood at the 1st tee, just as he had in the first three rounds. What did he have to lose? Finishing respectably in the top ten and earning a decent check held no appeal for him. Besides, he was in no humor to play conservatively.

Palmer was spitting mad. Furious about Bob Drum's dismissal of his chances, furious about his mediocre play throughout the championship, and furious about his past failures on this defenseless hole, Arnold took out his anger on the ball. This time he killed it. It soared all the way to the thick ring of rough protecting the front of the green, skipped out, and rolled onto the putting surface pin high, 20 feet from the hole—a prodigious drive, even accounting for the extra distance gained in Denver's mile-high elevation. The sizable gallery at the 1st hole roared its approval.

Twenty-five years later, recalling the moment in *Golf* magazine, Palmer wrote: "As I reached the green, all the anger melted away. Then, as I waited to putt, I began to feel very, very nervous. To this day, I don't know why. It was as if I were anticipating something that I *wanted* to happen." The tour's most aggressive putter left his eagle putt a foot short but did tap in for a birdie. When he and Paul Harney headed to the 2nd tee, few in the gallery trailed after them. Most waited to see Souchak, who was due up in about 15 minutes, and the other leaders yet to tee off—Finsterwald, Fleck, Barber, and Cherry.

As a nervous Mike Souchak prepared in the practice area for the most important round of golf of his life, the competitor uppermost in his thoughts was not Hogan or Nicklaus or Boros; it was Palmer. Souch had heard the crowd's roar and soon learned its cause, as word of Arnold's drive and near-eagle spread quickly through the grapevine.

In his first three trips around Cherry Hills, the four-wood had been Mike's judicious implement of choice at the first tee. This time, against his better judgment, he, too, pulled out the driver. Like Palmer in round one, he sprayed the ball off target into Little Dry Creek. The resulting bogey—the last thing he needed following his upsetting six at the end of his morning round—trimmed his two-stroke margin to one. Mike fought back admirably on number 2, however, holing an eight-footer for birdie. Meanwhile, cheers continued to ring out up ahead. Palmer was on a rampage.

Having finally conquered "that dinky little hole," as he later described the 1st, he had reached the 2nd tee energized and determined to go for broke. He left his approach shot at the 410-yard par four just in front of the green, 30 feet from the flag. Shooting three, he chipped dead toward the hole. The run-up nuzzled against the pin, and dropped in. Two birdies, each hinging on an electrifying shot, sent Palmer's confidence—and adrenaline—soaring.

On to the 348-yard 3rd hole. Palmer hit another huge drive. This one hooked slightly but it carried pin high. A splendid little pitch to the small elevated green died one foot from the flagpole. Arnold grabbed his beat-up blade putter—recently he'd welded lead to its back, almost ruining the club—

and tapped in. Three holes, three birdies—and he wasn't through.

A three-wood at the 426-yard par-four 4th hole split the fairway, a wedge covered the flag, a six-foot putt rattled the cup. With stunning suddenness, the golfer nobody had heeded for three days had propelled himself back into the tournament. In less than an hour he had advanced from two strokes over par to two under, and now, for the first time, the leaders hovered within his reach.

News of Palmer's blistering start blazed across Cherry Hills's sunny acres, and by the 5th hole he had attracted a throng of boisterous supporters. "Arnie's Army" had mobilized on the double. Reporters Jenkins and Drum, who'd remained behind in the locker room when Arnold stalked off to try for his 65, had planned to look in on leader Souchak going off at the 1st tee. Instead, they had hustled out to the 4th hole to see the Palmer charge in full flight. "By that time he was a wild man," Drum recalled later. "He nearly ran to the 5th tee, he was in such a hurry to get at it." Spotting Drum and Jenkins inside the gallery ropes, Arnold crowed, "I knew I'd get you guys back out here with me some way."

There, on the 538-yard par five, a hole he'd already birdied twice, his string ended, but not out of caution. Despite driving into the short rough to the right, he shot for the green with his three-wood and caught the deep bunker beneath the elevated green. Arnold couldn't do much with his sand shot and two-putted from about 20 feet for his first par.

When he planted a seven-iron 25 feet from the flag at the 174-yard 6th hole, it looked as though his game had returned to earth. He now faced a curving, side-hill putt, the kind that requires a player to read the break correctly and to apply the right amount of speed instinctively so that a miss won't drift beyond par range. Arnold rapped the ball decisively and watched as it curled straight into the hole. Again, thunderous cheers animated a small patch of Cherry Hills Country Club. To the ears of the Open contenders, spread out across the front nine, the distant roar sounded a siren. Whether they were near one of the four scoreboards out on the course or not, they *knew*—it was Palmer. Arnold Palmer was turning the course, and the shape of the championship, inside out.

The golfer, swigging Cokes, dragging on cigarettes, and hitching up his tan slacks in nervous energy, was back in orbit. By the time he reached the next tee, a large portion of the day's gallery of 15,258 (setting a tournament record of 43,878) had washed over the 7th hole and the 8th, where Hogan and Nicklaus were at work.

Stationed between the Hogan-Nicklaus and the Palmer-Harney twosomes, Gary Player was suffering through his worst round of the tournament. The feisty South African, itching to claim the lead role in the unfolding drama, had faltered and instead was relegated to the part of an extra. His fellow competitor, Julius Boros, remained in the thick of the competition even though he failed to post the low numbers with which he'd hoped to exert pressure on the other contenders. A bogey at the 6th hole offset his birdie at the 3rd. He was even par for the round and still three under for the tournament.

Palmer might very well have drawn every last spectator to his gallery were it not for Hogan and Nicklaus, who were playing their own lofty, if less rarified, level of golf. After parring the first five holes, Ben finally broke through with a birdie at number 6, then immediately reverted to pars at 7, 8, and 9. His remarkable streak of greens-in-regulation had now reached 27, yet he had only three birdies to show for it. He stood at three under par with nine holes to play. Parring in on the difficult home nine would produce a 281—a score, he knew, that was unlikely to win this Open.

As Hogan turned to the final nine, it seemed as though his most conspicuous obstacle to the title might be the young man walking right over there, right before his eyes. Amateurs were supposed to have bowed to the field's experienced professionals long before now; but as even the few remaining skeptics following the championship had to appreciate, Jack Nicklaus was not your typical amateur.

On the front nine, he hadn't merely held his own; he had lopped three strokes off of par. Jack made three steady pars after his eagle at number 5, and then drained a clutch 22-foot putt at the 9th hole to make the turn in 32. The fresh-cheeked kid was five under for the tournament and now tied with Mike Souchak. For the first time in his golfing career, he had a share of the U.S. Open lead.

Julius Boros, with pars at the 7th, 8th, and 9th holes, completed the front side in even-par 35. Though somewhat displeased with himself, he was still in strong position for his second Open title; he was tied with Hogan at three under par.

Palmer, two holes back on the 411-yard 7th hole, drove into the left rough but recovered beautifully with a wedge that settled some five feet from the hole. Arnold curled over the ball, but then backed away from it, something he rarely did. Then he stepped up and knocked it in. His enormous following went crazy, cheering wildly, almost giddily. Six birdies in the first seven holes! None of the fans could believe what they were seeing. Indeed, the U.S. Open had never seen anything resembling Palmer's fourth-round salvo.

It was just after 3:00 P.M. In the hour and 20 minutes since he had angrily driven the green with his first shot, Arnold Palmer had created a whirlwind of excitement at Cherry Hills Country Club. Onlookers, rubbing their eyes at the six red numbers signifying below-par scores alongside Palmer's name on the scoreboards, wondered, Could the Masters hero storm to victory again?

When Palmer reached the 233-yard 8th hole, Player and Boros had just gone off. "Looks like I finally got the wheels going on this thing, doesn't it?" he said. Soon frustrated by the delay, he paced impatiently back and forth on the tee. After a few minutes he grabbed a cigarette from his caddie, Bob Blair, and sat down to smoke.

Finally, the long par three, the third toughest hole during the tournament, was clear. Palmer went with a two-iron. He hooked the ball and it landed in the deep bunker left of the green. He visibly slumped, disappointed with his effort. Two pars and he would have a 29, a magical nine-hole score never before recorded in the National Open. Arnold wanted it badly.

As he reached the front of the teeing ground, a lone fan started to applaud lightly. A few others joined in, and that ignited it. As Arnold strode down the fairway, packed with spectators on both sides, the applause spread and deepened, swelling, escorting him all the way to his ball. By the time he arrived at the green, he was standing erect, his shoulders high again.

Palmer stepped into the bunker, planted his feet deliberately, and delicately popped the ball out to three feet from the hole. The gallery cheered warmly, and Palmer, who usually went bareheaded, tipped his red sun visor in acknowledgment. Then, up on the green, he blew the three-foot putt. Bogey. Now for a 29 he would need a birdie three at the uphill 430-yard 9th hole.

He regarded it, with good reason, as the course's toughest. There, he'd gone bogey, bogey, double-bogey—four over par in three rounds. This was no dinky hole. Starting at 240 yards out, the fairway sloped sharply to the right. To reach the green in two, the tee shot had to stay in the fairway and the approach had to avoid the sizable bunker guarding the most direct flight to the green.

Palmer's three-wood off the tee was perfect—right down the middle. "I'm going for the pin here," he said. Perhaps overly excited by the circumstances, perhaps a bit gun-shy of the bunker, he knocked his six-iron over the green. His chip coming back left him some eight feet for his par. So much for a 29; he had his work cut out for him now to make 30.

As he lined up the putt, the gallery grew deathly quiet; even the casual fans who rarely strayed from the clubhouse area interrupted their chatter. Palmer pulled back his putter, and with a confident rap buried the ball in the heart of the hole. His 30 tied the lowest nine in U.S. Open history, that of amateur James B. McHale, Jr., in the third round of the 1947 championship. Unlike McHale's 30, which had no bearing on the tournament, Palmer's thrust him into the center of the action. It carried his score to three under par for the championship, and moved him into a tie with Hogan and Boros, two behind Nicklaus.

Mike Souchak, playing two holes back, heard the uproar Palmer was creating—he could hardly ignore it—and had all he could do to stay composed. After his bogey-birdie start, he settled into a run of six straight pars. This was the kind of consistency that would please leaders in the last round of most U.S. Opens, but not Souchak, who had hemorrhaged his lead, and not at Cherry Hills, with its soft front nine.

Souch came to the tough 9th hole at the same five-under-par aggregate score with which he entered the round, tied with Nicklaus for the lead. His drive landed in an unplayable lie under a hawthorn bush, and he needed four more strokes to hole out. With this bogey he relinquished the lead he'd held since the tournament's beginning.

Twenty-year-old Jack Nicklaus now led the U.S. Open with nine holes to play.

Palmer and Nicklaus were not the only players to shoot low front-nine scores. Ted Kroll, one of the leaders at the halfway point, went out in 32, thanks to birdies at 1, 3, 4, 6, and 7. Two offsetting bogeys, though, left him a distant five shots behind Nicklaus at the turn. The amazing Dutch Harrison, six behind Souchak after 54 holes, refused to fade. With six pars and three birdies, including a big one at the 9th hole, he recorded a 32 as well, and trailed Nicklaus by only three strokes.

Putts finally started to fall for Jack Fleck. The hot round

he'd been waiting for arrived just on time. Fleck, playing directly behind Souchak, birdied the 1st hole, bogeyed the 2nd, and then ran off his own torrid stretch of birdies on each of the next four holes. He missed a seven-footer for birdie at 7, he bogeyed 8, and he parred 9. His 32 moved him into a tie for second with Souchak at four under par, and it kept him one shot behind Nicklaus with the back side yet to be played.

Fleck's fellow competitor, Dow Finsterwald, got off quickly, with birdies at 3 and 5, but then gave back a stroke at 6 and two more at 9, where he drove under a pine tree. As unhappy as he was with his double-bogey, with his front-nine 36 Dow had lost only one stroke on the lead. He stood three shots behind the new front-runner, Nicklaus.

Jerry Barber also went out in 36 and slipped from two shots out of the lead to three. It could have been worse. After playing the first eight holes without producing a single birdie, he made a rare three at the 9th. It was just what the doctor ordered.

When the 2:24 tee time for Sam Snead and Don Cherry finally arrived, the often hot-headed amateur resumed his eerily airtight, patient game. Cherry parred the first four holes and then alternated birdies and pars over the next four to get to three under for the first time in the championship. Like so many others in the field, though, he got the worst of it at number 9. He bogeyed, but even so shot 34 and joined Barber, Finsterwald, and Harrison at three strokes behind Nicklaus.

As expected, the inexperienced Johnny Pott did not have another below-par round in his bag. Like Gary Player, he fell off the leader board on the front nine and was not to reemerge on the back nine.

THE FRONT NINE HAD the stuff that thrilling telecasts are made of—Palmer's birdie binge, Nicklaus's poised advance to the lead, and Hogan's conquest of the fairways and retreat on the greens. But in 1960 the television technology and know-how were not up to capturing—"live" or on videotape—action unfolding all over a golf course. The day's newspapers enjoyed pointing out that fact.

"Did you see what NBC advertised and presented as the National Open golf finals Saturday night?" *Greensboro Daily News* sportswriter Smith Barrier wrote a few days after the tournament. "If you had not called your favorite newspaper or listened to your special radio sportscast beforehand, you were lost in the NBC-TV presentation."

NBC had come to Denver with nine cameras and a 39-member crew, not counting on-course spotters who reported details to the director using walkie-talkies. The plan was to cover five holes—1, 9, 16, 17, and 18—and to videotape the morning round for a 90-minute afternoon broadcast and the afternoon round for a one-hour evening show. Some live action was supposed to be mixed in along the way. But according to accounts in the *Philadelphia Inquirer,* as well as the Greensboro paper, the broadcasts were so chopped up that it was virtually impossible to follow what happened. A tongue-in-cheek story in the *Inquirer* the next day purported to be written for those who *watched* the telecast. It confirmed the name of the winner.

Despite NBC's best intentions, viewers glimpsed little more than sporadic highlights of the competition on Open Saturday. Ironically, the ever-changing scoreboards, like wire service ticker-tape machines, provided the best sense of the fourth round's swirling, convoluted developments. And what the scoreboards showed after nine holes was that the 1960 championship was shaking out to be the tightest, most hotly contested U.S. Open in history. Only the 1925 Open, in which any one of a handful of players had a chance to win in the final round, could rival it.

The Cherry Hills Open was still a ten-man competition, but with a difference. At the start of the final round, the top ten players were within five strokes of one another. Now, the top ten players—Palmer and Harrison having replaced Player and Pott—were bunched within three strokes of one another. Soon the number of contenders dropped to nine.

Dutch Harrison, the first contender to proceed to the back nine, parred the 10th hole. With a birdie at the par-five 11th, he reached three under par for the first time in the tournament. One more birdie over the final seven holes and he could par in for 280, which, he thought, might just be good enough to win. Sadly, the old-timer didn't get to find out. At the 12th, he lost a stroke to par, then another at the 14th. Another bogey followed at 18, but by then Dutch was out of the title picture.

IN HIS 18 PREVIOUS Open appearances, Ben Hogan had never played so masterfully from tee to green. On the home nine, he continued to reach green after green in regulation figures—10, 11, 12—and to give himself realistic birdie chances. The Hawk had hit 30 consecutive greens, but almost uniformly his putting had failed him hole after hole.

Jack Nicklaus matched Hogan at par over the first three holes of the back nine. With six holes left, he stated later, he knew he had sole possession of the lead and he wasn't a bit nervous. He believed he could play the final holes under par. He believed he was going to win the championship.

So did Robin Obetz, a teammate on the Ohio State University golf team who looked on. On Friday night in Columbus, talking to his father on the phone, he said he had a feeling that Jack was going to win the Open. Early the next morning, father and son hopped on a plane to Denver. They caught up with the Nicklaus-Hogan gallery as it turned to the back nine in the morning round.

Ohio State football coach Woody Hayes was back. Unfortunately, the brash coach had appointed himself a sort of personal marshal to Charlie Nicklaus. Dismissing Charlie's embarrassment, he asked fans to step aside so the golfer's father could see his son play, and he shooshed spectators who were noisy when Jack was preparing to shoot.

At the comparatively easy 384-yard 13th hole, Jack faced his first crisis of Open Saturday. It came out of the blue, following two faultless shots. He hit a perfect three-wood from the elevated tee that landed in the narrow fairway on level ground, not far from the creek that cut across the hole 20 yards in front of the green. He plucked up his ball with a beautiful nine-iron, and it braked 12 feet below the pin. The straight, uphill putt was about as good a birdie chance as Cherry Hills's last six holes were likely to offer. Jack went for it, but he missed his target and committed a cardinal sin in the process: he passed the hole by more than tap-in distance—his ball rolled 18 inches above the hole.

Lining up the short putt, Jack noticed an indentation in his putting line. In the searing pressure of the moment, he could not recall whether the rules allowed him to repair a ball mark (they did); and with the Hawk standing stonily nearby, he was too embarrassed to check the rule with a USGA official, a routine measure. So he putted, and the indentation deflected his ball just enough for it to miss the hole.

Hogan was distressed in his own right. His pitch to the 13th green had dropped just short of the flag, bounded into the pin, and ricocheted nine feet away. Disgusted with his bad luck, Hogan swore under his breath. If the ball had missed the thin flagstick, its backspin almost certainly would have stopped it much closer to the hole. Up on the green, he missed yet another birdie putt. All the same, he now trailed the kid by only one shot.

Nicklaus's timidity on the green dropped him to four under par and into a four-way tie for the lead. Boros had just birdied the par-five 11th hole, and moments later so did Palmer, who reached the green in two and two-putted from 25 feet. When Arnold learned that Jack had bogeyed 13 and he was tied for the lead, he said, "How sweet it is!" Fleck, with a par at number 10, remained at four under for the championship.

What about Souchak? Mike seemed on the verge of unraveling when he missed a 15-inch putt for par at the 10th hole. Once seven under par for the tournament, his aggregate score was now three under and his confidence seemed in shambles. Like the other long hitters in the field, though, Mike could reach the 11th hole in two, and with a birdie there he reclaimed a share of the lead—now a five-way share—with Nicklaus, Boros, Fleck, and Palmer.

Mike's recovery was short-lived. On the elevated tee of the 12th hole, Souchak's year-long dream of redemption at the U.S. Open nearly drowned with one swing—his tee shot sank in the lake, and the resulting double-bogey shoved him back, two strokes out of the lead. The picturesque par three that had enraged Tommy Bolt, tortured Deane Beman, and toyed with Arnold Palmer all but extinguished Souchak's normally buoyant reserves of optimism.

Finsterwald, meanwhile, was having his own problems. Hoping to blot out his ill-timed double-bogey at the 9th hole, Dow bogeyed the 10th. Like Souchak in the twosome in front of him, he fought back with a birdie at the 11th only to receive a staggering blow at the 12th. In Finsterwald's case it was only a bogey, but it left him barely alive at one under par. To get to 280, he'd need three birdies on the six holes remaining, a daunting task. Meanwhile, Boros and Palmer each had parred the 12th and 13th holes to remain at four under par.

Nicklaus, shaken by his three-putt at the 13th hole, three-putted the 14th green from 40 feet for a second straight bogey. Hogan made par yet again, and now he and Jack were tied at three under for the tournament. When Boros landed in the large bunker protecting the right front of the green and bogeyed the hole, he, too, stood at three under par. Next came

Palmer. He pulled his drive at the 470-yard hole into the left rough but still reached the green with a six-iron. He two-putted for par and now shared the lead with only one other man—Jack Fleck, who had parred both 11 and 12.

Jerry Barber, two under at the turn, closed the gap on the leaders with his own birdie at the par-five 11th hole, but then "the wheels stopped turning," as he put it for writer Ray Cave in a July *Sports Illustrated* profile. More than 30 years later, he could recount his play from this point on with passable accuracy.

At 12, he missed the green. The little master of chipping hit a run-up from just off the left front of the putting surface, then blew the remaining short par putt. After recovering with two routine pars at 13 and 14, he ran into serious trouble at the next par three, the 196-yard 15th hole. Jerry didn't want to leave this one short; the green being elevated, balls had to carry all the way in. The danger was Little Dry Creek—the same stream Palmer and Souchak had visited at the 1st hole—which ran only a few yards from the left side of the green.

"As I sometimes do when I try to hit the ball hard, I turned on it a little bit. It hit on the left edge of the green about halfway up, and the green was *as hard as a rock,*" Barber said, emphasizing each of the last five words. "The ball never saw ground again until it went into the water." He took a drop, pitched up, missed the putt, and made five. Bogey at 12, double-bogey at 15—the back nine's two par threes—knocked Barber back to even par, ending his title chances.

Eight men still remained in contention.

Don Cherry displayed his own Hoganesque consistency on the second nine—par at 10, par at 11, par at 12, par at 13, par at 14. The par at 14, actually, was spectacular, coming on a 40-foot putt. Years later, Cherry recalled to writer Curt Sampson in *Golf Journal,* "Sam [Snead] looked at me and said, 'You're gonna win the tournament.' " Holding fast at two under par, Don was tied with Souchak, one stroke behind Nicklaus, Boros, and Hogan, and two behind Palmer and Fleck.

Nicklaus's poise had finally been shaken: after three-putting his way to two straight bogeys, he badly needed to settle down on the 15th hole. And this he did with a par. Hogan left himself with a birdie putt that was reported variously as either 10 feet or 20 feet from the hole. This time he canned it—his second birdie of the round and first one since the 6th hole. It was 4:40 P.M. and there was a three-way tie for the lead, Hogan joining Fleck and Palmer. In the press tent writers speculated about a repeat of the Hogan-Fleck 1955 play-off.

As Souchak left the 12th hole, devastated over his double-bogey, he tried to regroup, to persuade himself that the tournament was not over. Even going bogey-bogey-birdie-double-bogey over the past four holes, he was only two shots out of the lead. Hadn't he rallied from behind for a few of his 11 career victories? But how much more difficult his task was here. After having set the pace for almost the entire championship, he first needed to stanch the bleeding. Souch did pull himself together and parred 13 and 14. Time was running out, but he hadn't quit. He was hanging in there, two back.

Jack Fleck had waited 54 holes to find a cure for his putting woes, and when he did the results were phenomenal. Were it not for Palmer's outrageous front-nine assault on Cherry Hills, Fleck's name would have been on everyone's lips. In fact, his round closely paralleled Arnold's. After laying down his own string of birdies, he'd bogeyed the par-three 8th hole and then settled into par golf. Through 66 holes, he was in excellent position. Par in and he had a four-under-par 280.

At the 13th, or 67th, hole, Fleck left himself a seven-foot birdie putt to take sole possession of the lead. He missed the putt, then botched the remaining short one for par. The horrible, almost amazing lapse bumped him one behind Hogan and Palmer, leaving him wondering whether his putting stroke had left him as suddenly as it had returned on the front nine. His fellow competitor, Finsterwald, parred the hole to remain three shots back with only five to play.

Up ahead, energetic members of the Hogan and Palmer galleries, situated one hole apart, were rushing back and forth to catch as much of the standoff as possible. At 16, Hogan and Nicklaus traded wonderful approach shots, Ben's stopping 12 feet from the pin, Jack's some 6 feet. Ben missed his birdie putt and then labored over his short par putt for many long moments before finally disposing of it. As he left the green, he pulled his white shirt away from the left side of his chest, shaking his head and smiling. The yips, he was saying. Some of his fervent supporters yelled, "Go get 'em, Ben!" Jack's birdie attempt then lipped out.

Two holes remained. Hogan, at four under par, clung to a share of the lead; Nicklaus hovered one stroke back. Meanwhile, Boros had parred the 15th hole. His round approached Hogan's in its steadiness—1 birdie, 1 bogey, 13 pars. With another par at 16, he was even with Nicklaus and Fleck at three under par for the championship, one behind Hogan and Palmer.

Arnold flirted with the creek near the 15th green when he pulled a five-iron tee shot and was fortunate to land in one of the two bunkers flanking the left side of the green. His sand play, which had been superb throughout the round, sustained him again. He blasted out to one and a half feet from the pin and holed out for his par.

Like many in the field, Palmer used a two-iron off the tee at the treacherous 16th hole and placed his ball safely in the fairway. An eight-iron approach shot landed 20 feet beyond the hole. Two putts and he had his fifth straight par to stay deadlocked with Hogan at four under par. Two more pars and he'd have his 65. Arnold's lunchtime rejoinder to writers Drum and Jenkins that a 65 would, too, win him the Open—

"Oh, yes it will. It'll put me at 280, and that's a play-off fig-ure"—was looking prophetic.

Souchak, at 15, parred his third straight hole. He was still two under par, and now his best hope was for a tie. He needed a couple of birdies and he needed the same kind of help from the leaders at the closing holes that he had given them. Fleck fought back from his three-putt bogey at 13, parring the next two holes to stay a thin stroke behind Hogan and Palmer. Fin-sterwald, needing a couple of birdies at once, was unable to break out of his own par streak. With three holes left, Dow was mired at one below par, three shots out of the lead. He was out of it.

It was just before 5:00 P.M. The leaders were down to their final few holes, and seven golfers still had a legitimate chance to win. Hogan and Palmer led Nicklaus, Boros, and Fleck by one shot and Souchak and Cherry by two. Dutch Harrison was in the clubhouse, enjoying his temporary perch as 72-hole leader. His one-under-par 283 would not hold up for long.

Hogan and Nicklaus moved on to 17, a taxing eight hours after teeing off for round three. With Ben's every weary step, supporters along the route shouted words of encouragement. For what it was worth, the count was now 34—he'd hit 34 straight greens in regulation. Nobody knew whether this had ever been done before. Of course, it was a statistic that would mean very little to the Hawk unless it contributed to earning him a fifth Open victory.

Hogan knew he was tied for the lead but, surprisingly, he didn't know with whom. Spotting a friend, he inquired; Palmer, he was told. Hogan was amazed. So engrossed was he in his own game that he wasn't aware of Arnold's charge. "*He's* not a contender, is he?" he replied.

Ben belted a wood down the long tree-lined 17th fairway and followed it with a strong, well-placed three-iron that came to rest about 50 yards short of the moat that fronted the island

211

green. Nicklaus laid up, too, and his ball sat nearby on the fairway. Each mulled over his strategy for hitting to the green.

The USGA had cut the hole some 12 feet from the front of the green, insuring that birdies would be few and extremely well earned. A narrow apron of grass fell off quickly from the green to a bank that dropped a few feet to the moat. The moat separating the green from the fairway was a shallow channel about 15 feet across.

Because the green was hard and fast, a golfer would have to land his ball softly on the front to keep it close to the pin. Even at only 50 yards, trying to do so would be extremely risky. Apart from having a tight landing area, Hogan and Nicklaus would not be able to take a full swing at such a short distance; a controlled, partial swing would be needed, and this was among the toughest to execute under pressure. Nicklaus decided it was too dangerous to shoot for birdie. His pitch landed pin-high and ran 18 to 20 feet past the hole.

Hogan, deep in thought, stood behind his ball and picked out a landing spot. He was going for the birdie. A slight breeze blew in his face—a modest aid. This was his biggest shot of the tournament. He stepped up to his ball and hit a half wedge, striking the ball crisply. Arching toward the green, the shot looked perfect, and applause began to build. Phil Strubing, the USGA referee, saw it differently and said, "Oh, no!"

The ball came down at the top of the bank with terrific backspin. It trickled down the bank and settled at the edge of the channel on the far side. The crowd groaned. Another foot or two—maybe less—and the ball would have hopped forward and crowded the pin. Hogan walked up to the green showing little emotion. He crossed the small causeway over the moat and turned around to examine his lie. The top quarter of the ball broke the water's surface.

It was a striking scene, a panorama for a pictorial history of the game. On the putting green, Jack Nicklaus looked on, as did Julius Boros and Gary Player out on the fairway, and Arnold Palmer and Paul Harney back on the tee. Spectators whispered among themselves as they watched Hogan stare at his ball. Everything stopped. And then Hogan sat down on the bank, took off his right shoe and sock, and rolled up the trouser leg of his mustard-yellow gabardine slacks. The crowd broke into applause when it realized Hogan's intent. He really didn't have much choice, though; he couldn't afford the loss of a stroke by taking a drop. He was going to splash it out and hope to get it close enough to save par.

Ben stepped down the bank and placed his bare foot into the cool water. The footing was slippery, so out he came to put on his shoe without the sock. Back down he went. This time, satisfied with his stance, he lashed into the ball, and out from a fountain of spray it hopped onto the green. Newspaper reports of the distance the ball rolled past the hole ranged from 4 to 20 feet. Whatever, all observers agreed: Hogan's par putt never had a chance. Stunned, he left the hole tied with Nicklaus, who barely missed his birdie putt.

Next came Boros, who made his own unsuccessful crack at birdie on 17. Then, facing a three-footer for par, he missed the putt and fell two strokes behind Palmer.

Hogan and Nicklaus both seemed spent. The 17th hole had taken a lot out of the kid as well as the veteran. Nicklaus acknowledged in his 1969 book, *The Greatest Game of All*, that his concentration was gone and that he assumed mistakenly that he was out of the tournament. In fact, a birdie would get him, and Hogan for that matter, back to four-under-par 280, forcing Palmer, who was then on the 17th fairway, to birdie one of the final two holes to win outright. Both golfers were shaky, but still in contention on the 18th tee.

Jack choked up on his driver, trying to fade the ball safely onto the fairway, but he pushed it and it landed in the right rough. Ben took the opposite approach. Trying to cut as much distance off the uphill second shot as possible, he navigated the shortest route to the green. Almost the entire flight of his ball would be over water—and there would be no pitching out of this hazard. He selected a landing spot that would give him the best possible approach shot.

His ball exploded off the clubface, as on all his drives, but this one he hooked slightly. It was going to be close. Just before reaching land, it dove into the pond, a foot short of the opposite bank. It was all over now. Walking up the fairway, young Nicklaus looked across at the great Hogan. All life seemed to have gone out of him.

Jack hit a four-iron into the rough to the right of the green. He now had a very difficult chip from near the scorer's tent. He played it wonderfully well, leaving himself some six feet below the pin. He didn't think it really mattered, but if he could sink this par putt it could tighten the screws on Palmer at the home hole. Nicklaus missed it. He finished at two-under-par 282, one shot better than Dutch Harrison.

Hogan's finish at 18 was painful to watch. It was reminiscent of his 1955 U.S. Open play-off against Jack Fleck, when he lost his footing on his final tee shot and then couldn't dig his ball out of the appallingly high Olympic rough. Only this time he didn't conclude on a long, long putt that carried a hint of defiance. At Cherry Hills he hit his fourth shot over the green, chipped on in five, and two-putted—once lifting his head while putting and topping the ball. Thinking 279 only moments earlier on the 17th fairway, he finished with a bogey six and a triple-bogey seven for an even-par 284.

At 18, Boros needed a birdie to get back to three under, a score that would give him a chance, albeit slim, to make a play-off. But Julius landed in a bunker and bogeyed his second straight hole. He finished at one-under 283.

Three men still chased Palmer: Souchak, Fleck, and Cherry.

Arnold did not receive confirmation of Hogan's bogey at the 17th hole until after he had hit his second shot there. "You mean I'm leading the tournament all alone?" he asked, surprised and delighted. "Well, now it's a different story." His layup had settled a few yards farther away from the green, and farther to the left, than Hogan's. He was taking no chances now, and his wedge carried some 30 feet beyond the hole. He coolly two-putted for his par to remain at four under.

One more par, just one more par—that's what he wanted at 18. He had a two-stroke cushion over Nicklaus and over Souchak, who had just parred number 16. Fleck, now playing the 16th, was his closest pursuer, just one stroke behind. Cherry, back on the 15th hole, faced a two-stroke deficit.

Palmer hit a one-iron from the 18th tee across the pond and safely onto the fairway. His second shot, a four-iron, came up short and to the left of the green. He was 80 feet from the pin and in the rough. If he took three to get down, one of his pursuers might still catch him. If he got down in two, he'd have his 280, and somebody would have to get hot to catch him. This was the moment he'd waited for all his golfing life.

Arnold hit the perfect chip shot. It ran up two and a half feet of the pin. Walking to his ball, he casually repaired a ball mark, then surveyed his line. When he bent over his ball to putt, he said later, it seemed like a 25-footer. In the long shadows of the late Denver afternoon, Arnold Palmer rolled it home. He took two quick steps forward, scooped it up out of the cup, and without breaking stride he peeled off his red sun visor and pitched it high in the air toward the gallery at the back of the green. Palmer, beaming, looked like some happy kid half his age. On NBC's videotaped broadcast, an announcer cried, "Palmer has won! Palmer has won!" But it wasn't over.

With cheers ringing in his ears, Arnold walked into the scorer's tent. "Hi, Chops," he said cheerfully to Ed "Porky" Oliver, sometimes known as "Ol' Porkchops," who was hanging out there. Arnold collapsed in a chair, threw out his arms to his sides, exhaled, and smiled broadly. After checking and rechecking his scorecard, he signed it. Yes, indeed; he'd just shot a 65 for a 280. His next stop was the press tent.

Back on 16, Fleck fell short of the birdie he wanted so badly. His putting had become a torment again, and he hadn't yet seen the worst. He blew a *one-foot* par putt. Two behind with two holes to play, Jack could do no better than a par at number 17.

Moments later, Mike Souchak arrived at the 18th green. He had parred his fifth straight hole at 17 to remain at two under par. No one expected Mike to make the miracle eagle he needed to catch Palmer, but no one wanted to see him finish the way he did, either. He was on the green in two, 45 feet from the flag. In a short while he would tell the press, "I really don't know why, but I've played harder for a dollar Nassau than I did here." Mike's 45-footer stopped 18 inches from the cup, and then he missed the putt.

Don Cherry, it seemed, could shoot nothing but pars, a peculiar problem he would have accepted willingly before the tournament. At 15 he missed a birdie putt of four feet. At 16 he faced an eight-footer for birdie and missed that one, too. He remained two under par, two shots behind Palmer.

It was almost 5:45 P.M. A portable bar had just been set up in the press tent, and for the moment, the scene was quiet. When Palmer entered, the place came alive. Arnold, still appearing to be extremely keyed up, sat on a dais and ran down his round, hole-by-hole, punctuating his monologue with drags from a cigarette and swigs of beer. His eyes returned repeatedly to a nearby scoreboard. "Who can do what?" he asked. "What can Fleck do?" Told Fleck needed an eagle at 18 to tie him, he seemed to relax a bit. A few minutes later, word arrived that Jack had bogeyed the hole. He had missed a six-footer for par, completing a collapse in his putting on the back nine.

Now only Don Cherry had any hope to catch Palmer. Out on the 17th fairway, he pulled his three-wood out of the bag. He was going for the island green in two. He topped the ball, and it ran into the moat. When he finally holed out, he had taken seven strokes. The thoughts of his fellow competitor, Sam Snead, the man with the "Open jinx," could only be surmised.

The last of the ten contenders had made his final bid. One by one, nine of them had fallen away. Palmer, with his final-round 65, had overtaken 14 players to capture the 1960 U.S. Open. His seven-shot comeback to win was the largest ever. His 65 was the best finish by an Open champion, one stroke better than Gene Sarazen's concluding score in 1932. His 280 was the second lowest winning score in Open history. Speaking with his wife, Winnie, on the phone after the press conference, Arnold skipped the details. "Hi, ya, lover. We won."

Soon it was time for the awards ceremony. Still out on the course, the final threesome of Rosburg, Johnson, and Johnston plodded on as announcements were made on a loudspeaker and tournament people started to tidy up the grounds. "They were already cleaning up all the Coke cups from the course. The goddamn Boy Scouts were out there cleaning up!" Howie Johnson would recall indignantly more than 30 years later. Afterward, Bob Rosburg complained to the USGA's Joe Dey that they weren't given a chance to play. It was the rare discouraging word sounded at Cherry Hills.

THE '60 OPEN LEFT a handful of players muttering to themselves that *they* should have won it, not Palmer.

"I *gave* him that Open," Jack Fleck said in Curt Sampson's *The Eternal Summer*. "If anyone blew it, I did."

Years later Jerry Barber bemoaned his "senseless bogey at the 12th hole" and added, "I always felt I could have easily won the tournament."

"I really thought this was going to be my big one," Dutch Harrison said after completing his round, with a chuckle. "Here I was three under and, man, all I needed was to stay there."

*   *   *

As OTHER PLAYERS CLEARED out, Mike Souchak sat motionless in the Cherry Hills locker room, his large hands cradling his head, shielding his disappointment. For the second consecutive year, he could have won the U.S. Open but tied for third place. His caddie, Babe Aranjo, passed by quietly; Mike didn't look up. Later, Palmer dropped by for a chat, and Souchak, as gracious as ever, said, "It couldn't happen to a nicer guy."

"There'll be another day, I suppose," Mike said to *Newsday*'s Bill Searby. "I don't understand the way it all finished, but I guess the good Lord does." Why the good Lord needed Souchak to blow his 18-inch putt at the very end was a mystery. The miss proved to be costly as well as extremely distressing. The par would have given him a share of second place with Jack Nicklaus and the runner-up's prize of $7,200. Instead he finished in a six-way tie for third place and won $3,950.

THE QUESTION ON EVERYONE'S lips was why had Ben Hogan risked all at the 17th hole? A par there and a par at the final hole would have given him a 280; Palmer would have had to birdie one of the two final holes—something he had not done in the first three rounds—to beat him. Hadn't Hogan's strategy always been to avoid high-risk shots, to let his opponents make the mistakes? Why not this time?

Hogan believed that Palmer would make at least par at each of the final two holes; and as brilliantly as he was putting, he stood a good chance to birdie the 17th. So, the Hawk reasoned, he needed a birdie there or at 18 to ensure himself of a tie, and at 18 he wouldn't get the close-up look at the pin that he had from the 17th fairway. The way he was putting, he knew he'd have to get the ball damn close to the pin for a birdie chance. And a birdie at 17 might put pressure on

Palmer. Besides, Ben never liked play-offs, and the thought of going head-to-head with Arnold for 18 holes the day after playing an exhausting 36 could not have been appetizing.

Afterward, though, Ben questioned his own reasoning before some golf writers in the locker room. "Maybe I should not have done it, but I wasn't more than this far from finishing with 279," he told Larry Robinson of the *New York World Telegram and Sun*, holding his hands five inches apart. "I'm just a dumb guy, I guess. I figured I needed to finish five under for 279 to win the tournament and gambled for a birdie four on the 17th. Maybe I should have played it safe."

But, then, in the same breath, he defended his decision. "You have to play it that way—short and trickle the ball toward the pin—if you are going to get the birdie there." Could Hogan have misjudged the shot and not aimed far enough over the bank to counteract his backspin? Doubtful. Hogan had practiced shots like that for 30 years. He was confident that he could execute it perfectly. And he came close to doing so. "I missed my spot by only 2 feet from about 50 yards out. I thought it was a good shot, a good shot," he insisted. Bitterly disappointed, he warned the circle of reporters, "Don't play golf. There are so many disappointments, you want to cut your throat."

Apparently, nobody inquired about his tee shot at 18, even though it was that shot, not his half wedge at 17, that had ended his bid for a fifth Open. The moat in front of the island green at the 17th—the very spot where he had lost his 1941 PGA quarterfinal match to archrival Byron Nelson—that's where Hogan's hopes died in the '60 Open, everybody would always say. As it turned out, the 1960 championship was his last serious bid for a fifth U.S. Open title.

It probably provided little solace, but it occurred to Hogan that he wasn't the only player who could have seized the crown for himself. Jack Nicklaus, who finished two shots behind the champion, had bogeyed three of the last six holes. In the locker room, Hogan said, "I played 36 holes today with a kid who, if he had a brain in his head, should have won this thing by ten strokes."

Jack Nicklaus was "sorta happy and sorta unhappy" about his performance, he told Paul Hornung of the *Columbus Dispatch*. Actually he had good reason to be thrilled. Jack's score was the lowest by an amateur in U.S. Open history, surpassing Marvin Ward's 283 in 1939. And he became the first amateur to break par since Billy Goodman in 1933.

What he was *not* happy about was how he had putted. He had failed on putting greens he called "my kind of greens. I really know how to putt these." He also blamed his failure to hold on to the lead on playing too conservatively. "I never went for broke the entire tournament," he told the press afterward. "I played very conservatively, or at least as conservatively as I could."

What did he learn playing with Hogan, he was asked. "He showed me that I'll have to learn to hit the ball better—at least put it where I want it—to win. He really hits the ball like it should be hit. I just scrape it."

Nicklaus didn't discuss with the writers what happened at the 13th green, but he would never forget it. He would never again hesitate to ask an official to clarify a rule. In later years he became such an exceptional student of the rules of golf that he rarely ever had to.

How did Arnold Palmer do it? the newsmen wanted to know. Answering their own question, they recounted dramatically how Palmer won by driving the 1st green and birdieing six holes on the front nine. This soon became scripture. In reality, Arnold's unforgettable outward nine thrust him back in the tournament; his steady but unspectacular home nine—one birdie, eight pars—won him the tournament.

Only Ted Kroll, among the top finishers, matched his 35 on the home nine. No one else even matched the par of 36. Nicklaus, Hogan, Souchak, and Fleck each brought in a 39; Boros, Barber, and Cherry, 38; and Finsterwald and Harrison, 37. And at the climactic final three holes, only Palmer among the contenders turned in rock-solid pars of 4-5-4. Nicklaus went 4-5-5; Boros, 4-6-5; Fleck, 5-5-5; and Hogan, 4-6-7.

Luck helped, too, as Palmer acknowledged. "I hadn't been getting the breaks until the last round," he said in the press tent, apparently forgetting a couple of long putts he had holed to avert disaster in the earlier rounds. "Then everything started going my way."

Others' opinions showed up in the papers the next day. "His strength, his driving," said Art Wall. "He's so long and so straight." Doug Ford turned to another Palmer asset: "His putting. He's the boldest putter I've ever seen. He's absolutely without fear."

Something inside also accounted for his triumph. He *believed* he could win no matter how unlikely the odds; he believed if he played his best it would be good enough to win. "My desire to win never left me," he said.

1960 U.S. OPEN RESULTS

1	Arnold Palmer	72-71-72-65—280	$14,400.00
2	Jack Nicklaus	71-71-69-71—282	Amateur
T-3	Julius Boros	73-69-68-73—283	$3,950.00
T-3	Dow Finsterwald	71-69-70-73—283	$3,950.00
T-3	Jack Fleck	70-70-72-71—283	$3,950.00
T-3	Dutch Harrison	74-70-70-69—283	$3,950.00
T-3	Ted Kroll	72-69-75-67—283	$3,950.00
T-3	Mike Souchak	68-67-73-75—283	$3,950.00
T-9	Jerry Barber	69-71-70-74—284	$1,950.00

T-9	Don Cherry	70-71-71-72—284	Amateur
T-9	Ben Hogan	75-67-69-73—284	$1,950.00
T-12	George Bayer	72-72-73-69—286	$1,240.00
T-12	Billy Casper	71-70-73-72—286	$1,240.00
T-12	Paul Harney	73-70-72-71—286	$1,240.00
T-15	Bob Harris	73-71-71-72—287	$840.00
T-15	Johnny Pott	75-68-69-75—287	$840.00
T-17	Dave Marr	72-73-70-73—288	$630.00
T-17	Don Whitt	75-69-72-72—288	$630.00
T-19	Jackson Bradley	73-73-69-74—289	$472.50
T-19	Bob Goalby	73-70-72-74—289	$472.50
T-19	Gary Player	70-72-71-76—289	$472.50
T-19	Sam Snead	72-69-73-75—289	$472.50
T-23	Al Feminelli	75-71-71-73—290	$390.00
T-23	Lloyd Mangrum	72-73-71-74—290	$390.00
T-23	Bob Rosburg	72-75-71-72—290	$390.00
T-23	Ken Venturi	71-73-74-72—290	$390.00
T-27	Claude Harmon	73-73-75-70—291	$367.50
T-27	Lionel Hebert	73-72-71-75—291	$367.50
T-27	Bob Shave, Jr.	72-71-71-77—291	$367.50
T-27	Dick Stranahan	70-73-73-75—291	$367.50
T-31	Chick Harbert	72-74-69-77—292	$360.00
T-31	Harold Kneece	76-71-71-74—292	$360.00
T-33	Rex Baxter	79-67-76-71—293	$330.00
T-33	Frank Boynton	73-72-75-73—293	$330.00
T-33	Dave Douglas	75-71-76-71—293	$330.00
T-33	Doug Ford	73-72-70-78—293	$330.00
T-33	Huston LaClair, Jr.	70-74-76-73—293	$330.00
T-38	Bruce Crampton	70-71-75-78—294	$300.00
T-38	Stan Dudas	71-74-73-76—294	$300.00
T-38	Al Mengert	75-71-74-74—294	$300.00
T-38	Dave Ragan	71-72-78-73—294	$300.00
42	Bill Johnston	73-74-73-75—295	$300.00
T-43	Cary Middlecoff	77-70-72-77—296	$270.00
T-43	Henry Ransom	69-76-73-78—296	$270.00

T-43	Art Wall	72-73-78-73—296	$270.00
T-46	Doug Sanders	70-68-77-82—297	$260.00
T-46	Charles Sifford	74-70-77-76—297	$260.00
T-46	Jim Turnesa	76-71-72-78—297	$260.00
T-49	Walter Burkemo	74-72-72-80—298	$240.00
T-49	Howie Johnson	72-75-74-77—298	$240.00
T-49	Sam Penecale	73-73-77-75—298	$240.00
T-49	Frank Stranahan	72-73-74-79—298	$240.00
53	Bob Verwey	75-72-79-75—301	$240.00
54	Bob Watson	72-73-73-84—302	$240.00
55	Bob Goetz	73-74-74-85—306	$240.00

CHAPTER 10

THE NEXT DAY, THE PHOTO OF THE EXULTANT ARNOLD PALMER SLINGING his visor into the air dominated sports pages across the country. As Americans read in their Sunday newspapers accounts of his sensational U.S. Open victory, Palmer boarded a plane en route to Ireland. The conqueror of American golf was headed for his first international competition, the Canada Cup, to be followed by the British Open.

Bob Drum, the Pittsburgh newspaperman who had inadvertently contributed to Arnold's ferocious charge the day before, was on board for the first leg of the trip to New York. Palmer had something on his mind and motioned to him, Drum recalled.

"What if I win the Open at St. Andrews and then I win the PGA?" Palmer asked.

"That would be a wonderful accomplishment," said Drum.

"No. That would be the Grand Slam. Bobby Jones did it in winning both Amateurs and both Opens. I plan to copy that feat as a professional with the four major titles." And so the modern Grand Slam became his immediate goal.

The Irish were thrilled to be hosting for the first time the eighth annual Canada Cup (later named the World Cup), a prestigious international tournament, and they were justifiably proud of the site, Portmarnock Golf Club, Ireland's St. Andrews. Hugged by Dublin Bay, Portmarnock typified the rugged, windswept links courses that seem the antithesis to America's manicured, tree-lined layouts.

Two-man professional teams from 30 countries would play 72 holes for the cup. Those teams not from the traditional golf-playing nations—England, Scotland, Wales, Ireland, Australia, South Africa, Canada, and the United States—did not have the slightest hope of winning. Like the Americans in a World Cup soccer tournament, they were happy merely to be competing. Irish bookmakers made the American team of Palmer and Sam Snead a 2–1 favorite. A week earlier, they had pegged Palmer, at 5–2, a slight favorite over four-time British Open champion Peter Thomson in the event's individual competition. By the time the new U.S. Open champion arrived in Ireland, however, some bookies were refusing to take bets on him at any odds.

Palmer had been an unpopular selection earlier in the spring, when he, rather than an established star, was chosen. In previous years veterans Cary Middlecoff, Jimmy Demaret, and Ben Hogan had teamed with Snead. Now, of course, the Irish and the Americans alike could not have been happier. At the Dublin airport, Palmer was mobbed by writers and fans. Despite only four hours of sleep in the last 48, he was in high spirits, and he expressed confidence that he could acclimate his game to tough Portmarnock and to the slightly smaller British golf ball (one-sixteenth of an inch smaller than the American).

The next day, after shooting a four-under-par 68 in practice, he raved about the small ball. "I can't drive it off line, and in putting, it makes the hole look big as a washtub," he said. On the final practice day, Wednesday, Palmer and Snead played together and left little doubt they were ready. Palmer shot a 66; Snead, a 65.

Sam's thoughts, though, weren't with the Canada Cup in Ireland; they were still with the U.S. Open in Denver. "I thought I had it going for me for a while on that last day," he said sadly, gazing out on Dublin Bay. "But then up jumped the devil"—the demon being the 9th hole of the last round, where he took a triple-bogey seven. "Sure, it took the heart out of me." Reminded that before the Open he had called Cherry Hills his "last big chance," he said, "It was just talk. I figured I might do it this time. I felt real good and I was playing right well." Snead faulted his lackadaisical preparation for the Open and vowed to mend his ways. "I figure I've got two more good chances," he said. In two years he'd be 50.

As predicted, the Americans won the team championship, overcoming two particularly strong duos: the defending champion Aussies, Peter Thomson and Kel Nagle, and the fascinating South African pairing of Gary Player and Bobby Locke, another four-time winner of the British Open. Although Palmer had ruined his chances for individual honors with uncharacteristically atrocious putting during a third-round 75, he dominated everyone's attention throughout the tournament. He was in no way a stylist like Snead, the Irish observed, but he had spirit and he never quit.

After three rounds it was Snead who looked to be the sure individual champion, but he frittered away a three-stroke lead, skied to a 75, and finished second to a 48-year-old Belgian known as much for his refined breeding as his fine golf, Flory Van Donck. Palmer, by rescuing the team with a closing 69, finished tied for third. He had performed well in his brief apprenticeship in British-style links golf, and he left Ireland as the man to beat in the British Open. Snead passed up St. Andrews to return to the States for the more lucrative Buick Open in Flint, Michigan.

Deciding to play the British Open was an act of imagination by Palmer. And announcing his goal to win all four major golf tournaments in 1960, more than hubris, also was an act of imagination. At a time when his peers disdained the British Open, he saw it as the entrance into golf history.

Earlier in the century, if you wished to prove yourself against the best shotmakers in the world, you made the voyage across the Atlantic, as Walter Hagen and Bobby Jones and Gene Sarazen did. But when Sam Snead played and won at St. Andrews in 1946 he chose not to return to defend his title. And Ben Hogan traveled to Britain for the Open only once, in 1953, following his Masters and U.S. Open triumphs.

The Open Championship had not drawn America's top golfers for years, and as a result the world's oldest golf championship had lost considerable prestige. The field that Gary Player led to win in 1959 was decidedly inferior. Besides, the championship offered a paltry purse compared with even a minor tournament in the States. The winner's share in 1960 was the equivalent of about $2,000, and only the top 11 finishers received prize money. And since few American golfers appreciated the remarkable British golf courses, and many loathed the British weather, they stayed home. That 1960 marked the championship's 100th anniversary, and that it was being played on the historic Old Course in St. Andrews, Scotland, didn't matter.

In 1960 the only top American player to join Palmer was Frank Stranahan. Sarazen made his 14th visit to the championship, and the 58-year-old delighted the large galleries by shooting 69 and 72 in the 36-hole qualifying stage; he withdrew, exhausted, from the championship after the first round.

Even though a full week remained before the championship's two qualifying rounds, Palmer headed directly from Portmarnock to St. Andrews. He knew he would need every minute available to prepare. For more than 400 years local golfers had spent a lifetime getting to know the Old Course, a bleak, treeless landscape with hard, undulating greens and

227

fickle North Sea winds. When Bobby Jones first set eyes on it he said it looked like a cow pasture. Later, he came to love it like no other place on earth.

Palmer's arrival in St. Andrews stirred up enormous excitement. Tales of his childhood prowess on his father's golf course and of his recent feats preceded him so that when he went out to practice, all eyes were on him. One stern Scot, responding to a Palmer enthusiast's prediction that the American would run off a string of threes on the front nine, was overheard to say, "He'll need them goin' oot; he'll no get them comin' back!"

Palmer, though never much of a student, practiced methodically. Aided by one of St. Andrews's extremely knowledgeable caddies, Willie Anderson, he drilled himself in aspects of the game players rarely exercised in America, such as landing approach shots well short of the green so they wouldn't bound right off the putting surface. At night, back in his hotel room, he buried himself in topographical maps of the course, memorizing the location of its hidden, deep-walled bunkers, mounds, and hollows.

All this preparation was evident in his play from tee to green during the championship's first two rounds, but not on the putting greens. Palmer simply couldn't read the breaks—not yet, at least. With rounds of 70-71, he stood in third place, but he was seven strokes behind Argentinian Roberto De Vicenzo (67-67), a perennial challenger for the title, and five behind Australian Kel Nagle (69-67), the 1959 Australian Open champion.

On Friday morning, in the first of two rounds to be played that day, Palmer sank four lengthy putts and seemed about to catch the leaders, only to three-putt the last two holes for a 70. Nagle, who played those same holes birdie-par, lost only one stroke of his advantage over Palmer, and with his 71 he overtook De Vicenzo, who crashed up against reality with a 75. Moments after the two leaders finished their round, a tremendous downpour pounded St. Andrews, flooding sections of the course and forcing officials to postpone the final 18 holes until the next day.

In the final round, visions of Cherry Hills descended on the Old Course. Brilliant approach shots on holes 1 and 2 left Palmer with only tap-ins for birdies. There, however, the charge stalled. Nagle, playing behind him with De Vicenzo, birdied 6 and 7, matching Palmer's front-nine 34. When Palmer birdied the 13th and Nagle bogeyed the 15th, the American had closed to within two strokes of the leader. By now, De Vicenzo had fallen out of contention. The centenary Open was a two-man match.

On 17, the famous Road Hole, Palmer scrambled from the tangled rough behind the green for a memorable par four, and then at 18 he ignited a roar of approval with a birdie three. Now Nagle needed pars on the final two holes to win by a stroke. Only moments after the spectators erupted around the 18th green for Palmer, the 39-year-old Australian stood over the key shot of the tournament, a six-foot par putt at 17, and holed it. Closing with a par four, he won the Open Championship. It was the greatest win of Nagle's career. De Vicenzo held on to tie for third, his fifth top-three finish in the British Open. His day would come.

Palmer's dream of winning the Grand Slam was over. But he had played remarkably well—his 279 tied the previous record at the Old Course—and he had won the admiration and affection of the British, as he had the Irish. "I see a wee bit of Hogan in the laddie," one Scot observed. "Aye, but he is a warm boy," his companion replied. Palmer had shown the world that he had the golf game to match his reputation for boldness.

Indeed, the next year Palmer returned and won the Open Championship at Royal Birkdale, England. There, he made one of the legendary shots of his career. Leading on the 15th hole in the last round, he put his tee shot in deep grass at the foot of a little bush 140 yards from the green. Clearly, all he could hope to do, playing into the wind, was advance the ball onto the fairway with a wedge. But he decided to go for the green. Lashing at the ball with his six-iron, he tore through the grass and uprooted the bush like a divot, reached the green, and held on for his first Open title. A plaque that was laid to commemorate the shot still lies where the bush once stood.

In 1962 Palmer defended his British Open crown successfully at Troon, Scotland; this time Nagle finished second. By 1966, when Jack Nicklaus won his first British Open, almost all the top Americans were entering the championship, even though the prize money was still nominal. The greatest symbol of the game's origins, the Open Championship, was well on the way to its former prestige. In the following years, the tournament direction of Keith MacKenzie and coverage by American television brought the championship to a position of importance equal to that of the U.S. Open.

WHILE PALMER WAS FLYING to Portmarnock for the Canada Cup, Jack Nicklaus was driving to Colorado Springs for the NCAA golf championship. During the Open, over dinner, he and Deane Beman had asked transportation committee chairman Bill Kindel whether they could drive the courtesy car assigned to them down to the NCAA championship. Word came back to Kindel from the Oldsmobile people: oh, no.

Somehow, at the championship, Jack shot the second best score, a 70, in the first of two medal qualifying rounds, but afterward he appeared spent. "I hope I can get myself mentally ready for this one before the match play begins," he said. "Right now I feel both physically and mentally pooped."

Although Nicklaus was returning to the golf course on which he had won the 1959 U.S. Amateur championship, the Broadmoor, he lasted only into the third round of the match-play tournament. "I've had too much golf the past two weeks," he said after his 4 and 3 loss. His pal, Beman, made it to the semifinals before losing on the 38th hole to the defending champion and eventual winner, Dick Crawford, of Houston.

Nicklaus had little time or inclination to dwell on his recent golfing exploits. For one thing, he genuinely seemed to be not at all impressed with his effort at Cherry Hills. "People ask me if I got a thrill out of finishing second in the Open this year. It wasn't a thrill. I didn't win. Nobody ever remembers who finished second at anything." Besides, the college junior had other things on his mind: in a month he was getting married.

On the morning of his July 23 wedding to Barbara Bash, his girlfriend at Ohio State, he played golf with his three ushers. At the 18th tee he announced dramatically, "Gentlemen, this is my last tee shot as a single man. Step back. I'm really going to crush it." Swinging fiercely, he barely nipped the top of the ball and watched as it dribbled into a creek 20 yards away. His marriage to Barbara, still thriving after 35 years, turned out much better.

By the time of the U.S. Amateur in September, the couple had moved into a new Cape Cod–style house in a Columbus suburb. Mindful that he could no longer expect his father's long-standing generosity to continue, he planned to complete his studies and enter the insurance business.

In the Amateur, played at the St. Louis Country Club, Nicklaus coasted through the first three rounds of the championship. When he dispatched future pro Phil Rodgers 6 and 5 in his third match, it looked as though there would be no stopping him. Charles Francis Lewis III a little known 19-year-old with an awkward, loopy swing, wasn't intimidated, however, and Nicklaus was forced, 5 and 3, to make another premature exit.

Again, Beman outlasted his friend, the tournament favorite. And this time, with unshakable, sound shotmaking and exceptional putting, he advanced all the way to the 36-hole finals. There, he clinched the title on the 32nd hole against Bob Gardner. In the award ceremony, the champion demonstrated some of the poise he would later need as PGA tour commissioner. "I feel very much like that old flag flying from the pole over there—limp, tired, tattered, but proud and flying high," he said.

Two weeks later, a dream team of Nicklaus, Beman, Gardner, and Bill Hyndman III overwhelmed four-man teams from 31 nations in the World Team Amateur Championship. Although the collective play of the Americans was remarkable—the team won the 72-hole tournament by 42 strokes over the second-place Australians—it received minimal comment because the level of Nicklaus's game was nothing less than amazing.

The tournament was played on the famous Merion Golf Club almost 30 years to the day after Bobby Jones completed his Grand Slam there in the U.S. Amateur. Jones also had won his first amateur championship there in 1924, so it was fitting that he was the guest speaker at a dinner honoring the golfers.

Merion, though not exceptionally long, was one of the country's toughest tests of golf. There, at the 1950 U.S. Open—scene of Hogan's unforgettable comeback victory following his crippling car accident—regulation play ended in a three-way tie for the lead at seven-over-par 287. Nicklaus, a decade later in 1960, shot a 269, 18 fewer strokes, mind-boggling even allowing for generally easier playing conditions than a U.S. Open course setup. Beman, with the second best individual score, finished 13 strokes back.

With his prodigious effort, Nicklaus was proclaimed the new Bobby Jones, a comparison that failed to daunt the young man. Intending to remain an amateur, his biggest wish was to duplicate Jones's Grand Slam, with a Masters title thrown in for good measure. "I'll never turn pro," he said. "It'd take the fun out of golf." But in 1961, after winning the NCAA individual championship and his second U.S. Amateur title, he turned pro.

NO TOURNAMENT WAS SCHEDULED the week after the U.S. Open, so Souchak went home to his family in Durham, North Carolina. A few days later, a subdued golfer told *Greensboro Daily News* columnist Irwin Smallwood, "I couldn't come up with the right shot at the right time that last day. I have just reconciled myself to the idea that destiny must have had a lot to do with it."

The PGA tour doesn't stop for anyone. The next tournament is never far off, and there other players will have their hearts broken. If you're a legend like Hogan, you carry your misery back home with you, replay your fatal errors over and over, and question whether there'll ever be another chance in a major championship. If you're a regular on the tournament circuit like Souchak, about all you can do is lug your misery to the next tour stop.

Mike entered the next tournament, the Buick Open, and he won it. Years later he recalled vividly the climactic last hole. Tied for the lead, he left a 50-foot approach putt six or seven feet short. Then, with the tournament on the line, he holed the putt for a one-stroke victory. "It took a lot of the disappointment out of Cherry Hills," he said.

THE 1960 BRITISH OPEN was not the end of the season for Palmer. Soon after returning home from St. Andrews his preparations began for the PGA Championship, the last of the year's four major golf tournaments. No player had ever won the Masters, U.S. Open, and PGA in the same year, so Palmer had enormous incentive to play his best, and the press still had a big story. A sizable part of the story turned out to be the golf course, the rugged 7,165-yard Firestone Country Club in Akron, Ohio. Recently redesigned by golf course architect Robert Trent Jones, Firestone was the toughest course the pros would play all year.

Palmer led the field with an opening-round 67, but in the second round he had to scramble for a 74 on the par-70 course. Then, in the third round, he became the victim of his own aggressive style. After putting his tee shot into a fairway bunker on the 625-yard 16th hole, he chose to use a wood from the sand and pushed his second shot behind a row of trees shaping the right side of the fairway. From there matters took a turn for the worse—he took a triple-bogey eight and closed out his round with two bogeys. His attempted heroics had backfired. This time, at six strokes back, he had dug himself too deep a hole; with a final-round 70 he had to settle for a seventh-place tie.

Meanwhile, a few Old Guard players attracted attention, not all for the same reason. Ben Hogan shocked many; he failed to make a single birdie over 54 holes and missed the cut for the final round. Equally stunning, 45-year-old Jim Ferrier, the 1947 PGA champion from Australia, delighted fans with the low round of the tournament, a 66, and a second-place finish. And ageless Sam Snead, seeking his fourth PGA title, actually led by one stroke after 70 holes, only to go bogey-bogey and finish tied for third with Doug Sanders. Ultimately, Jay Hebert, 37, won the title. A handsome war hero with a picture-perfect swing and a five-year tour record burdened by 16 second-place finishes, Hebert was an enormously popular champion.

TWO WEEKS LATER, PALMER was back to his old tricks. Entering the last round of the Insurance City Open five strokes behind the leader, Jack Fleck, Palmer shot a 66, tied Fleck and Bill Collins for the lead after 72 holes, and won on the 3rd hole of a sudden-death play-off. It was his seventh victory of the year, and his $3,500 winner's check brought him within $5,000 of the single-season prize-money record of $73,000 set by Ted Kroll in 1956. Third-place ties at subsequent tournaments in Milwaukee and Portland moved Palmer to within $1,000 of the record.

In mid-November, Palmer received the Player of the Year award at the PGA Annual Meeting in Phoenix. In a polling of the nation's PGA members, golf writers, and broadcasters, he won by the widest margin in the award's 13-year history. Then, late in the month, after having taken off much of the previous two months from the game, he charged to victory again at the Mobile Open. Tied with Johnny Pott after 70 holes, he chipped in from 30 feet for a birdie on the 71st and holed a 20-foot putt for a birdie on the 72nd to win by two strokes. It was his eighth, and final, win of the year, the most since Sam Snead had won nine times in 1950. When the long 1960 golf season finally ended two weeks later, Palmer had set a new prize-winning record of $75,262.85.

As Palmer's domination on the tour marked the changing of the guard in golf, America also prepared for a new generation to take power in the White House. In a month, John F. Kennedy, vigorous, charismatic, and 43, would replace the grandfatherly leader of the Allied forces in Europe during World War II.

The sporting year 1960 had ascended one peak after another, *Sports Illustrated* noted in its January 9, 1961, Athlete of the Year issue. It had featured the Squaw Valley winter Olympic games and the Rome summer games, Floyd Patterson's world heavyweight title win over Ingemar Johansson, and the memorable seven-game Pirates-Yankees World Series, captured by Bill Mazeroski and his Pittsburgh teammates. But it was Arnold Palmer whom the magazine's editors named Sportsman of the Year "for dominating the game of golf with a bold determination while adding to its splendor with genuine graciousness and charm."

Epilogue

So the Young Lions had finally displaced the Old Guard and Forgotten Middles—with the notable exception of Julius Boros, whose career enjoyed a delightful Indian summer that lasted late into the 1960s. In 1963, when the U.S. Open returned to The Country Club in Brookline, Massachusetts, 50 years after Francis Ouimet's momentous U.S. Open victory over Britons Harry Vardon and Ted Ray, 43-year-old Boros defeated Arnold Palmer and Jackie Cupit in an 18-hole playoff. Then, at age 48, Boros captured another major title, the 1968 PGA Championship, overcoming Palmer again. He won eight other tournaments between 1963 and 1968.

In the decade following Palmer's victory at Cherry Hills, the average purse on the tour climbed dramatically, from $29,000 in 1960 to $143,000 in 1969. The winner of a tournament in 1960 received on average $5,000; in 1969, $30,000. The tenth leading money winner in 1960, Doug Sanders, earned $26,470; Billy Casper, tenth in prize winnings in 1969, won $104,689. The sixties marked the first time the pro tour provided a good living for more than just the handful of top players. As a result, an increasing number of "investors" entered on the scene, providing financial backing for up-and-coming pros in return for a share of future earnings. Such largesse left some war-era golfers cold about their successors' accomplishments. "Try playing for money when you haven't got any," Lloyd Mangrum once remarked.

In 1965 the tour instituted a qualifying school because an unwieldy number of golfers was trying to qualify at tournaments each week. Deane Beman, the great amateur player, abandoned his modestly successful pro career in 1974 to become PGA tour commissioner, and directed the tour through two decades of remarkable growth before resigning in 1994. In 1983 he guaranteed that playing the tour would be a profitable occupation for more touring pros than ever before when he instituted the "all-exempt tour." Since then any golfer in the top 120 money winners was exempted the following season from having to qualify for any tournament sponsored by the PGA tour.

Playing for huge stakes and flying from tournament to tournament, the golfers became more distant from one another. Away from the course, they turned increasingly to big-name golf instructors and sports psychologists rather than to one another. How far away was the tour of 1958! That year, at the Houston Open, when Paul Harney was striken with appendicitis the tournament committee took up a collection for him among the spectators.

In the eighties, golf commentators blamed the all-exempt tour for undermining the competitiveness of American golfers against the nascent Europeans. With U.S. colleges serving as a minor league of sorts, an unprecedented number of superb golfers with textbook golf swings were playing on the tour, but few had the idiosyncratic and scrappy styles of those who preceded them. Compared to the likes of Snead and Palmer, Bolt and Sanders, they appeared homogeneous and bland.

Europe, on the other hand, produced throwbacks to the earlier American tour, gutsy working-class players like Spain's Seve Ballesteros, Wales's Ian Woosnam, and Germany's Bern-

JULIAN I. GRAUBART

hard Langer, all of whose modest beginnings provided extra incentive to succeed. With such stars, Europe had become at least the equal of the United States in the biennial Ryder Cup matches. And the British Open had regained its standing as golf's preeminent championship.

Following the 1964 U.S. Open, the USGA dropped the 36-hole final day. That year Ken Venturi finally won the major championship that he had had coming to him for a long time—and he did it the hard way, surviving the cut in both 36-hole qualifying stages. But on Open Saturday, the Washington, D.C., heat was brutal, and Venturi was so dehydrated after his morning round that he needed a doctor's attention to continue. For much of the final round his physical condition remained frighteningly tenuous, making his ultimate victory all the more inspiring. When his final putt rolled into the 72nd hole, his putter dropped from his hands and tears streamed down his face. Overcoming his exhaustion he raised his leaden arms and murmured, "My God, I've won the Open!"

Although the Open moved to the standard four-day format, it retained its reputation as a grueling test of golf. The USGA's uncompromising course setup continued to penalize severely imperfect driving and nervous putting. And it continued to offer thousands of nontour golfers for whom the ultimate thrill would be to qualify for the national championship the opportunity to give it their best shot. Amateurs, however, faded largely out of the picture at the Open, as fewer and fewer great golfers could withstand the allure of the professional tour.

THE GREATEST AMATEUR OF them all, Bobby Jones, died December 18, 1971, at the age of 69. Golfers on the Old Course in St. Andrews, Scotland, halted their play as the club lowered its flag to half staff. Jones had suffered severe pain from syringomyelia, an incurable degenerative disease that attacks the spi-

238

nal column, over the final 23 years of his life (the rare chronic disease takes most of its victims in about half that time). Even as he was made an invalid and wasted away to 90 pounds, he never lost his keen intelligence, his self-deprecating humor, or his deep involvement in life.

No figure connected to the game had ever inspired such adoration and respect and loyalty as Jones. He was the idol of both Palmer and Nicklaus when they were youngsters dreaming of golfing glory—and of countless less famous lovers of the game. When he knew his time had finally come, a few days before his death he told his family, "If this is all there is to it, it sure is peaceful." Almost exactly two years later, his son, Robert Tyre Jones III died of a heart attack at age 46. He never did qualify for the U.S. Open.

AMERICANS IN THE SIXTIES flocked to the game, inspired by Palmer's enormous charisma and the great Palmer-Nicklaus rivalry, both of which were increasingly on display over television. In 1960 4.4 million golfers played on the country's 6,385 courses; in 1969 the numbers had grown to 10 million golfers and 10,000 courses. Since then the game's popularity has grown unabated in the United States; in the mid-nineties 25 million Americans played on 15,000 mostly crowded courses.

Golf mania spread throughout the world, particularly in Japan, where millions played despite green fees that routinely exceeded $100. In 1984 the first golf course in China, Chung-Shan Golf Club, was designed—fittingly by Arnold Palmer's golf-course-design company.

Palmer's stardom and the game's rejuvenation thrilled not only golf fans but those who had been covering the game for the country's newspapers. "It was beautiful for golf writers because we had something to write about," said Ralph Moore of the *Denver Post*. Readers couldn't get enough of the game, and sports sections began to run golf-instruction pieces and to expand PGA tour coverage. Driven by such demand, more and more newspaper sports departments created a golf beat, and national golf-magazine circulations swelled.

Golf became big business in the nineties, and not just for the professional golfers. Weekend duffers who couldn't break 100 could recite like an equipment manufacturer's representative the specifications of golf clubs they had spent thousands of dollars to obtain. Many joined exclusive golf clubs that cost many thousands more. And some enjoyed expensive golfing vacations at resorts and famous courses in the United States and around the world. Americans in 1994, for example, spent $16 billion on golf fees and merchandise.

The experience of playing golf also changed—for the worse, many felt. Most golf courses became very crowded, particularly on weekends. Securing a tee time, waiting to get out on the course, and then waiting between every shot for the group in front to move out of range made taking up the game anything but a relaxing hobby.

At many courses players were required to rent a golf cart, a money-making accessory that course operators had players believe was intended to help speed up the snail pace of play. Not only did golf carts fail to expedite play, but they also removed a basic, pleasurable element of the game—walking. They also threatened with extinction the caddie, the traditional passport into the game for disadvantaged youngsters.

Movements were afoot in the United States to preserve players' option to walk and to rebuild the caddie ranks, but thousands of golfers new to the game had always ridden around the course and saw no reason to give up the privilege. Further, although the game in America was never as elegant as it was popularly portrayed, the standard of behavior nonetheless had been uniformly high. The combination of crowds and untutored beginners had at times compromised these standards.

Meanwhile, long-standing discrimination by private golf

clubs against blacks, Jews, and women came out of the closet. After protest erupted over holding the 1990 PGA Championship at the all-white Shoal Creek Golf Club in Birmingham, Alabama, many clubs reconsidered their membership criteria. Some sought minority members (or *a* minority member) because they otherwise would have been dropped as a national tournament sponsor; others, because they decided it was the right thing to do.

Most elite clubs made only a token effort, if that, to encourage African Americans to join. And women remained second-class citizens at many golf clubs across the country, consigned to restricted tee times and, if they objected, harrassed by male members. In 1995 a female member of Cherry Hills filed a complaint against the club with the Colorado Civil Rights Division, maintaining that the club gave women inferior tee times and amenities; the club responded that it is a private entity protected under the First Amendment's right of association, and the government had no right to interfere.

Charlie Sifford wrote in his 1992 autobiography, *Just Let Me Play*, "Underlying all of golf's generosity and good manners and traditions is an ugliness and an elitism that is hard to shake." Bill Spiller, the black golfer who took on the PGA's racial restrictions, experienced that ugliness firsthand. Giving golf lessons for three years at a driving range in Long Beach constituted the stunted peak of his golf career. A few years before his death he said, "I stuck my neck out and it destroyed my career." He had been told he could get a PGA membership if he worked five years in a pro shop. "But who was going to give me a job?" he asked. "I was the one who spoke up." He never did get into the PGA, but because of Bill Spiller more than any other man, in November 1961 the PGA finally struck the Caucasians-only clause from its constitution. Legally, nothing prevented African Americans any longer from pursuing their player's card, but, sadly, 30 years later, very few black golfers were seen on the tour.

Sifford, the other black man in the '60 Open, finally obtained his "approved PGA player's card" in 1960, but as in the fifties, he encountered crude displays of racism almost routinely on the tour. In 1961 he became the first black golfer to play a tour event in the South, the Greensboro Open. Racists taunted him on the course and threatened him by phone. Somehow, he finished in fourth place.

In 1967 Sifford won his first official tournament, the Hartford Open. He was almost 45. When he accepted the winner's trophy and $20,000 check, the gruff man wept. Slowly collecting himself, he murmured, "If you try hard enough anything can happen. Thank you."

A joyous party in his honor followed his only other victory on tour, the 1969 Los Angeles Open. Several of the black pros were present—Lee Elder, Pete Brown, and his nephew Curtis Sifford. Bill Spiller, who had followed the tournament on television at their old haunt, the Western Avenue golf course, joined the revelers.

After 1974, Sifford's final year on the tour, nobody would give him a club job, which retiring tour members usually have no problem finding. No doubt his well-deserved reputation for gruffness didn't help. Finally, he became the pro at a public course in Cleveland. Charlie and his wife, Rose, worked from 6:00 A.M. to after sunset during the golf season—not exactly restitution for past injustices. After the Senior PGA Tour got established in the 1980s he was able to leave this job behind and for the first time his life in golf was a happy one. In 1985, at age 63, he won $104,000, the most prize money of any year in his career. With the rugged, tapered build of a collegiate wrestler, he had years of golf ahead of him.

The couple moved to a pleasant suburb of Houston in 1988, and Charlie was made an honorary member of Deerwood Country Club. "That's the greatest thing that ever happened to me in my life," he told Jaime Diaz of the *New York Times*. "I'm a member of a country club. Accepted." At last, it seemed as though he could let go of his anger. "I'm not angry at anybody, but I never will understand why they didn't want the black man to play golf. Nobody ever loved this game more than me."

In 1978 A SMALL field of 22 older golfers came out of retirement for a week to play in the Legends of Golf tournament in Austin, Texas. Organized into two-man teams playing "best ball" (a format in which only the better of the team's two scores per hole is counted), Sam Snead and Gardner Dickinson won the inaugural event. The tournament, with its warm, nostalgic atmosphere, was an occasion to be savored by the players, spectators, and television viewers alike.

The 1979 Legends retained the inaugural tournament's rich flavor and added the ingredients of high drama and superb play. A sudden-death play-off between the teams of Roberto De Vicenzo–Julius Boros and Art Wall–Tommy Bolt went five memorable extra holes. The first of these was halved in par. De Vicenzo birdied each of the next three holes, but Wall or Bolt matched him. On the fifth play-off hole, the 56-year-old Argentine birdied yet again, and this time his opponents had no answer and the match was over.

Encouraged by the excitement the 1979 Legends event had produced, six of the tour's all-time leading money winners—Snead, Boros, Dickinson, Bob Goalby, Don January, and Dan Sikes—met in January 1980 and designed the blueprints for what became the Senior PGA Tour. The organizing group envisioned occasional tournaments and modest prize money for former tournament pros older than 50. But to everybody's surprise—most of all the senior golfers themselves—the Senior Tour became extraordinarily popular and soon resembled the regular tour as a major professional sports enterprise.

The players regarded the Senior Tour as the ultimate "mulligan," the second chance golfers in friendly matches allow their playing companions following a botched shot. Unlike the regular tour, it consisted mainly of 54-hole events in which there was no cut and everybody received a paycheck. The new tour was an opportunity to kibitz and compete with companions from earlier days, not to mention win some money, in a much less pressured situation than the regular tour. Onetime sourpusses like Billy Casper and Bruce Crampton found themselves relaxing, enjoying the play, and chatting with the spectators more than they ever had, all while winning sizable sums of prize money.

During the eighties, the number of tournaments and the prize money mounted rapidly, from two events offering $250,000 in 1980 to 41 tournaments worth more than $14 million in 1989; by 1994, the purses had almost doubled. In 1990 Lee Trevino joined the Senior Tour, and the 50-year-old rookie won seven tournaments and almost $1.2 million— more than even the leading money winner on the richer PGA tour. By then, the elders' circuit had lost some of its early relaxed charm. The big money had brought with it the pressures of old. But nobody was seriously complaining.

The transition from the regular tour to the senior circuit wasn't easy for everyone. Some top golfers of the fifties and sixties who had been away from tournament competition for years like Dow Finsterwald and Mike Souchak simply could not rebuild their games sufficiently to become competitive. And former champions like Bolt and Boros and Wall, who were in their late 50s or early 60s when the Senior Tour began, suffered the misfortune of bad timing. Had they been born ten years later, or had the tour started ten years earlier, they might have been the Trevinos of the day.

On the other hand, a number of lesser players on the regular tour came into their own only on the Senior Tour. "Chi Chi" Rodriguez, a modest success on the regular tour, became one of the Senior Tour's biggest winners, in addition to its most popular player. Orville Moody, who won just one tournament on the regular tour (albeit the U.S. Open), compiled 11 victories in his first nine years on the over-50 circuit. In addition, the Senior Tour provided a setting where dreams could be realized by obscure club professionals like Jim Albus and Larry Laoretti, who emerged suddenly with surprise victories.

Arnold Palmer won only ten senior tournaments, the last in 1988. But it is widely acknowledged that he, along with Sam Snead, helped "make" the Senior PGA Tour. He did this mainly by showing up regularly to play tournaments during the tour's first few struggling years. Tournament organizers claimed that the difference at the gate between a field with and without Palmer was 10,000 spectators. But he didn't play only to help the cause; he played regularly, despite a busy and profitable business empire, because his love for the game and thirst for competition never waned.

Jack Nicklaus reached the age of 50 in 1990 but he tended to limit his play on the Senior Tour to only the top tournaments. In a few early wins he was fearfully dominant, like the younger Nicklaus had been. But the man regarded as the greatest golfer of all time seemed to lack the same zest for senior golf as his old rivals Palmer and Trevino.

Sam Snead, like Palmer, was a frequent participant on the Senior Tour from the beginning, and he remained active—and remarkably gifted—right into 1986, when he was 74. Although his best days lay behind him after the 1960 season, at times, when his unpredictable putting allowed, he still could be an extremely potent force against golfers 20 years his junior. At age 50 he almost won the 1963 Masters; leading going into the final nine, he was overtaken by Nicklaus and finished third. Then in 1965, 29 years after his first victory, Sam won for the last time on the regular tour. Just shy of age 53, he became the oldest player to win a tour event, the Greensboro Open. This was a fitting last hurrah, because he had monopolized this tournament during his career with eight victories, the tour record for most wins in a single event. His 81 U.S. wins is a record unlikely ever to be challenged on the PGA tour.

Actually, we still had not seen the last of Sam on the regular tour. At the 1974 PGA Championship, the 62-year-old Snead finished in a tie for third place. Then, in 1979, he became the youngest player on the tour to shoot a score lower than his age. Playing in the Quad City Open, the 67-year-old shot a 66.

The Slammer played in the U.S. Open for the final time in 1977. The USGA had granted him an exemption to play on the 40th anniversary of his first appearance in the national championship. Shooting 74-78—152, he bowed out of the tournament that almost always tormented him. Over the years, Snead had finished second in four Opens, third once, and fifth twice.

Right into the 1990s, Snead was doing 40 golf outings a year, earning $15,000 for each appearance. To a player whose entire career winnings totaled $620,000, this was a considerable amount. But certainly a man reputed to never part with his money willingly must have wondered at times what his 81 tour victories would have paid him in today's dollars. One writer figured this out in 1992 and came up with $28 million. The all-time leading money winners wouldn't even have been close.

UNLIKE SAM SNEAD, BEN HOGAN, resisting the urging of his peers, declined to put his game on display for old times' sake on the Senior PGA Tour. Golf fans would have to satisfy themselves with his memory.

In rare instances, the reclusive Hogan was willing to reminisce. He indicated, for example, that two failed shots above all others in his career ate at him. The first was his tee shot on the last hole of his 18-hole play-off in the 1955 U.S. Open. Needing to keep the ball in the fairway for any chance to catch Jack Fleck, he lost his footing while swinging and buried his hopes in the Olympic Club's thick rough. The second was his third shot on the 71st hole of the 1960 U.S. Open.

"I find myself waking up at night thinking about that shot right today," Hogan told Ken Venturi in a 1983 television interview. "It's been 23 years ago and there isn't a month that goes by that that doesn't cut my guts out." In the early 1970s, Hogan's portrait was unveiled at USGA headquarters. Phil Strubing of the USGA mentioned to Hogan he had cried out "Oh, no!" after the shot, and he confessed he wasn't sure he'd have had the nerve to call a penalty if, on the next shot, Hogan had touched the water on his backswing. "You wouldn't have had to," Ben replied. "I'd have called it myself."

Two scenes involving the Hawk after the 1960 U.S. Open demand replay. The first is his unforgettable appearance at the 1967 Masters. In the third round the 54-year-old took apart the back nine of Augusta National. Despite a painful left shoulder that would be operated on three times in the next two years, he struck the ball impeccably, landed it close to the hole, and putted with the authority of the Hogan of the early 1950s.

At number 10: a seven-iron to five or six feet and a birdie putt; at 11: a six-iron that flew right at the flag and left him with a one-foot tap-in for birdie; at the perilous par-three 12th over Rae's Creek, a 14-foot birdie putt; at the par-five 13th, a fourth consecutive birdie after a four-wood left him a 15-foot eagle putt. After parring number 14, he reached the par-five 15th in two, again using his four-wood, and two-putted from 25 feet for birdie. Holes 16 and 17 he parred. Finally, at the tough, uphill 18th, he followed a perfectly placed drive with a five-iron that stopped 15 feet from the hole.

Trudging up the steep hill to the 18th green, the small figure in the familiar flat-billed hat was greeted as a hero returning home after a long journey. Following such an emotional welcome, could Hogan possibly collect himself and sink the putt for his sixth birdie on the back nine? He did. His record-tying 30 coming home gave him a 66, the low round for the tournament. A disappointing final-round 77 and a tenth-place finish hardly mattered. The 66 would be re-counted as long as Hogan's name was remembered. He shot it in his 25th, and final, Masters.

The second scene takes us to Hogan's last competitive tournament, the 1971 Houston Open. Following the 1967 U.S. Open, his last, he did not play in another tournament until the 1970 Houston Open. There, he had an impressive ninth-place finish. The next year he returned to the tournament, played at the Champions Golf Club co-owned by his old friends Jimmy Demaret and Jack Burke, Jr.

In the first round he knocked the ball all over the course, completing the turn in a horrid 44. On the 11th hole, his game deteriorated even further. Climbing down a ravine following another errant shot, he hurt his knee. After completing the hole, mortified and in considerable pain, he withdrew from the tournament. "Sorry, fellas," he said to his fellow competitors, Charles Coody and Dick Lotz. As he got into a cart that would carry him back to the clubhouse, he told a friend, "Don't ever get old."

So Hogan returned to Fort Worth and ran the Ben Hogan Company, the golf equipment manufacturing firm that he founded in the early fifties. Bringing his devotion to perfection to the making of clubs, he was very successful at business, too. When the company's first clubs were ready to be shipped in 1954 he decided they weren't up to his standards, discarded the $100,00 in merchandise, and started over. As he neared 50 he sold the company for a small fortune, but continued to serve as its chairman. He and his wife, Valerie, never had children—some speculated that Ben had ruled out having a family so he could devote himself to his career—but throughout more than 60 years of marriage they remained practically inseparable.

Although Ben never played in another tournament, he did play a lot more golf. The game was still his life. At age 64, he is said to have shot his age. And up until an arthritis condition intruded in his late 70s, he took enormous pleasure practicing most days at his home course, Shady Oaks Country Club. There, in a secluded area, he would experiment with his swing as he always had, and he would punch out crisp, controlled shot after shot, again as he always had.

NINETEEN SIXTY-TWO WAS ANOTHER marvelous season for Arnold Palmer. As in 1960, he won two of the four major championships, the Masters and the British Open. Again, he won eight tournaments, three of them consecutively. And again he was the tour's leading money winner. He was at the top of his game and adored by golf fans everywhere. Yet by season's end his throne was far less secure than it seemed. Jack Nicklaus, in his first full season as a professional, already had demonstrated that he had designs on it.

At the 1962 U.S. Open at Oakmont Country Club, in Palmer's native western Pennsylvania, Nicklaus had fought back from five strokes behind in the final round to tie the local hero. Jack's greatest test came on the 17th green, on which he calmly rammed home a devilish four-footer through a double break to stay even with Arnold. Bobby Jones, who watched the tournament on television, fully appreciated the putt's difficulty, and he later wrote to Jack, "When I saw the ball dive into the hole, I almost jumped right out of my chair."

Facing an 18-hole play-off against the upstart the next day, Palmer tried to mask his anxiety with humor. "I'd rather it was anybody but that big, strong, happy dude," he reportedly said. Journeyman Fred Hawkins recalls telling Arnold in the Oakmont locker room that Jack could be defeated and being told, with a laugh, "Well, then, you play him!"

In the play-off, Nicklaus refused to crack. He was so solid

that he did not three-putt any green—he did so only once in 90 holes—and ultimately he won by three strokes with a 71. The U.S. Open was his first professional victory on the tour.

All the more remarkable was that in winning the title, he had had to withstand sporadic rude, jeering comments from members of the pro-Palmer crowd. The victory was an early example of Jack's prodigious powers of concentration, judgment, and courage—attributes that remind one of Hogan. The jeers were an expression of many fans' resentment that a pudgy, expressionless prodigy was stealing glory that belonged to their swashbuckling hero. They would have to get used to Jack Nicklaus, however, because he was here to stay.

With time, Nicklaus relaxed more on the course and more of his natural warmth shone through. At the end of the decade he took off 30 pounds and doffed the porkpie hats and baggy slacks in exchange for a stylish wardrobe and more flattering hairstyle. "Fat Jack" was becoming the "Golden Bear," a nickname coined by the Australian press that grew into a term of endearment for American golf fans.

The jeers of the early sixties were succeeded first by grudging respect, then admiration. But this evolution did not come easily. It was after Tom Watson defeated him in 1977 in both the Masters and the British Open that his graciousness amid heavy disappointment stirred in golf fans a passionate support that never waned.

The Palmer-Nicklaus rivalry in the sixties, analogous to the Hogan-Snead duel in the fifties, provided the game of golf a magnificent attraction. The two men downplayed the rivalry publicly, but each acknowledged that he dearly loved to beat the other. In eight seasons, 1962 through 1969, each player's fans had plenty to crow about. Nicklaus won 29 tour events, including three Masters, two U.S. Opens, and one PGA Championship, plus one British Open; Palmer took 28 titles, including two Masters, plus one British Open. Although the sixties are thought of as Palmer's decade, Nicklaus possessed a decided edge.

This became evident in 1965 when Jack won his second Masters. He did so by hitting the ball higher and farther, with accuracy, than anyone before him. He reached Augusta's long, difficult par-five holes easily in two, and he set a new Masters scoring record of 271, three better than the mark Hogan had set in 1953. Bobby Jones marveled. At the award ceremony he observed, "Jack is playing a different game—a game I'm not even familiar with."

Defending champion Palmer, who finished tied for second with Gary Player, helped his foe on with the victor's traditional green jacket. The year before it was Palmer who had the pleasure of receiving the jacket, his fourth, from defending champion Nicklaus; in 1964 it was Jack who had tied for second place. Then, in 1966, Nicklaus became the first player to win the championship in consecutive years. He also won his first British Open.

The 1966 U.S. Open at the Olympic Club in San Francisco, without doubt, was the most bitter defeat of Arnold Palmer's career. Having lost the Open in 1962 and 1963 in 18-hole play-offs and won only one tournament on the tour in 1965, he badly wanted to prove he still had many more victories in him, including major championships. In the first three rounds he thrilled the galleries with long straight drives down Olympic's narrow tree-lined fairways. With nine holes to play, he held a seven-stroke lead over his nearest challenger, fellow competitor Billy Casper. The only question in many people's minds—Palmer's most of all—was whether he could beat Hogan's Open scoring record of 276, set in 1948.

Then, suddenly, Arnold's swing broke down, and his brilliant championship became a nightmare. Casper, a vastly underrated golfer who ultimately would win 51 tournaments in his career, took full advantage of his opportunity with superb clutch play. Five strokes behind with only four holes remaining, Billy birdied the 15th and 16th holes while Arnold bogeyed them. The lead was now one stroke. One hole later, another Palmer bogey evened the match. At the 72nd hole, Palmer put his tee shot into the rough but managed to reach the green with his next shot and match Casper's par. For the third time in five years, he would be competing for the U.S. Open title in an 18-hole play-off.

The next day Palmer appeared ready to right his wobbly game, taking a two-shot lead into the back nine. But, with a Casper birdie and a Palmer bogey at 11, suddenly the match was deadlocked. At 13, Billy administered the mortal blow, a 50-foot birdie putt. Although putts of such length obviously require luck as well as skill to fall, a putter as good as Casper couldn't be begrudged his magic on the greens. In fact, he did not three-putt one green in the tournament. Further, Billy had only used the same brand of magic that Arnold had been practicing for years. Casper, with a 69 to Palmer's 72, was a deserving champion, but the 1966 U.S. Open would always be remembered as the championship that Palmer lost, not the one that Casper won.

Many observers believe that Palmer was never the same after Olympic. "It did affect him down deep; I know it did," Casper would say almost 30 years later. Palmer denied it, categorizing the 1966 Open as a painful loss like many others in his career, but no more than that. His subsequent record of 15 more victories on the tour and several more fine performances in the major tournaments would seem to support his contention. So would his personal makeup. Not the type to over-analyze or sulk or second-guess himself, it is quite likely that he was mad as hell at himself but never psychologically wounded over his collapse.

And Palmer came back strong in the 1967 U.S. Open at Baltusrol. Paired with Nicklaus in the third round, he was just where he wanted to be—in prime position to erase memories of his collapse at Olympic. Could he redeem himself against his top rival? In the third round, Palmer and Nicklaus, playing sloppy, indifferent golf, caught themselves playing one another as though it were match play; in fact, several other players were very much in the running.

Their play reached its comical nadir when Jack knocked a putt well beyond the hole. It was as ugly a putt as Jack had ever made, and Arnold said, tongue-in-cheek, "Nice shot." The opponents broke down in laughter. "What do you say we play the course, rather than one another, for a change," Jack suggested.

In the final round, paired once again, the twosome put distance between themselves and the rest of the field, and now the championship had indeed come down to match play between the two greatest players of the time. Hole 7 marked a crossroad in the match—and maybe in golf history, too. With a slim one-stroke lead, Jack faced a 30-foot putt; Arnold had a 10-footer. Standing off to the side behind the hole, Palmer leaned on his putter and watched, frozen, as the Golden Bear ran his putt into the cup. He then proceeded to miss his far easier putt.

Just like that, Nicklaus had turned his opponent's opportunity on its head. At another time Palmer's fine closing round of 69 would have been sufficient to win the Open. But not this year. Sinking a birdie putt on the final hole, Jack shot a 65 for a 275, setting the Open scoring record that had seemed securely in Palmer's grasp at Olympic.

Never again did Palmer and Nicklaus go head-to-head in a major championship. And Arnold, whose last win in one of the game's great championships had been the 1964 Masters, never won another. He desperately wanted to win the PGA Championship, the one tournament among the four majors that had eluded him. Only Gene Sarazen, Hogan, Gary Player, and Nicklaus had won each of the four. Arnold came close— he was a runner-up in both 1968 and 1970, as he was in 1964—but as the game headed into the 1970s and he into his forties, his chances faded as the latest pride of young lions surpassed their elders.

In late November of 1969, as the golf circuit wound down to its final two tournaments, Palmer faced the prospect of not winning a single tour event in a season for the first time in his 15-year career. When he entered the inaugural Heritage Golf Classic no one could have wanted to win more than he. And win he did there at Hilton Head, South Carolina, and then, for good measure, again the following week in Memphis, Tennessee. So Arnold Palmer brought down the curtain on the decade in golf with the same wonderful flair with which he had raised it.

Jack Nicklaus's 1967 U.S. Open victory at Baltusrol was his seventh major professional championship, equaling Arnold's career total. But Jack went on to win 11 more. And where Arnold's failure ever to win the PGA Championship had blocked his completing the "Grand Slam," Jack achieved the milestone three times. Counting his two victories in the U.S. Amateur, he captured 20 major tournaments, 7 more than the next closest golfer, Bobby Jones, his boyhood hero.

The Nicklaus confidence from the mid-1960s to the late 1970s was intimidating. Leading comfortably in a four-ball match during the 1973 Ryder Cup competition, he and his partner, Tom Weiskopf, faced comparable birdie putts of about ten feet. Jack, whose ball was a bit closer, said, "Rack your cue." Tom said he didn't understand.

Jack replied, "Pick up your coin."

"Oh, you want me to move it," Tom said.

"No, I mean pick it up. I'm not going to miss this putt." He didn't.

So many triumphs at the game's greatest occasions over so many years place Nicklaus in the pantheon of the world's greatest athletes in history—boxing's Joe Louis, Olympic runner Jesse Owens, tennis's Bill Tilden, soccer's Pele, baseball's Joe DiMaggio, and basketball's Bill Russell. Such a rarified caliber of play, though, also entailed more bitter disappointment than lesser golfers ever face. Nicklaus finished in second place 19 times—in the major championships!

In defeat, Jack was often as impressive as he was in triumph. In the 1972 season, were it not for Lee Trevino's lackadaisical greenside chip that went in at the British Open, Jack could have held all four major championships simultaneously. But he never denigrated Trevino's victory.

At the 1977 British Open—quite possibly the most exciting battle of titans in golf history—he traded Tom Watson spectacular shot for spectacular shot in a head-to-head duel over the final 36 holes. He shot 66-66 to Watson's 66-65, a one-stroke loss. As they walked off the final green together, Jack draped his arm over Tom's shoulder in a generous expression of respect. Charlie Nicklaus, his father and best friend who died of cancer in 1970 at age 56, would have been proud.

Most painful of all was the 1982 U.S. Open, an experience reminiscent of Hogan's at the 1955 Open. The leader in the clubhouse, seemingly about to win the record-breaking fifth Open victory that Jack Fleck had snatched from Hogan, Nicklaus watched on television as Tom Watson turned disaster into triumph. His ball perched in thick rough just off of the 17th green at Pebble Beach, Watson delicately chipped the ball onto the green and leaped joyously as it rolled into the hole. When Tom walked off the final green, having finally won the National Open, Jack was waiting for him with a handshake, a smile, and words of congratulations.

Like Hogan's, Nicklaus's greatest moments emerged from intimations of golfing mortality. From 1962 through 1978 Jack had never gone a year without a tour victory. In fact, for those 17 seasons he had never won fewer than two tournaments or finished worse than ninth in prize money—even though, like Mike Souchak and Gene Littler before him, he refused to stay out on tour, away from his family, for more than a few weeks at a time. Indeed, his schedule was so selective that Chi Chi Rodriguez called him "a legend in his spare time." Then came 1979—a disastrous season in which he not only failed to win on tour but finished 71st on the money list.

Could he be washed up at age 39? In the winter he worked with Phil Rodgers on the weakest part of his game, chipping, determined to prove that he wasn't. The U.S. Open was returning in 1980 to Baltusrol, the 1967 Open site where he had set apart his game from Palmer's once and for all. When he broke the Open scoring record to win his fourth Open, linking him with his forebears, Jones and Hogan, the crowd chanted, "Jack is back! Jack is back!"

By 1986, though, Jack's game had grown so ragged that he called on his old tutor, Jack Grout, for a remedial course in the golf swing. His subsequent Masters victory at age 46 was perhaps the most emotional day in American golf since Bobby Jones withstood weeks of unbearable pressure to win the Grand Slam in 1930—or perhaps since Francis Ouimet conquered Vardon and Ray in 1913.

Is Jack Nicklaus the best in history? It's possible that at his best he was not quite the equal of Ben Hogan, Byron Nelson, or Bobby Jones—maybe Arnold Palmer, as well—when they were at their best. But judging his career as a whole, one can only conclude that he is the greatest golfer of them all.

TOMMY BOLT DIDN'T SEE it that way. No man—not Snead, not Palmer, not even Nicklaus—could strike a golf ball, or control the flight of a golf ball, like Hogan, he believed. And to support his opinion he remarked, "People are always wondering who's better, Hogan or Nicklaus. Well, I've seen Jack Nicklaus watch Ben practice, but I've never seen Ben watch anybody else practice. What's that tell you?"

In his 60s and 70s, Tommy received some belated recognition of his own as one of his era's most elegant shotmakers. He acknowledged that his temper tantrums had compromised his ability and fans' appreciation for his skills, but he also believed that his club-throwing antics attracted attention that helped him make a good living. Besides, he noted in the August 1994 *Golf Digest*, "I never threw a club that didn't deserve it."

"Ol' Dad," as he liked to call himself, mellowed somewhat and lived a comfortable life in Arkansas on a 600-acre ranch run by his son. He was undiminished as a colorful character whose florid style and unconventional opinions never failed to provide great copy. Ultimately, it was impossible to tease out his true feelings about his golf career and himself, except that he believed he was, above all, an entertainer; provoking a response from the audience was the thing. Asked in a 1989 *Golf* magazine interview if he would do anything differently if he had another chance, he answered, "No. It was better than being a caddie."

DOUG SANDERS BECAME MORE famous for his showy, multicolored outfits and reputation as a Lothario than for his extremely successful golf career. (Tommy Bolt, who prided himself on his attire, enjoyed lobbing one-liners at Sanders for his wardrobe, such as "The man looks like a jukebox with feet.") He burst into stardom the year after his collapse at Cherry Hills, winning five times and finishing in third place on the money list. Although he collected 20 career victories between 1956 and 1972, the tournament he is best remembered for is the big one he bungled.

Bent over a three-foot putt on the 72nd hole at St. Andrews's Old Course, he stopped to pick up a strand of grass that was distracting him. Rather than back away and set up again, he straightened up and putted at once. It was a shove of a putt that had no hope of dropping. The next day Jack Nicklaus defeated him in a closely contested 18-hole play-off to win the 1970 British Open.

Doug also finished second or tied for second in the 1959 PGA Championship, the 1961 U.S. Open (he was the leader after three rounds), and the 1966 British Open (Nicklaus won that one, too).

JULIUS BOROS, THE SON of a Hungarian laborer, continued to play the tour and earn substantial prize money into his 50s. Asked when he planned to retire, he replied, "Retire to what? I already play golf and fish for a living." At age 53, the man with the ideal game and temperament for the U.S. Open shared the 54-hole lead in the 1973 championship; he ultimately finished tied for seventh.

Boros played the Senior Tour regularly until the late 1980s, when his health declined. Toward the end of his life, when he no longer could play golf, he'd take a fishing rod and drive a golf cart around Coral Ridge Country Club, near his Fort Lauderdale, Florida, home. Away from his wife Armen, with whom he raised seven children, he'd sneak a smoke. Julius had a favorite spot—a bridge near the club's 16th hole that was shaded by a willow tree. Sitting there in his cart one day in 1994, he suffered a heart attack and died. He was 74.

DON CHERRY IS THE only man who has ever had a top-ten song on the American popular music charts and a top-ten finish in the U.S. Open. The 1960 Open was like no other for him. He competed in the next three, but each time missed the cut. In 1962 he turned pro, but he never made much money from his golf. His silky voice remained his meal ticket. Thirty years later, sounding as good as ever, he had a regular gig at the Desert Inn in Las Vegas, Nevada, and a new recording with the popular country singer Willie Nelson. The title song was "Augusta."

*   *   *

ALTHOUGH HE MISSED THE cut at the Open, onetime hockey enforcer Bill Ezinicki enjoyed his best golf season in 1960. That summer he won the state opens in Massachusetts, Rhode Island, Maine, and New Hampshire. Five more times he qualified for the U.S. Open, the last being in 1968, but he never did make the cut. Three times in the 1980s he won the New England PGA Seniors. A good life at several clubs in Massachusetts culminated in the head pro position at The International, a posh golf club and conference center outside Worcester, Massachusetts (whose yardage of 8,325 earned the course a place in the *Guinness Book of World Records* as the longest). Approaching 70, Ezinicki retired and became the club's teaching pro, a position he appeared to love.

DAVIS LOVE, JR., WHO qualified for the '60 Open and almost made the cut despite a serious finger injury, fought hard to make a go of it on the tour in the sixties, but poor driving distance and a low, weak hook pushed him into club positions. He did win several regional tournaments, however, and one year at the Masters, 1964, he shared the lead after the first round. Like his onetime mentor, "Mr. (Harvey) Penick," what fame he achieved was as an outstanding golf instructor. His prized student was his own son, Davis Love III, who was born on the last day of that 1964 Masters. Davis Love, Jr., died in a private plane crash in the fall of 1988 at age 53, but he lived to see his son become a star on the tour.

BOB VERWEY, GARY PLAYER'S brother-in-law who left his home in South Africa for the United States at age 19, played the PGA tour from 1960 until 1971. He won just one tournament in the States, the 1965 Almaden Open, but another dozen in Europe and South Africa. At age 30 he returned home and over the next 20 years raised three sons, bought a couple of driving ranges and racehorses, and entered tournaments on the Sunshine Circuit, which ran three months of the year. Far less driven than Gary, but equally lively and engaging, he thoroughly enjoyed his life away from the world's major golf tournaments. Then in 1991, at age 50, revived by a new marriage and the spread of senior professional tournaments worldwide, he picked up his clubs again full-time and won the Senior British Open. Afterward, when people would ask him, "Are you Gary Player's brother-in-law?" he would answer, "No, he's *my* brother-in-law."

VERWEY'S BROTHER-IN-LAW WON THAT same British Senior championship in 1990, but, unlike Bob, Gary had never stopped playing, and never stopped winning, all over the world. In the 40 years since he left South Africa to play professional golf in Britain, he traveled farther than any golfer ever had—an estimated 7 million miles—winning more than 150 tournaments in Australia, Europe, North America, South America, and South Africa. Nine of these victories were in the major professional championships, two more than Arnold Palmer's total.

Player rose to stardom in 1961, the year after the tumultuous 1960 Open, when he became the first non-American to win the Masters and led the PGA tour in prize money. The next year he won his third major championship, the PGA. In 1965 he became the first foreign player to win the U.S. Open in 45 years, joining Gene Sarazen and Ben Hogan as the only men to win each of the major professional golf championships. (Nicklaus would join this exclusive club the following year.) In the middle sixties, when he, Palmer, and Nicklaus were the dominant players in golf, they were called the Big Three.

Sometimes Gary tended to rub people the wrong way, coming off as overly dramatic or as a bit sanctimonious about one or the other of his passions—his faith, his physical conditioning, his faddish diets, or his golf. But he was a major sports star all over the world, and if he acted like a celebrity, he also accepted all the demands that went with it. In the late sixties, when he absorbed the wrath of civil rights demonstrators because of his homeland's apartheid policies, he held up with extraordinary grace and dignity. During the 1969 PGA Championship, despite having protesters throwing ice in his face and shouting "Miss it!" Player finished in second place. It was a courageous performance.

In the 1990s his life showed no signs of slowing down. Approaching age 60, but looking 10 years younger, he still played in tournaments regularly on the U.S. Senior PGA Tour and he still won occasionally. When not competing, he designed golf courses around the world, manufactured golf clubs, bred thoroughbred racehorses in South Africa, and enjoyed life with his wife, Vivienne, their six children, and a growing brood of grandchildren. A strikingly handsome man, strong and fit, a dab of white coloring his temples, he was a dynamo of energy, exuding self-confidence. He was justifiably called the greatest international golfer in history. The small man also was described justifiably as the golfer who got more out of his natural abilities than any other.

Player announced that his last tournament would be the British Open at St. Andrews in the year 2000. By the looks of him, that seemed a safe bet.

JERRY BARBER, RIGHT INTO his 70s the small, wise, sometimes caustic man, played the game of a master craftsman, and he cultivated aspects of his craft almost until the day he died. "I don't think I know it all, but I know enough to make it work," he said in 1991, then the oldest regular player on the Senior Tour. He also cultivated a lifetime of golf course one-liners. Praised for a well-struck shot, he replied, "Results of a misspent youth." Pretending to have lost sight of a perfectly placed drive, he asked his small gallery, "Did anybody see it . . . I mean, did *everybody* see it?"

He still used the same short, heavy blade putter he carried at the 1960 U.S. Open and at the 1961 PGA Championship. There he conducted probably the greatest demonstration of pressure putting in golf history. Trailing Don January, his fellow competitor, by four strokes with three holes to play, Jerry holed putts of 25, 40, and 52 feet to force an 18-hole play-off. The next day he won the major title he let slip away at Cherry Hills. He was a very young 45.

In his last years, he fought the Senior Tour's use of career earnings on the regular tour as a major eligibility criterion. "Now there are guys taking my spot who have never won a tournament—and never will," he told *Golf Digest* in October 1992. Jerry won seven times. Two weeks before he died unexpectedly in 1994, the 78-year-old was at his usual post—the weekly Senior Tour event. No one made much of his opening round, a 70 that was only two shots off the lead, because Jerry regularly posted scores lower than his age.

PAUL RUNYAN, ALREADY A senior golfer in 1960, seemed out to prove that one could go on forever. In 1961 and 1962 he beat renowned peers such as Jimmy Demaret and Dutch Harrison in the PGA Seniors Championship. Thirty years later, as the 1934 and 1938 PGA champion approached age 90 and could find no tournaments in which he could compete against other pros his age, he continued to play a brand of golf most players half his age only aspire to. At 87, hitting his tee shots only 200 yards, he shot a 73 at his home course, par-70 Annandale Country Club in Pasadena, California. His mind remained so sharp that his golf recollections amounted to oral history. And his passion for teaching, combined with his unparalleled experience and knowledge on the practice tee, kept him as one of the most sought after golf instructors in the United States.

SOME YEARS AFTER TELLING the young Billy Casper that he would never make it on the tour Runyan acknowledged to him how wrong he was. Casper, of course, went on to be one of the greatest winners in tour history. And yet Billy never did receive his due. Regarded as a refreshing newcomer who'd rather go fishing than practice when he won his first Open in 1959, he became hard on himself in the 1960s and irritable on the course. As a result, the media and much of the public spurned Billy for Arnie, Jack, and Gary—in spite of his profusion of victories, his three major titles, his winning the Vardon Trophy five times, and his appearances on eight consecutive Ryder Cup teams. Did this diminish his sense of accomplishment? "No. All who mattered to me knew [what I accomplished]," he answered many years later.

From 1975 to 1980, Casper's game collapsed. Then, with the arrival of the Senior Tour, the heavy-set man worked hard to rebuild his game and his confidence. During most of the 1980s, he reclaimed his rightful place as one of his age group's top players. Billy won the 1983 U.S. Senior Open and, just as notably, he lightened up, took to wearing plus fours and argyle socks, and mixed happily with the spectators. "We're having more fun now than we've ever had in our lives," he said, while out on the graybeards' tour.

MIKE SOUCHAK THREATENED AGAIN at the 1961 U.S. Open, at Oakland Hills. But after pulling within one stroke of the 54-hole leader with a 68, he trailed off to a 73 and tied for fourth place with Jack Nicklaus. In the 1959, 1960, and 1961 championships, he had taken only a combined eight shots more than the victors. He never contended for the Open again.

Souchak, having promised himself and his wife, Nancy, that he would get back home when their three children were growing up, quit the tour in 1966 and took a club job at Oakland Hills. He finished his playing career with 15 victories but he never did win a major championship. In 1972 he latched on to what he called "the best job in America"—running the golf program at the Innisbrook Resort in Palm Harbor, Florida. Ten years later he and two partners started a successful golf-cart-leasing company called Golf Cart Systems.

More than 40 years after he shot the lowest 72-hole score in PGA tour history, a 257 at the Texas Open, the record still stood; his nine-hole record of 27 was matched (by two-time Open champion Andy North), but not broken. Souchak pleaded guilty to the charge that he could have made himself into a better player but lacked the desire. Asked what he was most proud of in his playing career, he answered, "That I got away from it when I needed to and went home."

AFTER 1960 THE TEACHING reputation of Souchak's onetime boss, Claude Harmon, continued to grow inside and outside the sphere of professional golf. His students included American presidents Eisenhower, Kennedy, Nixon, and Ford. He was a mentor not only to a number of the top touring pros of the 1950s and 1960s, but to four of the top teaching pros of the 1980s and 1990s: sons Bill, Butch, Craig, and Dick. He died in 1989, at age 73, after undergoing heart surgery.

KEN VENTURI CAPPED HIS fourth season on tour, 1960, with his tenth career win (the Milwaukee Open), and he finished the year second on the money list behind Palmer. But a back injury in 1961 started a three-year professional and psychological tailspin. The fluid swing Byron Nelson had helped him refine fell apart, and his once brilliant career tumbled into a free fall until the spring preceding his stirring 1964 U.S. Open victory. By 1965 a serious circulation problem in his hands appeared, and by the time it was diagnosed correctly he had exchanged his tournament career for a long, successful tenure as the chief golf commentator on the CBS television network. In a poetic flourish, Ken claimed his last tour victory, his 14th, in 1966 at San Francisco's Harding Park, the course on which he played his first round of golf.

On the 30th anniversary of his Open triumph, he mused on a golf career cut short. "It would have been wonderful to keep my talent for 25 years instead of 10," he said in the May 1994 *Golf Digest*. "Who can say what I might have done? But I was there once. I passed there once."

BYRON NELSON, THE UNPRETENTIOUS Texas golf champion, became one of the game's beloved elder statesmen. He was introduced to many golf fans for the first time in the 1960s and 1970s when he was a golf commentator on the ABC television network. Others met him through the annual Dallas golf tournament named in his honor and through his close relationship with the great American golfer Tom Watson. On the 50th anniversary of Nelson's fantastic 1945 golf season, the 83-year-old legend recalled, and golf publications commemorated, the year he won 18 tournaments, 11 in a row.

DAVE MARR, PERHAPS THE tour's most urbane figure in the 1960s, transcended his journeyman's skills and record through the wit he brought to the game and through his gritty victory in the 1965 PGA Championship. In 1973 he began a long connection with ABC as a popular golf announcer. Later he worked in the same capacity for the BBC and NBC.

JULIAN I. GRAUBART

* * *

BOB ROSBURG ALSO TURNED from a career playing on tour to one announcing golf on American television. In 1975 he became an on-course commentator for ABC, a position he still held more than 20 years later while mixing in an occasional Senior Tour event. He won six tournaments on the regular tour, the final victory coming in 1972, 11 years after his previous win, at the age of 46. A U.S. Open title, which barely eluded his unconventional baseball-style grasp in 1959, came tantalizingly close ten years later when he again finished runner-up. Rosburg, mellower and warmer but still a forceful man in his 60s, commented on his erstwhile temper on the regular tour: "I wasn't the most congenial guy on the golf course, but I don't think I ever bothered anyone else."

GENE LITTLER, THE FIVE-TIME winner in 1959 who missed the cut at the '60 Open, won 29 tournaments on the regular tour—more than all but the dozen or so top players in tour history. But, being a family man of few words and playing in the expansive shadow of Palmer, Nicklaus, and Player, he never attracted the spotlight for long. Years later, asked for an interview for a book on the 1960 Open, the quietly dignified man replied, smiling wryly, "Why don't you do it on the '61 Open?" That one, Littler won—his only major professional championship. He lost two "majors" in play-offs: Casper topped him in the 1970 Masters (it was the tournament's last 18-hole play-off), and Lanny Wadkins got some felicitous bounces to edge him in the 1977 PGA Championship, when Gene was 47.

In April 1972 Littler underwent surgery for melanoma, but returned courageously to tournament golf that October. "Gene the Machine" won five more regular tour events before turning to a winning career on the Senior Tour in 1981. Years later, fighting a nagging back problem out on the tour, he chuckled about the nickname coined for him by the *San Diego Union*'s Jack Murphy in praise of his rhythmic swing. "It's not as a propos right now as it used to be."

BOB GOALBY WON 11 tournaments in his career, including the 1968 Masters—a bittersweet victory for which he never received full credit because Roberto De Vicenzo would have met him in a play-off were it not for his signing an incorrect scorecard. Afterward, Bobby Jones wrote Goalby "a beautiful letter at home. He said I played the finest long iron he's ever seen at 15 and that it [the scorecard incident] was unfortunate not only for De Vicenzo but for me," Goalby said. En route to winning the St. Petersburg Open in 1961, Goalby set a tour record for shooting the most birdies consecutively—eight. In 1973 he retired from competition to become a golf analyst on NBC. One of the founders of the Senior Tour—and extremely proud of that role—he left broadcasting after 13 years to round out his life in golf as a player. Reminiscing one day in 1992 about the players of his day, Goalby, a handsome, salty raconteur, said, "Hell, when I think back, I must have been a dumb son of a bitch to think I could beat those fellas."

DOUG FORD'S RECOVERY GAME was never well suited to the U.S. Open course setup, but he shared with Casper and Littler a superb playing record and an underappreciated reputation. In his 70s, when he continued to play in the Masters—the privilege of all past champions—he became the target of some golf writers who complained he was wasting a space better occupied by a player with a chance to win. But from 1952 to 1963 he won more than almost any contemporary Masters contestant could boast of—the PGA Championship and 17 other tournaments, in addition to the 1957 Masters—and he finished among the top-ten money winners ten years in a row. A down-to-earth man with a solid build, he never elevated the game to a life-or-death experience. "I've never been the Palmer-Nicklaus type, who, if you didn't win, you couldn't sleep. I was a plugger, a journeyman," he said in 1991, while still touring as a senior.

DOW FINSTERWALD PLAYED ONLY three more years full-time on the tour after 1960. In December 1963, at the age of 34, he accepted a position at the Broadmoor Golf Club, in Colorado Springs, Colorado, where he remained director of golf into the 1990s. Finsterwald was a consistent winner between 1955 and 1963, claiming 11 titles; but he was hounded by many more near-misses, including a play-off loss to Arnold Palmer in the 1962 Masters (Gary Player made that play-off, too). Years later, he blamed his tendency to finish as the runner-up—he did so in 30 tournaments—on being too conservative on the greens.

Could he have won more tournaments if he had remained on tour longer? While making an infrequent appearance on the Senior Tour in 1993, Finsterwald seemed wistful about what might have been. But the trim, sophisticated-looking man with eyes that sparkle with intelligence had no regrets about his golf career. "My father told me, if you can make a living doing something you enjoy, the chances you'll be happy are great." A close friend of Palmer's when they both were young touring pros, he remained so many years later, owning a Florida condominium in the same building as Palmer. "He's a very good friend, a true friend," Finsterwald said. "Those are the guys who are there when you need them."

ART WALL WON HIS 14th and final tournament in 1975 at the age of 51, nine years after his previous tour victory. Appearances on the Senior Tour were interrupted repeatedly by physical problems, but when he got out on the golf course he continued to demonstrate an uncanny ability to fire holes in one—at last count, 45. In 1995, a shoulder injury finally corrected through surgery, one of the game's true gentlemen returned to the tour even though he needed a five-wood where once he used a mid-iron. Two grandsons looked forward to seeing him play for the first time.

ALTHOUGH GEORGE BAYER WAS among the tour's top-60 money winners each year from 1955 to 1964, he never overcame his image as the Paul Bunyan of the links. Golf fans watched him for one reason only—to see how far the 6-foot 5-inch, 240-pound giant would drive the ball. He joined the Senior Tour at its inception, but in 1981 his right hip deteriorated so that he could barely climb in and out of a golf cart. After the 1982 season, he underwent surgery to have an artificial joint in his hip implanted, and the procedure was so successful he rejoined the tour in a few months; later it was a knee replacement. He was still playing more than ten years later.

PAUL HARNEY, PALMER'S FELLOW competitor on Open Saturday at Cherry Hills, was one of the top-60 money winners on the tour each year from 1956 to 1965. He capped his playing career with his seventh win on tour in 1972. In 1983 he finished ninth on the Senior Tour money list, had another fine season the next year, then tapered off.

TED KROLL, WHO SNUCK into a third-place tie in the '60 Open with his final-round 67, won his eighth and last tournament in 1962. Already in his 60s when the Senior Tour rolled along, he played regularly during the tour's first six seasons with modest results.

DUTCH HARRISON REFUSED TO hang up his clubs. The year after one of the game's most colorful characters finished tied for third in the '60 Open as a 50-year-old, he came in tied for 17th. Although he complained about the championship's qualifying requirements, he entered the 1967 Open and, at age 57, not only qualified but finished tied for 16th. He died in 1982.

CARY MIDDLECOFF'S BRILLIANT PLAYING career wound down abruptly in the early 1960s after a back operation. In 1961 he won his 39th and last tournament—fittingly, the Memphis Open, played in his hometown. The 1960 Open was the final time he made the cut. Later he served as a golf commentator on NBC. Asked in the November 1996 *Golf Digest* if he worried that people don't remember his superb record, the 75-year-old former dentist said, "No. I played a lot. I won a lot. I am very pleased."

LIKE OTHERS WHO HAVE won the U.S. Open and little else, 1954 champion Ed Furgol perhaps was accorded less respect than if he had never won the Open at all. But the man with the withered, crooked left arm won five other tournaments in his career, finished in the top ten of 123 tournaments, made the top-ten money list for 1947 and 1956, and played on the 1957 Ryder Cup team. In 1993, when the U.S. Open returned to Baltusrol, the place of his greatest triumph, he attracted some widely scattered attention. Then a 76-year-old teaching pro living in Florida with Helen, his wife of 48 years, he defended his career with characteristic modesty. He told *New York Times* reporter Jaime Diaz, "What I did with what I had to work with, I think I did pretty good. I worked very, very hard, and I was blessed."

JACK FLECK HAD HIS best year as a pro in 1960 with six top-five performances, including his third-place tie in the Open. The next year he won the Bakersfield Open, his third tour victory. As it turned out, it was his last. In 1963, putting atrociously and earning peanuts, he took a club job outside Chicago. For the next 13 years, he lost it completely as a tournament player. "Then I started pounding balls, pounding balls . . . and I'm still searching for it," he recalled in 1991, laughing. He found it sufficiently to win the 1979 PGA Seniors Championship and the 1979 World Seniors title. At age 59, he joined the Senior PGA Tour when it began, and he played actively and well into his 70s. His best year was 1984, when he finished 20th on the money list with $65,000.

Everything Jack did in golf after 1955 paled in comparison to his victory over Hogan in the U.S. Open. (Jack qualified for the 1966 Open, back at the Olympic Club, but he missed the cut.) His triumph was regarded by many as almost a mystical moment, as though he had been touched by some divine power. Years later he put up for sale the Hogan irons he used in winning the Open, seeking an amount "well into six figures."

THE '60 OPEN PROVED to be the last one for Lloyd Mangrum, a great Open player who had six top-five finishes including the 1946 championship, which he won. Mangrum, who was wounded twice in World War II, survived 11 heart attacks before succumbing to the 12th in 1973 at age 59. After his seventh heart attack, which coincided with President Eisenhower's second, he telegrammed the President, "Dear Ike, I'm five up on you."

* * *

Johnny Bulla, Sam Snead's sidekick on the road in the 1930s and the medalist in the '60 Open's Denver sectional qualifier, won only one tournament in his career, but he carried a couple distinctions with him long afterward. He was the first to play and promote an inexpensive golf ball sold outside the pro shop; because the Walgreen's ball competed with the more expensive balls sold by the club pros, Johnny raised the ire of the PGA. After the war he became the first golfer to fly his own plane from tournament to tournament; sometimes he transported some of his colleagues for a fare. After missing the cut in the 1960 Open, Johnny did not make it back into the Open for six years. The 1966 championship was his last one, and at 52, he made the cut.

Fred Hawkins, the journeyman who faced Hogan in the 1959 Colonial play-off that culminated in Ben's final career victory, won only one tournament in almost 20 years on tour; he was the bridesmaid 19 times. But he won a long bout with the bottle, and despite looking older than his age, he played for a dozen years on the Senior Tour. Summing up his career in 1991, he said, "Well, I didn't have good luck in golf. I've always said I've been lucky in life in general, which is more important."

Johnny Pott, who went into the final round of the 1960 Open with hopes of collecting his first professional victory, didn't have to wait long. He won a couple months later at the Dallas Open and repeated in December at the West Palm Beach (Florida) Open. He played on three Ryder Cup teams in the mid-1960s and won three other tournaments, but like Hawkins and Finsterwald, his career suffered from "bridesmaid syndrome." He finished second 17 times. In 1972 he began a long, high-flying, sometimes turbulent second career as a real estate developer. The Senior Tour never tempted him.

Bruce Crampton, the young Australian who played amid the leaders for the first two rounds of the '60 Open, won the first of his 14 American tour events in 1961. In 1973 he became the first non-American to win the Vardon Trophy since Harry Cooper of England in 1937, and he repeated in 1975. Playing week in, week out, Crampton earned a reputation as an "iron-man," which continued on into a very successful career on the Senior Tour. Asked during the 1992 season what was his best round of golf, he answered, "When asked that, I say, 'Whenever I win.' I savor my wins richly and I think about them later for nourishment."

Arnold Palmer returned to Cherry Hills Country Club in December 1966 to accept an honorary life membership at a testimonial dinner. No native son could have been greeted more warmly, and Palmer responded in kind.

Meanwhile, Denver's sports fans started to welcome an influx of professional teams. Years later, Ralph Moore, the head golf writer for the *Denver Post* in 1960, said that the Cherry Hills Open hastened this development. "The 1960 Open was Denver's post-war entry into big-time sports."

In 1960 the Denver Broncos, of the new American Football League, broke through the barrier depriving the city of a major-league team. Later, basketball's Nuggets followed. Denver saw a National Hockey League team move in and move out, and after a 13-year hiatus, another team (the Avalanche) arrive. In the nineties Coloradans embraced the baseball Rockies passionately, turning out in record numbers, delighting in the launching-pad effect that mile-high baseball has on hitting.

Cherry Hills Country Club remained enthusiastic about hosting major golf tournaments, and the game's key organizations continued to favor the course. The USGA brought back the Open to the club in 1978 (Nicklaus finished tied for sixth and Palmer missed the cut), the PGA chose the course again for its championship in 1985, and the USGA returned with the Amateur in 1990. As wonderful new golf courses such as Jack Nicklaus's Muirfield Village evicted venerable clubs from rankings of the greatest golf courses, Cherry Hills held fast to its top-50 ranking in America and top-100 position in the world.

The USGA, well pleased with the course and the club during the Amateur, selected Cherry Hills to host the 1993 U.S. Senior Open.

As SENIORS, ARNOLD PALMER and Jack Nicklaus remained adversaries, though usually friendly ones. They competed in the golf-course-design business, they competed in hosting a PGA Tour event (Palmer's Bay Hill tournament, Nicklaus's Memorial Tournament), and, thankfully, they competed on the golf course. In 1993 Palmer began the Masters with three straight birdies, inspiring Nicklaus to shoot a 67. "I guess we still compete," Jack said.

That year some real warmth returned to their relationship. Jack's Memorial Tournament selected Arnold as the year's honoree, and Jack played at Bay Hill. And at the Tradition, an important Senior Tour event, Palmer asked a surprised Nicklaus for the first time ever to critique his swing.

In July, Palmer, 63, and Nicklaus, 53, returned to the place of the 1960 U.S. Open to compete in the U.S. Senior Open. Sentiment aside, both men were long shots. Palmer hadn't won a tournament in five years, and Nicklaus had played so poorly in 1992 that his enormous pride was the main reason he hadn't retired.

As he did three decades earlier, Palmer went with his

driver off the first tee each round, hoping to reward his fans for their years of devotion. Despite a still powerful swing and the fervent support of his followers, he couldn't duplicate his opening drive of the 1960 Open's fourth round—a feat Cherry Hills members had commemorated nearby on a brick monument. One had to look hard for a tournament highlight involving the King, the nickname given Arnold by golf writers and his peers. But it was there all the same—a gritty second-round performance in which he overcame painfully feeble putting to make the cut.

After botching three straight four-foot putts to start the round in bogey-bogey-double-bogey, Palmer looked certain to miss the cut. But he bore down grimly and played the next 14 holes in even par. At 18, needing a par to secure a place in the final two rounds, he landed in the huge bunker at the right front of the green. His sand shot came out high and soft and landed seven or eight feet from the pin. Now for the scary side-hill putt. He holed it. Leaving the green, he smiled warmly, seeming completely relaxed. For those who walked in his gallery, it is hard to imagine Arnold ever having played harder than he did that day.

Just as he was completing his round—right to the minute—Jack Nicklaus was scheduled to tee off at the 1st hole. Again, as in the 1960s, the torch was being passed from Palmer to Nicklaus.

Two days later, Jack came to the 18th hole needing a par for a one-stroke victory over his long-time foe, Tom Weiskopf. A pure one-iron from the tee and a faded five-iron left him 35 feet to the left of the hole. As he strode up the 18th fairway, a television microphone picked up his remarks to his caddie, his eldest son, Jackie. The left side—that's where he wanted to be, he said. "I've been right—in 1960—and made bogey."

This time, at Cherry Hills, the magic Arnold Palmer had found at the 1960 U.S. Open was captured by Jack Nicklaus.

Bibliography

Books

Barkow, Al. *Gettin' to the Dance Floor: An Oral History of American Golf.* New York: Atheneum, 1986.

———. *The History of the PGA Tour.* New York: Doubleday, 1989.

Bisher, Furman. *The Birth of a Legend: Arnold Palmer's Golden Year—1960.* Englewood Cliffs, NJ: Prentice Hall, 1972.

Gregston, Gene. *Hogan: The Man Who Played for Glory.* Englewood Cliffs, NJ: Prentice Hall, 1978.

Grimsley, Will. *Golf: Its History, People, and Events.* Englewood Cliffs, NJ: Prentice Hall, 1966.

Guest, Larry. *Arnie: Inside the Legend.* Orlando: Tribune Publishing, 1993.

Jenkins, Dan. *The Dogged Victims of Inexorable Fate.* Boston: Little, Brown, and Company, 1970.

Johnson, Salvatore. *The Official U.S. Open Almanac.* Dallas: Taylor Publishing Company, 1995.

Jones, Robert T., Jr. *Bobby Jones on Golf.* New York: Doubleday, 1966.

———, and O. B. Keeler. *Down the Fairway.* London: A & C Black, 1990.

McCormack, Mark H. *Arnie: The Evolution of a Legend.* New York: Simon & Schuster, 1967.

Nelson, Byron. *How I Played the Game*. New York: Dell Publishing, 1993.

Nicklaus, Jack, with Herbert Warren Wind. *The Greatest Game of All: My Life in Golf*. New York: Simon & Schuster, 1969.

Norland, Jim. *Fifty Years of Mostly Fun: A History of Cherry Hills Country Club 1922–72*. Englewood, CO: Cherry Hills Country Club, 1972.

Penick, Harvey, with Bud Shrake. *Little Red Book*. New York: Simon & Schuster, 1992.

Peper, George, et al., eds. *Golf in America: The First One Hundred Years*. New York: Harry N. Abrams, Inc., 1988.

Sampson, Curt. *The Eternal Summer*. Dallas: Taylor Publishing Company, 1992.

_____. *Hogan*. Nashville: Rutledge Hill Press, 1996.

Scharff, Robert, et al., eds. *Golf Magazine's Encyclopedia of Golf*. New York: Harper & Row, 1970.

Sifford, Charles. *Just Let Me Play*. Latham, NY: British American Publishing Ltd., 1992.

Snead, Sam, with Al Stump. *The Education of a Golfer*. New York: Simon & Schuster, 1962.

Sommers, Robert. *Golf Anecdotes*. New York: Oxford University Press, 1995.

_____. *The U.S. Open: Golf's Ultimate Challenge*. New York: Atheneum, 1987.

Wind, Herbert Warren. *Following Through*. New York: Ticknor & Fields, 1985.

_____. *The Story of American Golf*. New York: Alfred A. Knopf, 1975.

Periodicals

MAGAZINES

Golf Digest
Golf Journal (formerly *USGA Journal*—Joseph C. Dey, Jr.)
Golf Magazine
Golf Monthly (British)—Joe E. Doan
Golf World—Mark Schreiber
Newsweek
Professional Golfer (1958 through 1960)—Jim Gaquin

Saturday Evening Post—Will Grimsley
Sports Illustrated—Herbert Warren Wind
Time

NEWSPAPERS *(JUNE 1960)*

Augusta Chronicle—Johnny Hendrix
Chicago Tribune—Charles Bartlett
Cleveland Press—Jack Clowser
Colorado Springs Gazette Telegraph—Tom Cushman, Loy Holman
The Columbus Dispatch—Paul Hornung
The Commercial Appeal (Memphis)—Cary Middlecoff
The Daily Oklahoman (Oklahoma City)—Wally Wallis
The Dallas Morning News—Frank Reece, Bill Rives
The Denver Post—Harry Farrar, George Franco, Chuck Garrity, Willard
    Haselbush, Ralph Moore
The Des Moines Register—Bert McGrane
The Detroit News—John Walter
Fort Worth Press—Dan Jenkins
Fort Worth Star-Telegram—Jim Trinkle
Greensboro Daily News—Irwin Smallwood
The Houston Post—Tom Davison
Los Angeles Times—Braven Dyer
Newark Evening News—Des Sullivan
Newsday (Long Island)—Bill Searby
New York Herald Tribune—Al Laney
New York Post—Gene Roswell
The New York Times—Lincoln Werden
New York World Telegram and Sun—Larry Robinson
The Philadelphia Inquirer—Fred Byrod
The Pittsburgh Press—Bob Drum
The Plain Dealer (Cleveland)—John Dietrich
Rocky Mountain News (Denver)—Dorothy Jane Burke, Leonard Cahn,
    Dolores Johnson, Warren Lowe, Maxine Lowry, Bud Maloney,
    Al Nakkula, Chet Nelson
St. Louis Post-Dispatch—Robert Morrison
The Salt Lake Tribune—Jack Schroeder
The San Diego Union—Jack Murphy

San Francisco Examiner—Phil Norman
The Toronto Daily Star—Gordon Campbell
Washington Star—Merrell Whittlesey

WIRE SERVICES

Associated Press—Harold Claassen, Don Weiss
United Press International—Oscar Fraley

Also, the AP and UPI provided localized coverage in the hometown newspapers of 1960 U.S. Open contestants.

Videotape

United States Golf Association. "The 1993 U.S. Senior Open: Golden Again at Cherry Hills." Far Hills, NJ: USGA, 1993.

Index